BRITISH AND AMERICAN PLAYWRIGHTS
1750–1920
General editors: Martin Banham and Peter Thomson

Charles Reade

OTHER VOLUMES IN THIS SERIES

Already published

TOM ROBERTSON edited by William Tydeman
W. S. GILBERT edited by George Rowell
HENRY ARTHUR JONES edited by Russell Jackson
DAVID GARRICK AND GEORGE COLMAN THE ELDER
    edited by E. R. Wood
WILLIAM GILLETTE edited by Rosemary Cullen and Don Wilmeth
GEORGE COLMAN THE YOUNGER AND THOMAS
    MORTON edited by Barry Sutcliffe
ARTHUR MURPHY AND SAMUEL FOOTE edited by George
    Taylor
H. J. BYRON edited by J. T. L. Davis
AUGUSTIN DALY edited by Don Wilmeth and Rosemary Cullen
DION BOUCICAULT edited by Peter Thomson
TOM TAYLOR edited by Martin Banham
JAMES ROBINSON PLANCHÉ edited by Don Roy
A. W. PINERO edited by George Rowell

Further volumes will include:

SUSAN GLASPELL edited by C. W. E. Bigsby
HARLEY GRANVILLE BARKER edited by Dennis Kennedy

11 95p

Plays by
Charles Reade

MASKS AND FACES
THE COURIER OF LYONS
IT IS NEVER TOO LATE TO MEND

Edited with an introduction and notes by
Michael Hammet

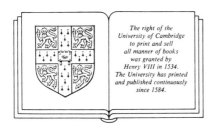

The right of the
University of Cambridge
to print and sell
all manner of books
was granted by
Henry VIII in 1534.
The University has printed
and published continuously
since 1584.

CAMBRIDGE UNIVERSITY PRESS

Cambridge

London   New York   New Rochelle

Melbourne   Sydney

Published by the Press Syndicate of the University of Cambridge
The Pitt Building, Trumpington Street, Cambridge CB2 1RP
32 East 57th Street, New York, NY 10022, USA
10 Stamford Road, Oakleigh, Melbourne 3166, Australia

First published 1986

Printed in Great Britain at
the University Press, Cambridge

British Library cataloguing in publication data

Reade, Charles
Plays by Charles Reade. – (British and American playwrights 1750–1920)
I. Title   II. Hammet, Michael   III. Moreau, Eugene. The courier of Lyons
IV. Reade, Charles. It is never too late to mend   V. Series
822′.8   PR5212

Library of Congress cataloguing in publication data

Reade, Charles, 1814–1884.
Plays.
(British and American playwrights, 1750–1920)
Bibliography: p.
Contents: Masks and faces – The courier of Lyons – It is never too late to mend.
I. Hammet, Michael.   II. Title.   III. Series.
PR5212.H36   1986   822′.8   85-29089

ISBN 0 521 24361 0 hard covers
ISBN 0 521 28627 1 paperback

GENERAL EDITORS' PREFACE

It is the primary aim of this series to make available to the British and American theatre plays which were effective in their own time, and which are good enough to be effective still.

Each volume assembles a number of plays, normally by a single author, scrupulously edited but sparingly annotated. Textual variations are recorded where individual editors have found them either essential or interesting. Introductions give an account of the theatrical context, and locate playwrights and plays within it. Biographical and chronological tables, brief bibliographies, and the complete listing of known plays provide information useful in itself, and which also offers guidance and incentive to further exploration.

Many of the plays published in this series have appeared in modern anthologies. Such representation is scarcely distinguishable from anonymity. We have relished the tendency of individual editors to make claims for the dramatists of whom they write. These are not plays best forgotten. They are plays best remembered. If the series is a contribution to theatre history, that is well and good. If it is a contribution to the continuing life of the theatre, that is well and better.

We have been lucky. The Cambridge University Press has supported the venture beyond our legitimate expectations. Acknowledgement is not, in this case, perfunctory. Sarah Stanton's contribution to the series has been substantial, and it has enhanced our work. Later volumes in the series have benefited from the care and attention of Kevin Taylor.

Martin Banham
Peter Thomson

CONTENTS

ILLUSTRATIONS

The first illustration and nos. (1)–(9) are taken from *Charles Reade as I Knew
Him*, by John Coleman. No. (10) is from *Wilkie Collins and Charles Reade*,
by Morris L. Parrish.

Photos: The British Library

ACKNOWLEDGEMENTS

Thanks are due first to the staffs of those institutions who have made this volume possible: the British Library, the British Theatre Museum, and the British Theatre Association. To the many people with whom I have discussed the Victorian theatre, both colleagues and students, thanks are also due, and especially to Martin Banham and John M. Pick in respect of this edition of plays. I am grateful, too, to Judith Greenwood for her precise and careful correction of the typescript of the introduction.

M.H.

Charles Reade, aged 45

INTRODUCTION

It is impossible to speak simply about Charles Reade's character or his career, for both embraced paradoxes with enthusiasm and energy. He published twenty-seven novels as well as serials, short stories, pamphlets and journalistic pieces. He wrote twenty plays, some original, some adaptations from the French, collaborating with Tom Taylor, and with Dion Boucicault. He supplied serialized stories for Charles Dickens, and theatrical pieces both for Henry Irving and Ellen Terry. He engaged in theatrical management, promoting Ellen Terry's return to the stage. His dramatic forte was a melodramatic sentiment, and yet he professed realism, even naturalism, and an adherence to carefully researched fact. His plays remained in the professional repertoire for decades, and his novels and short stories sold in their hundreds of thousands, yet he had no high regard for his readers or audiences. He was often to be found in the Garrick club, and gave regular luncheon parties at his house in Knightsbridge, yet he is not recalled by actors and managers as a centrally important character. His evidence was sought by a parlimentary select committee on censorship, and his indefatigable campaigning for authors' rights led to his being proposed for a royal commission on copyright; yet his efforts on their behalf did not make him a favourite of authors, and, indeed, publishers were reputed to be afraid of him.

His mother intended him for the church, yet he avoided it, and took to religion only shortly before his death. He spent a year in Edinburgh trying to train as a physician, but could not stand it, and took to the law. He was called to the Bar, but never practised, though he was an ardent litigant in matters of libel and copyright. He was reputedly irascible and arrogant, a hard bargainer for his financial dues, and proud of his economic success; yet his plays aspire to a compassionate sensibility, a sympathy for society's underdogs and outcasts that cannot be feigned. He publicly campaigned against social and legal injustices, devoting much energy to the causes he adopted – an energy which spilled over into calvinistic moral denunciations, which his contemporaries found hard to support.

In that he could make a comfortable living by his pen, he was a mirror to his age; and even though he was accused of exaggeration, his bombastic and splenetic letters to the press, and his ready resort to the courts reflected, too, the ethos of his times. His literary income was more secure than that from his theatrical speculation, as his cultural climate dictated, yet he was continually drawn back to the theatre in the face of prudence, just as his sympathetic heroine was a central idea upon which the dramas of a life-long bachelor hung.

Reade both loved and hated his readers, just as he was a man in the theatre, but not of it. He might have been a clergyman, a doctor, or a lawyer, but chose to live by writing. He was a fellow of Magdalen College, Oxford, at various times its Junior Dean of Arts, its Bursar, and its Vice-President, yet despite his mother's Calvinism, he chose to follow actresses, and lived for many years in an uncertain relationship with Mrs Seymour, styled his housekeeper, confidante, and companion.

He cannot, therefore, simply be seen as a don who took to writing; or as a novelist who took to turning out plays; nor can he be regarded as an author who took to management, as a vexacious litigant, as a comfortably-off reformist, as a reclusive misanthrope, as a misogynistic stage-door-johnny, or as a moralizing gold-digger. As his plays attest, he was all of these things at the same time, and yet none of them quite; his cast of mind reflected that of the theatre industry of his time, which it is a commonplace to observe was then at its greatest extent; and the complex intertwining of the strands of his career, so energetically pursued, reflected the opening up of possibilities brought about by the development of industrial capitalism and of the means of communication, both physical and in the realm of ideas. If, like the aboriginal, Jacky, in Reade's most successful work, *It Is Never Too Late to Mend*, our first reaction is to break the mirror which presents an uncongenial image, we should remember that he later causes Jacky to return to a re-examination of the fragments, under the wryly amused but sympathetic and beneficent gaze of the piece's hero. Reade slips like a wraith through the cultural history of his age, from time to time raising demons which, if his critics hated them, his audiences, his readers, and his leading actors understood.

Charles Reade was born at Ipsden House in Oxfordshire on 8 June 1814. He was the youngest of ten children, three of whom were sisters, and he never knew the eldest three brothers, who went to India. His father seems to have been a conventional country squire, and to have been largely preoccupied with his own affairs. Though educated, he seems to have had little interest in literature or the theatre. Reade's mother, though strongly interested in religion, appears to have had wider aesthetic tastes, and it seems it was through her that he became introduced to literature. He was sent to school first under a Reverend John Slatter, then under a Mr Hearn at Staines, and finally to a crammer, with the result that a young man, already thought precocious, matriculated to Oxford in July 1831 as a 'demy' at Magdalen College. It was not to be expected that Reade's father could support him, so it was clear that he would have to earn his own living, and it was his mother's ambition that he become a clergyman.

At Oxford Reade was regarded as eccentric. He dressed according to his own tastes, rejected alcohol, and kept a squirrel and a robin in his room. He was neglectful of his lectures, and though fond of reading, followed his own inclinations in his studies. He was never ordained, and took a third class degree in 'Greats', but in the year in which he graduated he began to make notes with a view to writing fiction. He preferred the notion of freedom and a literary career to holy orders.

His parents could not support him, and so he needed the college fellowship which he obtained in July 1835. He attempted to study medicine at Edinburgh, but was repulsed by blood. He took to law instead and was entered at Lincoln's Inn in November of the same year. There he became acquainted with Samuel Warren, already a novelist.

A pedantic and eccentric don in embryo, he greatly enjoyed London, books, trade, commerce, and galleries, and the law courts, as he said in a letter to his father, and he 'fixed upon a study of all [literary] masterpieces in all languages, and all recorded times'. He first saw Mrs Seymour in a performance of *The Bridal*, with Macready, while he was studying law.

Reade took an M.A. degree in April 1838, and in the following year, touring on the continent, he became greatly interested in the Parisian theatre and its management arrangements. After his return he became a member of the Garrick club, in December 1839. In 1841 he was made Junior Dean of Arts at Magdalen College, and in 1842 he was both called to the Bar, and elected Vinerian Fellow at Magdalen. The Vinerian fellowship, which was worth £80 per annum, added to his fellowship which was worth £250 per annum, gave him a modest independent security. He subsequently held college posts, no-one disliking him, despite his remarked eccentricities. He was an accomplished amateur violinist, and thought to enhance his income by importing violins from the continent. He visited Paris and Germany for this purpose, and perhaps Holland, but following the violent political events in Paris in 1848, he had to depart, leaving his stock behind. In 1849 he became Bursar at Magdalen, and attended his father during the last days of the latter's life.

In 1846 Reade had been introduced to Mrs Stirling. In 1850 he offered to her his play, *Christie Johnstone*. She showed it in turn to Tom Taylor, who judged it unfit for the stage, and recommended that it be turned into a novel. In 1851 he was more successful with his first acted piece, *The Ladies' Battle*, which he had adapted from Scribe and Legouvé, and which was presented at the Olympic Theatre by William Farren and Mrs Stirling in May, and later by Benjamin Webster and Mrs Stirling at the Haymarket Theatre in November. In 1851, too, he published at his own expense *Peregrine Pickle*, which was not to be performed until 1854. As soon as he had finished writing *The Ladies' Battle*, in April 1851, he began upon his collaboration with Tom Taylor to write *Masks and Faces*. Thus within five years of his introduction to Mrs Stirling, his career as a dramatic author was

Ben Webster as Triplet and Mrs Stirling as Peg Woffington in the original production of *Masks and Faces*

begun, in advance of his career as novelist and writer of short stories. It is not too fanciful to see some of Reade's condition in the dependence of Triplet in *Masks and Faces* on the recommendation of the famous actress, Peg Woffington, who was played by Mrs Stirling.

Admirer of Mrs Stirling though he might be, however, and presumably glad to see *The Ladies' Battle* transferred to the Haymarket, Reade none the less observed at the time that French actors respected authors, while English actors did not, and that he feared for his own 'credit' because actors 'did not believe authors knew their own meaning'.

The Ladies' Battle at the Olympic Theatre was successful enough for Farren and Mrs Stirling to take another French adaptation from him: *Angelo*, from Victor Hugo, in August of the same year. Given the source of his first two successes, therefore, it is not, perhaps, surprising, that Reade should compare the French and the English theatre. The commencement of *Masks and Faces* with Tom Taylor, however, marked an important departure. Taylor was three years Reade's junior when Mrs Stirling effected their introduction, but five years his senior in experience. The partnership was to produce four plays: in addition to *Masks and Faces* they were: *Two Loves and a Life*, which Webster presented at the Adelphi Theatre in March 1854; *The King's Rival*, for Mrs Seymour and Isabel Glyn, which was presented at the St James's Theatre in October 1854; and *The First Printer*, which was presented by Charles Kean at the Princess's Theatre in March 1856.

Two adaptations produced, and work begun with Tom Taylor in 1851 might have seemed a sufficient launch into the theatre; but Reade was not content, for in April of the following year he undertook his first venture in theatrical management. He adapted a French play by Annicet Bourgeois, giving his version the title *The Lost Husband*; he took the Strand Theatre, and there presented it with Mrs Seymour on 26 April 1852, together with another piece by him, *A Village Tale* (which was to resurface, revised for Ellen Terry, in 1874). It did not, however, find favour, and closed after a few days.

In August of that same year he finished writing *Peg Woffington*. *Masks and Faces*, whose central character is, of course, Peg Woffington, was produced on 20 November, and his novel on the same subject was published one month later. The close coincidence is not coincidence at all; it would be a mistake to regard Reade as creatively ambidexterous, working both in the medium of the novel and the theatre, for he exploited his ideas and his material in both media, and at the same time. The formal distinction is more apparent than real; just as it would be ultimately impossible to distinguish some absolutely original ideas from those of his peers, and, indeed, those of his culture. The persona of the famous actress, exploited as the main theme of *Masks and Faces*, was no novelty or rarity in nineteenth-century theatre,

Sir Squire Bancroft as Triplet in a revival of *Masks and Faces*

Lady Bancroft as Peg Woffington in the same production

of course, but Reade seems to have felt that in the play itself he had lost some of his *amour propre*, and that Taylor had adapted it to suit Webster, who, he noted, was not so good a writer as he was an actor. In his private notebooks Reade wrote long critical reviews of his works, solely for his own enlightenment.

As soon as he had finished his *Peg Woffington*, in August, he began upon his play, *Gold*, which he finished at Oxford in September, the month before *Masks and Faces* was produced. *Gold* was to be produced in January of the following year, 1853, at the Theatre Royal, Drury Lane, and to resurface later both as his novel and his play, *It Is Never Too Late to Mend*. Once *Peg Woffington* was published, in December 1852, Reade embarked at once on the writing of his novel, *Christie Johnstone*, which was published in 1853. In 1852, it seems, Reade was persistently hawking his adaptations from manager to manager; but it is also the year in which his association with Mrs Seymour began. *Gold*, on completion, had been offered to Charles Kean, but he declined it. It was Reade's first original piece (neither an adaptation nor a collaboration) and he hoped it would prove that he was an author as well as an adaptor. *Peg Woffington*, published by Richard Bentley, brought Reade £10 for the first edition, owing, Reade maintained, to an unjust contract. *Masks and Faces* was a success; Taylor and Reade received £150 between them for it, though it was a 'gold-mine' to Webster, possessing 'the elements of eternal success' according to Lewes in the *Leader*. *Gold* was a lesser success, though its reworking was to establish Reade; and *Peg Woffington*, though no great sensation, was kindly reviewed.

January 1853, then, saw the production of *Gold* by E.T. Smith at Drury Lane. *Christie Johnstone*, begun in December 1852, was completed in June 1853, and Reade began immediately upon his novel, *It Is Never Too Late to Mend*. For the writing of it he visited gaols in Durham, Oxford, and Reading, because, he said, 'I propose never to guess where I can know.' His working method is further elucidated by another comment in the same context:

> My story must cross the water to Australia, and plunge after that into a gold-mine. To be consistent with myself, I ought to cross-examine at the very least a dozen men that farmed, dug, or robbed in that land. If I can get hold of two or three that have really been in it, I think I could win the public ear by these means. Failing these I must read books and letters, and do the best I can. Such is the mechanism of a novel by Charles Reade. If I can work the above great system, there is enough of me to make one of the writers of the day; without it, no, no!

He had begun a collection of notebooks and scrapbooks in 1848, which, as Reade described it in 1871, required an index to the indices. Such an encyclopedist's collection of detail, to be turned eventually to account, prompts the image of Conan Doyle's literary detective haunting Baker Street a couple of decades later: he too a bachelor, a violinist, and possessed of a vigilant sense of public morality.

In August 1853 Reade went to live in chambers in Piccadilly, and began writing short stories which were to be published in *Bentley's Miscellany* from November 1853 to September 1854, initiating another remunerative strand to his career.

Reade's theatrical campaign was now to come to its first climax, for 1854 was to see the production of his second and third collaborations with Tom Taylor, and of a staple of his dramatic works, by Charles Kean, before he embarked on a season of management with Mrs Seymour at the St James's Theatre.

Two Loves and a Life, which he wrote with Tom Taylor, was produced by Webster at the Adelphi Theatre on 20 March 1854. It was described by Henry Morley as 'an absolutely commercial composition, every part being written for an actor'; the Adelphi audience was 'fitted to perfection'. Taylor and Reade received £100 between them for it, though, Reade observed, in France it would have been worth £5,000.

Charles Kean had enjoyed a great success in *The Corsican Brothers*, in which he played two roles as the brothers. Perhaps influenced by the success of *Two Loves and a Life*, which fitted parts to their actors, and impressed by Moreau, Siraudin, and Delacour's piece, Reade offered a free adaptation of the French play to Kean as *The Courier of Lyons*. Kean accepted, and, indeed, chose the play for his benefit night. The Queen and the Prince Consort were present at the play's opening night on 26 June 1854. It ran for twenty-six nights to the end of the season, and was resumed in the winter season. It became one of Kean's stock pieces. Many pirated versions were done, and, indeed, in 1855 Reade could claim that *The Courier of Lyons* had been seen in nearly every London theatre. It had an enduring popularity, and Reade later did a revised version for Henry Irving in 1877, then entitled *The Lyons Mail*.

The Courier of Lyons did not contain a particularly strong female leading part, but in the characters of Peg Woffington, Christie Johnstone, and Susan Merton in *It Is Never Too Late to Mend*, all of which he had then recently been creating he did have such a character, and he wanted to promote plays with a leading actress. Mrs Stirling was his first, and now his natural choice, but, rebuffed by her, he turned to Mrs Seymour, with whom he had mounted a none-too-successful venture at the Strand Theatre two years before. They took the St James's Theatre for the season in October 1854, and opened with Reade's third collaboration with Tom Taylor, *The King's Rival*. Their company included Tom Mead, who had played in *Gold* at Drury Lane, Lydia Thompson and J. L. Toole, who had acted in the previous season with Mrs Seymour at the Haymarket Theatre under J. B. Buckstone's management, and George Vandehoff with Isabel Glyn who had acquired Shakespearian reputations at the Sadler's Wells Theatre under Phelps.

The King's Rival was not a great success, according to J. L. Toole, because Mrs Seymour was not great enough to sustain a star role as Nell Gwynne. On the third night *Honour Before Titles; or, Nobs and Snobs*, a one-act comedy by Reade, and with J. L. Toole in it, was introduced. The following month another of Reade's pieces, previously rejected, *Peregrine Pickle*, failed. The fortunes of the theatre were not flourishing by Christmas, and in January 1855 an operatic version of Euripides' *Alcestis* was tried, but proved an utter failure. Ingloriously and unprofitably the theatre struggled on till the spring, when Reade presented it with an adaptation from Fournier, *Art*, which he had already used as a short story in *Bentley's Miscellany* in December 1853. The same play was later to be revived as *An Actress of Daylight* for Mrs John Wood in 1871, and as *Nance Oldfield* for Geneviève Ward in 1883, but on this occasion it was not sufficiently successful to retrieve the finances of the season which closed with Reade, very probably, out of pocket.

The result of so unsuccessful a season was to cause Reade to draw in his theatrical horns for a while, and apart from his final collaboration with Tom Taylor, *The First Printer*, which was presented by Charles Kean at the Princess's Theatre in March 1856, he produced nothing else for the stage for a period of nine years, but devoted his energies to literature.

Nicholas Trübner persuaded him of the potential value of the American literary market. A Boston firm, Ticknor and Fields, were immediately offered, and accepted, the American rights to *Peg Woffington* and *Christie Johnstone*. The unexpected, successful result of their publication opened Read's eyes to America. The novel, *It Is Never Too Late to Mend*, was advertised before publication in the United States as *Susan Merton*, the name of its principal female character. It had however, changed its name by the time it got to the press. It was published on 1 August 1856 in London, where the reaction was not very great, though a second edition published in October of that year drew generally favourable critical reviews. Reade wrote to Fields, his Boston publisher, that he hoped for a great success in America where 'I know my success is really great . . . [in England] the book is a dead loss to me'. So depressed a tone was not ultimately justified, for his market was expanding. Bernard Tauchnitz published him in Leipzig, and a translation of *Christie Johnstone* was done in France.

It Is Never Too Late to Mend contained a damning evocation of Victorian prisons, and Reade energetically stimulated press correspondence about their conditions, arguing from his press cuttings and scrapbooks, and from his research, with those who denied that his picture was true. It was a novelty for a novelist to beard critics, and to argue upon facts. It had, of course, a great publicity value. When charged with melodramatic exaggeration, he responded with bombast. He became hated in Fleet Street because, according to 'Q' in *Dramatists of the Present Day* in 1871, journalists regarded him as a 'literary fusée. You have only to touch him and he goes off.'

In the late 1850s and 1860s much of Reade's leisure time was spent at the Garrick club, where, according to Edmund Yates, he changed into slippers and perambulated the coffee-room. Here Squire Bancroft met him, and remembered seeing him playing whist with Trollope and Lever. Here, too, he dined with Millais, who wrote, 'He is delighted with my pictures, and regards all criticism as worthless. He has never been reviewed at all in *The Times* although his book [*It Is Never Too Late to Mend*] has passed through more editions than most of the first class novels.'

Reade's only dramatic work to get onto the stage for nine years after the season with Mrs Seymour was *The First Printer*, which, like his other three collaborations with Tom Taylor, was an original piece. Kean complained that it suffered from an excess of poetic licence, but Reade, though he admitted having taken liberties with history, defended it. The piece was received well by audience and press, but it was withdrawn after nine performances because of falling receipts.

It was not his only theatrical project, however, for he bought the English rights to, and adapted, *Les Pauvres de Paris* by Edouard Brisebarre. In a new departure, instead of seeking a manager who would take his adaptation he advertised it. Before any manager applied for it, however, a pirate version of the piece appeared at the Strand Theatre. Reade took legal action against Payne, the manager, and the authors of the piece, Ben Barnett and J. B. Johnstone. The French Society of Dramatic Authors offered to pay one-half of Reade's costs in the action, which amounted to £270. The action fizzled out, but the defendants were ordered to pay Reade's costs. They could not, however, though Barnett finally paid £60 after arbitration.

At this period, also, Reade fell into dispute with the publisher, Bentley, who offered a cheap edition of *Christie Johnstone*. Bentley seemed to think that in the light of the success of *It Is Never Too Late to Mend* Reade was his best author after the loss of Dickens and Harrison Ainsworth. The dispute was over copyright, and Reade issued an injunction restraining Bentley. Bentley still had the copyright of *Art*, and *Clouds and Sunshine*, which he published together with several short stories in September 1857. These, said Reade, 'By the light of *It Is Never Too Late to Mend* . . . sold twenty-five thousand copies in a few months.' Bentley now proposed two-shilling editions of *Peg Woffington* and *Christie Johnstone*. Reade then went to court seeking a declaration of his rights, which found in his favour to the extent that Bentley's interest was adjudged to be ended. Both parties had to bear their own costs, however, as the court decided that the fault lay with both of them in making a defective agreement.

Trübner then published *White Lies* in three volumes in December 1857. The story had been serialized in the *London Journal*, which, according to R. L. Stevenson, 'nearly wrecked it'. Reade's relations with his editors were not of the smoothest. Whereas, for example, Dickens and Ainsworth collaborated closely with their illustrators, Reade boasted that he did not know his, John Gilvert, 'even by sight', and on one occasion insisted on a prefatory heading which announced that the piece was published without illustration at the author's expressed wish. *White Lies* was based upon a stage adaptation of a French play, *Le Chateau Grantier*.

After his dispute with Bentley, who was by others regarded as 'an ornament to publishing', and was 'publisher in ordinary to Her Majesty', Reade was compelled to publish his next five books, including *The Cloister and the Hearth*, which may claim to have proved his most enduring success, on a commission basis. The action over *Les Pauvres de Paris*, which amounted to a stand for international copyright, gained little public sympathy, no doubt because the theatre profited so much by adaptations from the French. Similarly, his stand for authors' rights against Bentley received little sympathy, perhaps from authors' fears for themselves. Like *White Lies, Art* and *Clouds and Sunshine* were taken from French originals.

Reade did not contend only with managers and publishers. In July 1857 Fitzjames Stephen published an attack upon *Little Dorrit* and *It Is Never Too Late to Mend* in the *Edinburgh Review*, accusing them of sensationalism, and Reade of distorting his scrapbook research to that end. There followed an exasperated guerrilla correspondence which only attracted the jeers of Reade's contemporaries. Thus he felt that he had been unfairly used by Bentley; he had seen his painstaking research methods accused of distortion; and his attempts at copyright reform had attracted only odium.

That Reade possessed a talent for self-publicity is undeniable, and certainly, also, he was capable of choosing themes for his books and plays which would arouse controversy, thereby bringing them to public attention, but this is not to deny that he possessed both a social conscience and a reformist spirit. His novel *Hard Cash*, published in 1863, for example, mounted an attack upon abuses in private mental asylums, just as he had attacked degrading prison conditions in *It Is Never Too Late to Mend*. He was a crusader for *realism* in art, and was happy to use it as an instrument of social reform. 'Justice is the daughter of Publicity', he said, and devoted himself to novels of purpose, which he thought could be achieved through sensation. *The Eighth Commandment*, published in 1860, was another such novel. At the same time, he could privately admit that *White Lies* and *Love Me Little; Love Me Long*, published in 1859, had been written for the pot.

The dividing line between self-interest and public interest is very difficult to draw. Following the publication of *Hard Cash*, Reade kept up an angry correspondence in the press about the mental asylums; and later he wrote about miscarriages of justice, taking up the cudgels on behalf of those he thought unfairly done by. At the same time he would engage in litigation against Lacy, the publisher of plays, for a pirate version of *It Is Never Too Late to Mend* written by Colin Hazlewood. Hazlewood seems similarly to have pirated Reade's *The Double Marriage* to which he gave the title, *The Forlorn Hope*. Reade calculated that between 1660 and 1815 258 adaptations and imitations had appeared on the London stage. Bulwer-Lytton, Ainsworth, and Dickens all suffered dramatic piracies. He initiated legal proceedings against Benjamin Oliver and his son George (whose stage name was Conquest) for a pirate version of *It Is Never Too Late to Mend* at the Grecian Theatre. In this action he was successful, not because the play infringed his rights in the novel, but because it infringed the novel's theatrical antecedent, *Gold*.

Reade could say of *The Cloister and the Hearth*, which had its origins in *A Good Fight*, serialized in *Once a Week* in 1859, that 'My medieval story has been interrupted by cruel lawsuits in defence of my copyright which have laid me on a sick-bed, as well as hindered my work.'

Nor did he hold an unduly modest opinion of himself. By his own estimate he was three times better received in America than in Britain, and the second most celebrated sensational novelist after Dickens. He argued with Samuel Lucas, his editor for the serialization of *A Good Fight*, saying that if Lucas insisted on changing his text, he would publicly disown the serial and supply no more manuscript. Lucas refused to accept the condition, and Reade brought the serial to an abrupt end.

Reade's quest for authentic detail led him to employ hacks, for example to devil in the Bodleian for the background to his 'medieval story', *The Cloister and the Hearth*. He observed, 'Sometimes I say it must be dangerous to overload fiction with facts. At others, I think fiction has succeeded in proportion to the amount of fact in it.'

It was alien to Reade to assume the dignity of silence. He would not tolerate the slightest suggestion of injustice or inaccuracy, or resist the smallest opportunity of putting the world straight. Thus in the hey-day of his career he roused enmities, and as he grew older he alienated younger critics like William Archer. Though he seems to have been respected by artists of his time, few figures of the 1860s left any record of their acquaintance with him.

Reade was introduced to Dickens by Bulwer-Lytton, and remained on cordial terms with him for the last decade of his life. Publishers seem to have ranked him second only to Dickens as a shrewd bargainer. In 1862 he was offered £2,000 for a novel, with an additional £1,000 if it was published in the *Cornhill Magazine*. Reade, however, considered that twice that sum would not compensate for the periodical market. He expected *Hard Cash* to bring him £5,000.

After the publication of *Hard Cash* in 1863, he found himself for the first time with more than enough money for his needs, and his mind directed itself back to the theatre as though by instinct. When dealing with theatrical affairs he was not, perhaps, the shrewd man of business dreaded by publishers. He wrote a draft stage version of *It Is Never Too Late to Mend* which he showed to Dion Boucicault. Boucicault said that it needed much reduction.

The play was first produced in Leeds by John Coleman in March 1865, went to Manchester, and then on 6 April began a provincial tour. Coleman thought it not a success, with no chance of a London showing, but Mrs Seymour persuaded George Vining, who had then recently gone into management with Boucicault, and was specializing in sensational melodrama, to see a performance by Coleman's company.

Vining decided that he would produce it at the Princess's Theatre, and did so on 4 October 1865. According to Coleman, Vining allowed Reade to include scenes which he himself had rejected as too revolting for presentation. One critical notice described the play as a 'weak, three-act piece ... with only a chance gleam here and there of the genius that produced, in conjunction with Mr Tom Taylor, one of the best dramas of our time – *Masks and Faces* – and to which we owe so admirable a novel as *The Cloister and the Hearth*'.

None the less, in London the play received 140 consecutive performances, helped, quite possibly, by Frederick Guest Tompkins. Reade hankered after *realism* in his stage effects, and supervised the creation of a treadmill for the prison scene. Tompkins, on the first night, rose from his seat and loudly protested at the 'brutal realism' of the treatment of the boy, Josephs, in the scene (as G. R. Sims recalls in his *My Life*, 1917). Louisa Moore, who played the boy, confessed that perhaps she 'entered too thoroughly into the spirit of the part' when she allowed herself to fall upon the stage with an apparently alarming bang. Vining altered the scene for the second night.

It Is Never Too Late to Mend, according to Coleman, brought Reade in its first eighteen performances more money than all his previous theatrical work. He had accepted a new financial arrangement proposed by Boucicault under which he received a percentage of the profits rather than a single sum. The play was performed continually in the provinces for the remaining nineteen years of his life.

The novel, *Griffith Gaunt*, was published in 1866. In October of 1884 W. L. Courtney, in the *Fortnightly Review* could describe it as Reade's 'masterpiece', though posterity seems not to have kept it in print. It was much praised by A. C. Swinburne, but charged with indecency and

Edward Coleman, who played the
original George Fielding in *It Is
Never Too Late to Mend* at Leeds

Grace Leigh (Mrs John Coleman),
the original Susan Merton in *It Is
Never Too Late to Mend*

Stanislaus Calnaem as Jacky in the
Princess's Theatre production of *It
Is Never Too Late
to Mend*

George Vining as Tom Robinson
in the same production

immorality in the United States of America, where it received a ferocious attack in the *Round Table* of New York. When the *London Review* echoed that attack, Reade started legal proceedings against it, though other critics were kinder. Reade sued the *Round Table* itself; he was awarded six cents' damages, but galloping sales were a greater financial compensation, no doubt helped by the attendant publicity. Within a few weeks of the novel's appearance, Augustin Daly staged an adaptation in New York. That other managers competed to secure it indicates the measure of its anticipated popularity.

Thus to charges of exaggeration and distortion were added, at least in some critical minds, those of indecency and immorality. Reade rebuffed such charges with epistolary polemic, and with litigious vigour, yet when called with Boucicault, Taylor, Shirley Brooks, and Hollingshead as literary witnesses before a parliamentary select committee inquiring into theatrical censorship, he, with Boucicault, was in favour of it (though the others were opposed). Perhaps typically, his support was qualified by the stipulation that there should be some right of appeal.

The success of *It Is Never Too Late to Mend* brought Reade's attention back to the theatre. Mrs Seymour, with whom he had gone to live in Mayfair in the autumn in 1856, had not been as good as he had hoped, and she was now too old to play Reade's ideal leading roles. His election lit upon Kate Terry who appeared to be similar in style and circumstances to the Mrs Stirling of 1851. Kate Terry was a protégée of Tom Taylor, and had played under Kean in *The Courier of Lyons*. Through Kate, Reade was to meet her sister, Ellen.

With a new leading actress in mind, therefore, Reade set about the adaptation of Tennyson to produce *Dora*, and of Maquet to produce *The Double Marriage* in the spring and summer of 1867, together with a stage adaptation of *Griffith Gaunt* which was tried out in Newcastle, though it was not to be produced in London until 1874, when Ellen Terry took the leading role. The Terrys, therefore, seem to have been in the front of Reade's creative imagination in 1867.

Dora, a free adaptation of *The Promise of May*, with Kate Terry in the lead, was presented at the Adelphi Theatre on 1 June 1867. It was not a success. Kate Terry married and left the stage two months later.

The Double Marriage was a revised version of Reade's adaptation of *Le Chateau Grantier*. It was presented on 24 October 1867 under the management of Wilfred Wigan at the new Queen's Theatre opened by Henry Labouchère. Ellen Terry and Fanny Addison took the leading roles, but it, too, failed utterly, in Coleman's view because of the part played by Ellen Terry.

Inspired by Daly's success in New York, Reade adapted and himself produced a version of *Griffith Gaunt* in Newcastle towards the end of 1867.

It was entitled *Kate Peyton; or, Jealousy*, and though local reviews, while suggesting that it required condensation and quickening of action, were encouraging, it was not to appear in London.

While achieving no great success himself in 1867, Reade decided to ally himself with Dion Boucicault. In 1864 Boucicault had successfully staged a version of *Les Pauvres de Paris* as *The Streets of London*, following a similar adaptation in New York. The two men therefore had a certain theatrical taste in common, and Boucicault had made a profession of playwriting, maintaining a prodigious output. Further, he had a businesslike approach which may have appealed to Reade, who certainly had benefited from Boucicault's profit-sharing scheme.

Their collaboration began in the autumn of 1867. In the spring of 1868 Reade completed *Foul Play* as a serial in *Once a Week*, which ran from January to June of that year, and was published in three volumes in June. Boucicault produced a dramatic version at the Holborn Theatre on 28 May 1868. It seems to have been assumed that Reade was generally responsible for the novel, and that Boucicault was the principal partner in the stage version. Critics regarded the collaboration with doubtful favour. It was a pity, said Dickens, that Reade 'did not stand upon his own bottom'; the novel was felt to be 'Frenchified' with trivial and unnatural chapters designed solely for the drama. *Foul Play* suffered from 'sheer sensationalism', and was thought less ambitious in design, sentiment, and style than Reade's previous novels.

The serial ended on 20 June 1868; Bradbury and Evans issued the novel at the end of May coincident with a provincial production in Leeds by Coleman (it appeared in Manchester in the third week in June), and Boucicault's production at the Holborn Theatre. The timing was calculated by Boucicault for the sake of achieving the greatest measure of publicity. Coleman regarded the Holborn production, which proved a failure, as entirely Boucicault's doing. On 20 June the play was satirized in a burlesque at the Queen's Theatre by F. C. Burnand entitled, *Foul Play; or, a Story of Chicken Hazard*.

'Boucicault produced the greater part of it in pure dramatic dialogue', noted Reade, 'which makes an excellent backbone for me.' 'Mr Reade writes the story, while Mr Boucicault regulates the action and the development of the plot', wrote a critic in the *Imperial Review* on 6 June 1868. The authors received £2,000 from Bradbury and Evans for a limited copyright.

Reade's next project was to write *Put Yourself in His Place*, which he began in June 1868. The story was serialized in the *Cornhill Magazine* from March 1869 to July 1870. It was published in three volumes in June 1870, thus bringing Reade approximately £4,000. He decided that he would take the Adelphi Theatre to present its stage version with Henry Neville. As *Free Labour* it opened on 28 May 1870. It was a long presentation, beginning at

George Vining in Reade's adaptation of
Molière's *Le Malade imaginaire*

7.30 p.m. and going on till past midnight. Reade's penchant for *realistic* detail led to the claim that Neville 'actually forged a knife on the stage'. *Realism* or no, however, the production was a comparative failure.

On 15 June Reade added an afterpiece. It was *The Hypochondriac*, originally taken from Molière's *Le Malade imaginaire*, now revised and called *The Robust Invalid*. George Vining gave his last performance in it. Mrs Seymour appeared in it, as did Florence Terry, who, coached by her sister Kate, made her theatrical début.

Dulton Cook, writing in the *Pall Mall Gazette*, said of the play that it was 'a far more faithful rendering of Molière's comedy than the English stage [had] hitherto known', and that Reade's adaptations 'were not the commercial cobblings of the theatrical hacks but scholarly and discriminating efforts to preserve the spirit of the original'.

Reade's tenure of the Adelphi Theatre came to an end, and he transferred the production to the National Standard Theatre on 1 July 1870. The season, however, was not on the whole a success, and Coleman believed that it lost Reade about £5,000.

None the less, at the close of the London season 'Mr Charles Reade's

London Company', headed by Henry Neville, took *Free Labour*, now renamed *Put Yourself in His Place* after the serial and novel, on a provincial tour. Although the London production had been mounted before the end of the *Cornhill Magazine* serialization, and Coleman had presented the play in Leeds even before that, the pirates were not forestalled. A pirate version, entitled *The Union Wheel*, toured in advance of Reade's company in several northern towns, including Sheffield, in which the piece was set.

The tour was not a success, and during its course *Put Yourself in His Place* was withdrawn from the bill, and replaced with *It Is Never Too Late to Mend*.

In October 1870 Reade called a halt to theatrical speculation, signing a contract for a novel with Cassell's. It was called *A Terrible Temptation*, and was serialized in *Cassell's Magazine* beginning in April 1871. It was published in three volumes in August 1871, provoking some vigorous critical comment: 'the most indecent book lately issued from the press', was one comment; 'a mass of brothel garbage' was another; and Reade was described as a 'narrator of vice'. Reade responded, lamely one might think, that he 'wrote of vice only to expose it', and he also observed that 'three United States publishers had already sold 370,000 copies' which, he added, he 'took to be thirty times the circulation of *The Times* in the United States, and six times the circulation of *The Times* in England'.

It had been difficult to find a publisher in London to take the novel. George Smith said that he was afraid to. Frederick Chapman eventually agreed to do it, but offered only £600 for a three-volume edition of 1,500 copies. Reade noted that this represented a 'pitiable decline' on former sales. He had been given £1,500 for a limited copyright of *Griffith Gaunt*, and £2,000 for a limited copyright of *Foul Play*. He considered, then, that the serial in its first form would soon be the only considerable market open to him. A similar reflection found its way into Trollope's mind at the same period.

His suspension of theatrical activity held while the controversy over *A Terrible Temptation* raged, and he engaged in his next serial, *A Simpleton – A Story of the Day*. In the mean time, however, he took but a 'personal', and no financial, interest in Mrs John Wood's management of the St James's Theatre when on 8 June 1871 she presented Reade's reworked version of *Art*, entitled *An Actress of Daylight*. Mrs Wood was a first cousin of George Vining.

A Simpleton was begun in Oxford in November 1871, and finished in London in April of the following year. It was serialized in *London Society* from August 1872 to August 1873, and simultaneously in *Harper's Magazine* in the United States of America. It was published as a novel in 1873 at the end of its serialization.

Meanwhile, on 1 April, John Hollingshead produced *Shilly-shally* at the

Gaiety Theatre. Reade had adapted it from Trollope's then recently published novel, *Ralph the Heir*. J. L. Toole and Nellie Farren were in the company. It was an 'unpretending little comedy' in three acts, and its production was a comparative failure. Trollope, however, publicly disclaimed responsibility for it, instigating a hostility between Reade and himself which endured for five years.

Richard Lee, a minor critic, writing in the *Morning Advertiser*, charged the play with indecency on scant grounds, but the charge was echoed in other papers, and Reade sued *Zig-zag*, the *Orchestra*, and the *Morning Advertiser* for libel. Though he transformed but a molehill into a mountain, Reade won, and the *Morning Advertiser* had to pay him £200 in damages.

In June 1872, at the age of fifty-eight, Reade wrote in his notebook: 'With the proceeds of a pen that never wrote a line till I was thirty-five years of age I have got me three freeholds in the Brompton Road, a leasehold in Albert Terrace, a house full of rich furniture and pictures, and a few thousands floating, and so I can snap my fingers at a public I despise, and at a press I know and loathe.' His novels achieved enormous sales, and he must have been wealthier than his own estimate if he had not suffered in theatrical speculation.

Reade's story, *The Wandering Heir*, was completed in December 1872 when he published it on the eighteenth of the month as a play, and as a story in the Christmas edition of the *Graphic*, of which it was the sole feature. He estimated that 200,000 copies were sold in Europe; while in the United States Harper's sold 150,000 copies in their *Weekly*, and 80,000 in book form; and in Canada Hunter Rose of Toronto sold 10,000 copies in their journal, and a further 5,000 in book form.

The play was tried out in Liverpool, at the Amphitheatre, early in 1873. Mrs John Wood took its principal role in Liverpool, but she was replaced by Maggie Brennan while the play toured, only to return when the play came to London, where it was presented at the Queen's Theatre under Mrs Seymour's managment on 15 November 1873. It opened in London to a 'rarely more brilliant audience', and drew Mrs Wood much critical praise. For Reade, its success was the greatest he had experienced since *It Is Never Too Late to Mend*. Another engagement caused Mrs Wood to leave a successful run.

Reade therefore had a proven, new success with which to relaunch Ellen Terry in London after an absence of six years from the stage which began shortly after her appearance in *The Double Marriage*. Reade managed her return with flair, announcing an important return, but not saying of whom till just before the night, in essential melodramatic style.

The play opened at the Queen's Theatre under Reade's management on 28 February 1874. In her autobiography Ellen Terry recalls that she was 'received with great acclamation'. On 9 March she appeared in *Rachel the*

Reaper which Reade had reworked from his *A Village Tale*, first performed at the Strand in 1852.[1] It was played in 1874 before *The Wandering Heir*, its leading actor being Charles Kelly, who, of course, became Ellen Terry's second husband. Before the season closed *The Wandering Heir* was withdrawn and replaced by *Griffith Gaunt*, still with Ellen Terry in it, and finally Reade presented her in April 1874 at Astley's Theatre in *It Is Never Too Late to Mend*.

The London season closed in April, and Reade then promoted Ellen Terry in a provincial tour with a repertory of *It Is Never Too Late to Mend*, *The Wandering Heir*, and *Our Seamen*, his own newly made version of *Foul Play*. Reade considered Ellen Terry his best interpreter of Philippa Chester in *The Wandering Heir*, and much admired her genius. She was to him a wonderful artistic medium in the making.

Boucicault tried to tempt her to America, but Reade dissuaded her. He was, she said, 'her nurse and mentor', and she was a frequent visitor to his house in Albert Gate for regular Sunday parties, and to Tom Taylor's house with Reade and Mrs Seymour.

The tour ended in August 1874. A month later Ellen Terry played opposite Charles Wyndham at the Crystal Palace, and the following year she joined the Bancrofts with whom she played Mabel Vane in *Masks and Faces* in November 1875. Her only other professional association with Reade was when in the autumn of 1878 she made a provincial tour with Charles Kelly in *Dora*.

Having enjoyed a measure of managerial success with Ellen Terry, Reade proposed a new development. He wrote to John Hollingshead, manager of the Gaiety Theatre, on 20 July 1874, suggesting a collaboration in management. Reade had a number of plays, and was prepared to advance capital for big pieces. He did not, however, wish to go directly into management, he said, as the loss of time for other things which this entailed would 'cost him many thousands of pounds'. He offered seven 'masterpieces': *Our Seamen, Two Loves and a Life, Masks and Faces* (he had then recently bought the rights of these last two from Webster), *Dora, Rachel the Reaper, The Wandering Heir, The Robust Invalid* (he had remodelled and strengthened the female interest of *Masks and Faces*, he said). For *Rachel the Reaper* and *The Wandering Heir* he already had scenery in store. He suggested that they take the Princess's Theatre, for being in a large thoroughfare it drew many people; its capacity would take lots of money, and it had paid with big pieces. Further, he said, it was then 'down in the market, and might be had for three months with the right of going on'. He even proposed that they might mount *Macbeth* with George

---

[1] Reade had adapted *A Village Tale* from George Sand's *Claudie*, which he also used for the basis of his story, *Clouds and Sunshine*.

Honey and Helen Faucit. Hollingshead, however, was unimpressed, and turned the offer down.

The scale of the proposed enterprise, and his desire to be free of the detail of management, signify a change which was overcoming Reade, now in his sixtieth year. His novelist's career had effectively ended with the publication of *A Simpleton*, and he now devoted an increasing proportion of his energies to pursuing public cases and *causes célèbres*. He intervened to free people from asylums, and wrote diatribes to the *Daily Telegraph* and to the *Pall Mall Gazette*. He wrote lettters on the celebrated 'Tichborne case', which mystery he claimed to have solved, and he became occupied with another legal cause, the 'Lambert affair'.

In 1873 he became a founder member with Tom Taylor of the Authors' Protection Society, which proposed to protect authors from unauthorized dramatizations. In 1875 he wrote *The Rights and Wrongs of Authors*, and was proposed for membership of a royal commission on copyright. The commission recommended protection from dramatic piracy, but despite a campaign for an international copyright in respect of America, it did nothing about this latter.

Reade was in fact to write only three new pieces for the theatre, and he was to be largely concerned now with reworking old material. The Bancrofts' revival of *Masks and Faces* was considered the event of the season at the Prince of Wales Theatre. It was now, however, materially altered from the original: there were three acts instead of two, a new opening scene, and a pathetic ending. Reade had to be persuaded, according to Bancroft, but eventually was brought to discard the old book in favour of the new.

In 1875, too, Reade became acquainted with Robert Buchanan. A genuine friendship seemed to develop between them, and they enjoyed a common public image of ferocity, pugnacity, and spleen. Buchanan's young sister-in-law, Harriet Jay, was responsible for *The Queen of Connaught*. Reade assisted in its production by Henry Neville at the Olympic Theatre in January 1877. On the completion of its run it was followed, on 2 April 1877, by Reade's reworked version of *Foul Play*, now under the title of *The Scuttled Ship*, with Henry Neville. The critics' reception was generally lukewarm or unfavourable, objecting to its length and its *realism*. On 30 April 1877 Mrs John Wood revived *The Wandering Heir* at the St James's Theatre, but the reviewers regarded it as a mere stop-gap.

On 19 May 1877 Henry Irving produced *The Courier of Lyons*, revised and restyled *The Lyons Mail*. Irving persuaded Reade to make some alterations to the original, in particular in the second act where Joseph Lesurques has the interview with his father. It is a scene with a clear bearing on the plot, and might seem necessarily strained for the sake of preserving a melodramatic dénouement. Dulton Cook considered that Irving's greatest success was attained in this second act. If so, then it must seem that what modification of Reade's original version there was, was for the sake of fitting the part to Irving.

Though at this period Reade may seem to have been living principally off his literary capital, by adapting old works to the requirements of modern producers, he was still creatively active. He projected a play about Voltaire, and a novel about the railways, though nothing came of either of these. However, *Good Stories of Man and Other Animals* was published in *Belgravia* from June 1876 to June 1877, and a serial entitled *A Woman-hater* was published by Blackwood at the same time. It was issued in three volumes in June 1877. In July and August of 1876 Reade conducted a legal action against the *Glasgow Herald*, and in September 1877 he wrote *Hang in Haste: Repent at Leisure*, securing, it is said, the reprieve of the Penge murderers.

In January and February of 1878 he agitated against the demolition of Albert Terrace, where he lived, writing *Private Bills and Public Wrongs*, and *The History of an Acre*. In February, also, of that year, he published a pamphlet defending his adaptation of Tennyson in *Dora*. On the dramatic front in 1878 he obtained the rights of Sardou's *Andrée*, which he adapted as *Jealousy* for Henry Neville, who produced it at the Olympic Theatre on 22 April. The production contained what the *Theatre* of 24 April 1878 described as 'realistic effects . . . unfitted for the stage'.

Mrs Hodgson Burnett's *That Lass o' Lowrie's* had been successfully adapted and presented at the Opéra Comique in 1877. Reade saw it, and, greatly admiring Rose Leclerq, its leading lady, made his own version the following year. No London manager, however, would produce it, and so Reade engaged Rose Leclerq in a company of his own, and presented the piece entitled *Joan* at the Liverpool Amphitheatre in September 1878. Neither there, nor later in Manchester, was it a success.

Its production was not without result, however, for Mrs Hodgson Burnett accused Reade of piracy. His consistency and integrity were impugned; but he riposted that, as with *Shilly-shally*, he had offered payment to the despoiled authors.

On 26 December 1878 Charles Warner revived *It Is Never Too Late to Mend* at the Princess's Theatre, as he was again to do at the Adelphi Theatre on 8 September 1887. He thus established himself in 1878 as a powerful actor of Reade's roles, which led to his election as the leading character of Reade's final major theatrical piece.

After *Joan* had failed, Reade, in his sixty-fifth year, possessed little enthusiasm for further theatrical projects, which at this period he seems to have regarded somewhat as a harmful addiction, but which, like an addiction, could not be resisted if the prompting was too strong. Hollingshead, perhaps regretting his rejection of Reade's offer of four years before, proposed to Reade that he make an adaptation of Zola's

L'Assommoir. Hollingshead had seen the piece in Paris, and concluded that Reade was Zola's nearest spiritual kin in England. Reade was at first disinclined to do it, but was eventually persuaded.

He made no attempt to Anglicize the scenes as Boucicault would have done and, indeed, as he himself had done in *Les Pauvres de Paris*. He worked, it was said in the age of Aestheticism, as an artist rather than as an adaptor, catching Zola's *spirit*. He offered the play to Walter Gooch at the Princess's Theatre, and he readily accepted. However, in the course of rehearsal Gooch developed cold feet, perhaps influenced by a violent antipathy to Zola which existed in some critical corners. Nothing loth, Reade entered into partnership with him, taking a large share of the financial risk. In consequence, according to Hollingshead, when the play proved a success, Reade received £20,000 from it instead of the usual, and much smaller, royalties.

Drink, Reade's title for Zola's piece, was produced on Whit Monday, 2 June 1879. The critics were shocked and enthralled, or dismayed. Three years later, writing in *Dramatists of Today*, William Archer observed: '*Drink* was an instructive play of distinctly moral tendency ... It rose in several respects above the level of a conventional melodrama, and was a more or less truthful illustration of life ... If ever there was a drama which could cause instant conversion from evil ways, *Drink* was that drama.' Reade was, of course, himself a teetotaller.

Reade published a threat to prosecute the authors of any pirate version of *Drink* which appeared, but this did not deter E. Romaine Callender who quickly produced *D.T.; or, Lost by Drink*, which began touring in the provinces almost as soon as Reade's own company. Indeed, in some towns the pirate version preceded Reade's authentic production.

Reade did not prosecute, however. He was now five years from his death, and suffering from asthma. Further Mrs Seymour, who had been his companion for twenty-four years, and had attended every first night of Reade's plays, was terminally ill. The first night of *Drink* was the only such which she missed, and she died on 27 September 1879. She had been ill for two years, and Reade, who had been gloomy throughout the rehearsal of *Drink*, anticipating its failure, was said to be prostrate with grief at Mrs Seymour's death.

In December 1879 Reade met the Reverend Charles Graham, who later wrote an account of Reade's religious conversion. He passed June and July in 1880 with his brother, William, in Margate, and in August tried to resume work. In the spring of 1881 he moved to Blomfield Villas, in the Uxbridge Road, and wrote *Singleheart and Doubleface*, and other short stories. *Singleheart and Doubleface* was produced in Edinburgh at the Royal Princess's Theatre on 1 June 1882. It was serialized in *Life* from June to September 1882, and published in the year of his death as a novel.

Reade's final theatrical venture was not well-fated. He collaborated with

Henry Pettitt to write *Love and Money*, which was presented under Reade's management at the Adelphi Theatre on 18 November 1882 with John Ryder and Sophie Eyre. His play, *Nance Oldfield*, which had previously been *An Actress of Daylight* for Mrs John Wood, and before that, *Art*, and which would be revived by Ellen Terry in May 1891, was acted by Geneviève Ward at the Olympic Theatre on 24 February 1883.

In March of 1883 Reade was almost fatally ill. He revived enough, however, to make a visit to the continent in the summer, and made his last visit to a theatre on 4 August. In that autumn he completed *A Perilous Secret*, which was published by Richard Bentley in two volumes in 1884, and which was serialized in *Temple Bar* from September 1884 to May 1885; in the *Dublin Weekly Freeman* from 25 February 1884; and in America in *Harper's Bazaar*. His last literary work was *Bible Characters*, which was completed in the autumn of 1883, but published posthumously in 1888. In early December he went to Cannes for the winter. He returned to London in late February 1884, and died on Good Friday, 11 April, at Blomfield Villas.

To be born a tenth son was to be born without capital, for there were elder sons aplenty to live from his father's estate. Moreover, it was to be born into a large world, his eldest brothers so remote that he never met them. They had gone to the other side of the world to make what fortune they could. Struggle as he might with his inheritance, like George Fielding, the hero of *It Is Never Too Late to Mend*, Reade could not make his living, let alone his fortune at home. By an irony, Reade makes Fielding hand over his farm to his younger brother to make what he can of it, while he himself goes to Australia hoping to make his fortune from sheep, but by accident finds gold. The young Reade, however, was not author of the plot of his own life, and had to set out on the course his mother had charted for him, to Oxford, to become a cleric. He was born into a family where, by accident, he was of necessity closer to his sisters and his mother than to his father and his brothers. He must leave sisters and mother at home while he went to make his way in the world, just as George Fielding had to leave his Susan Merton. The celibacy enjoyed as a condition of his fellowship was a pointed reminder of the injustice into which he was born, and he railed against it in *The Cloister and the Hearth*.

The fellowship gave him a much-needed security and, a precocious youth, Reade took to studying, if not to his studies. He could not bring himself to become a clergyman, to follow the Reverend Eden's course in *It Is Never Too Late to Mend*, even though the latter is treated with nothing but admiration and respect. He must have a professional career, none the less, and, medicine tried but rejected, he chose the law. Crawley's profession (Crawley is an attorney in *It Is Never Too Late to Mend*), though it gave Reade a legalistic sense of right and wrong, seemed for 'little men', as

Crawley described himself, and in the year of his graduation Reade began to do what he could to build up his capital by collecting a stock of notes, of ideas which he might invest in a career as an author.

Just as he went to Oxford to become a cleric out of duty, and perhaps because he could think of nothing else to do, but switched career at the last moment, so he studied law, and was called to the Bar, but avoided practice. His encounter with Mrs Stirling was perhaps fortuitous, but it was certainly fortunate. Just as the country gentleman, Ernest Vane, in *Masks and Faces* had gone to London and become enthralled by an actress, so Reade was deeply impressed by Mrs Stirling – enamoured of her, it is suggested. Unlike Vane, however, Reade was not blown about by circumstances, but saw opportunity in his new acquaintance, and began to write plays. He accepted without difficulty two conventions of the time: firstly, that of the leading female character; and secondly, that of adaptation from the French. If the first suited his own emotional disposition, the second very practically gave him an easy route to the rapid production of pieces. He began work as an adaptor in a congenial milieu, with the advantages that adaptation gave: he need only choose what were established successes as plays so that there was little chance of any major defect in the piece, and it had a reputation to commend it; and he had largely only to translate, often with a high degree of literalness as can frequently be felt in *The Courier of Lyons*. For a young man of reasonably agile mind, the process need be neither slow nor particularly difficult. The only major task was to Anglicize those parts which English managers thought in need of it. Moreover, to the extent that a craft can be learned by copying out models, he learned his trade in the process. He needed only a brief apprenticeship to be able to produce a serviceable product.

With Mrs Stirling's patronage he was able to meet Tom Taylor and Mrs Seymour, both of whom were of immediate service to him, and both of whom proved enduring friends. While he gained experience he could learn an advance in the adaptor's art, which was to fit the piece not only to the manager's requirements, but also to the actor. With relatively little experience he was admitted to the profession of dramatic author, and taught the techniques of the time.

After he had learned to write *for* the managers and actors, and as his own confidence and ideas developed, he grew impatient of the subordination of authorial integrity or originality. Yet the techniques, once learned, were not lost, and after his period of greatest creativity, he could adapt and re-adapt both new pieces and his own earlier works for actors and managers. He became an author *through* the theatre, but also made himself independent of it, because he could employ his material in serialized stories and novels. The character Peg Woffington, in *Masks and Faces*, is central to his career. Not only was she Mrs Stirling to Reade's impressionable Ernest Vane, she was the *angel* to Reade's Triplet, the man without resources but a family to support who would turn his hand to anything artistic: comedies, tragedies, verse, eulogies, or portraits, for the sake of financial survival. Ernest's wife, Mabel, did not exist to Reade: the good country wife to the squire could not arrive to rescue him from sophisticated entanglement, but he might avoid becoming a Snarl, the arrogant and graceless critic in the play, or a Colley Cibber, the elegant and graceful roué, by his own independence. *Peg Woffington* became a novel which began a train of literary publishing which would keep the theatre's uncertainties and vices at a distance through a financial security, while his various positions in Magdalen College gave him an intellectual security.

Triplet, in *Masks and Faces*, was an amateur violin player, just as was Reade, and his early efforts in trading in violins offer a valuable key to his commercial character. Not only did he set out to trade in the import of violins, he published a paper about them. A practicable trade and publishing were not separate in Reade's mind. That he should leave his stock of violins in Paris as a consequence of French revolutionist behaviour was emblematic of the vicissitudes of commercial management. What he could export from Paris without difficulty he could contain in his head: the Parisian theatre. Here he had no novelty or originality. Others had done it before him, and did it with him. He regarded the Parisian theatre with respect, not least of all because of its profitability to successful authors. Nor can he be the only man to have thought that a system of international copyright was desirable. He did, however, distinguish himself by making a stand for it. While his actions against English pirates of his own works can be seen as merely self-interested, and his desire to maintain a copyright in America similarly so, it was not to his advantage to attempt to preserve the rights of French authors, except to the extent that it would reinforce a general principle from the adoption of which he might benefit in the long run. In fact it was a matter of legal principle to him, and perhaps more than a legal principle, a trait of character. That it was a legal and commercial principle seems indicated in that he felt his financial offers of compensation to Trollope and Mrs Hodgson Burnett permitted any artistic liberty or violence. Infatuated as he might be with the theatre, Reade wrote for it for profit.

If he was cavalier with dramatic writings, his standing on principle was not simply legalistic. That he should sue so easily was perhaps a consequence of his legal education, but his ferocious press correspondence, his adoption of causes, and his writing with a purpose, were more than devices for the gaining of publicity. That he should defend himself, and support causes with a splenetic polemic might be specially his own, but that he did so at all was also his own.

In *It Is Never Too Late to Mend* he castigates Merton, a farmer and Susan's father, for folly and inflexibility, but above all for ingratitude.

Crawley, the weak and corrupt lawyer, he drives to an alcoholic verge of insanity. He makes of Hawes, the prison governor, a monster of depravity whom with historical perspective we should probably now call a Fascist. But the real villain is the corn-factor, Meadows, a man generally respected in his community throughout the play, but whose status is only created by the wealth he can generate through dealing, and whose wealth thus gained allows him, if not leads him, to be corrupt, and to corrupt others.

Colley Cibber in *Masks and Faces* is a roué, but a principled roué, and treated with some sympathy, while Sir Charles Pomander, who aspires to the same kind of life which Cibber's older generation enjoyed as natural to them, uses wealth vulgarly, and to corrupt. Pomander belongs in the same class as Meadows; without roots to anchor them in a morality, they float in society, dangerous like sharks, with wealth lending them teeth. Hundsdon, Pomander's unscrupulous servant, is, like Meadows's creature, Crawley, a weak man corrupted. Theirs is a simple case, however, compared with the brutal prison governor, Hawes; for they are corrupted by their condition which leaves them prey to bad men. Hawes is different: he is a man made evil by an ideology willingly adopted, and it is not an ideology deep-rooted in a morality however ancient and retributive, but a shallow ideology which treats society's accidental outcasts with mechanical harshness that becomes its own *raison d'être*.

Reade's is by no means an unusual moral view. Robinson, a professional thief, and George Fielding in *It Is Never Too Late to Mend* both rediscover and reaffirm their own essential honesty through hardship and effort in the new world opened by imperial exploration. The values which they reaffirm are ancient values rooted in a natural morality of landed stability and religion. Isaac Levi, the rootless Jew in *It Is Never Too Late to Mend*, who in the latter part of the play acts like a *deus ex machina*, personifies and articulates that ancient morality. The new order, which now would be identified with capitalism, imperialism, and the industrial revolution as glibly as familiarity with the concepts allow, was giving scope in Reade's imaginative world for a whole class of injustices and evil abuses which he sought to stigmatize in his novels and plays, and in his pamphlets and letters to the newspapers.

The Courier of Lyons is starkly simple by comparison. It opposes men made criminal by circumstances, and of varying degrees of ruthlessness, to honest folk. But only Dubosc is tainted with a genuine evil, and that an ancient evil. The play's dilemma springs from the difficulty of recognizing truth in the midst of accident and confusion. There *are* new men who bring moral uncertainties with them, and they are the product of the revolution and of revolutionist thought. The wake of the revolution bankrupts the hero's father and creates a moral disorder which allows the scheme of the drama to exist. But Jerome's financial difficulties may be no more than the ordinary vicissitudes of commerce, and very little is made of new ideological thinking. Circumstantial detail apart, *The Courier of Lyons* takes place in an ancient world indeed.

Dubosc is simply depraved. He knows it; and to know it he must know that there is a moral alternative. He can distinguish between good and bad, and chooses the latter. His confederates have made a similar choice, even though they are driven by poverty. One of them, who by the way has received a college education, in the end chooses to betray Dubosc when the superior ethic intervenes in his conscience. That there is a superior moral course even in financial ruin is demonstrated by Jerome, the hero's father. Jeanne, the real victim of Dubosc's depravity and of poverty acting together, is caused, like Triplet in *Masks and Faces*, to review her condition in the face of her child's hunger, and to conclude that every honest means to salvation has been exhausted. Both are rescued by *angels* just before they take the fatal step into depravity.

Events must be manipulated by the dramatist to bring about their relief, to be sure, but persons are the agents of relief, through their own moral choice. The author guides the evolution of conscience, whilst implying or proposing that it is a natural morality, to bring about a satisfactory conclusion in *Masks and Faces* and *The Courier of Lyons*. The process is acutely obvious in the latter case, for in the actual events upon which the play was based the hero was *not* saved; Reade's manipulations to secure the happier moral outcome appear very crude compared with the machinations he was able to devise to suit other cases.

In the later play, *It Is Never Too Late to Mend*, however, a distinct change is marked. George Fielding is not driven to similar extremities before a remedy must be found; and, moreover, the worst parts of his misfortune are consciously and deliberately engineered by Meadows by economic means. Fate deals Lesurques a blow in *The Courier of Lyons* by making him resemble the villain; and fate deals Triplet a blow in *Masks and Faces* by making his theatre management unsuccessful. Fielding is brought low by a subtle and secret manipulation of economic forces for selfish ends. The economic and legal system allow such a manipulation; just as the penal system permits Hawes's brutal abuses of the prisoners in his charge. The systems are at fault, and it is beyond individual morality to rectify them. Reade is quite clear about this with regard to the prison system, and he is compelled to invent an intervention by the Home Secretary, by the government, therefore, to relieve the abuse of the prison system. In his life outside art Reade campaigned against abuses in mental asylums in the hope of precipitating a similar intervention.

But in the economic sphere he is much less clear, and in *It Is Never Too Late to Mend* he dodges the question, first by proposing that enterprise in the new world of America and Australia can solve it, and when this fails (again through malicious machination), he solves it by leading the hero to stumble upon a gold nugget of miraculous proportions. That the gold nugget is deserved is not to be doubted; but it is found more by magic than by the deliberate action of conscience. The theories of Marx were not available to Reade, and he tended to regard economic forces as akin to natural forces. That they could be manipulated he made clear, but on the whole he treated them as the agents of fate. Thus while the good conscience of the author could compensate for the individual abuse of wealth, Reade could not conceive of the general relief of poverty by a deliberate, systematic intervention.

This is not to say that his own conscience did not revolt at the injustice of it, nor that he did not think poverty an evil; for he showed in methodically expounded detail how it led to moral degradation, and then inexorably to depravity in the general case. His heroes and heroines were chosen for the resilience of their moral conscience, which could hold out in adversity until a *deus ex machina* could come to their aid. It is a moral solution to a material problem, just as the use of Reade's pen compensated for his lack of capital, and solved his material problem.

But it is not logically satisfying. Lesurques's physical possession of his head in *The Courier of Lyons* is threatened by the guillotine, and he keeps it in the play only because of the intervention of the author's moral conscience. In reality he lost it; and the end of the play must seem improbable, for we know it, as did Reade's audience, to be unreal. Peg Woffington, in *Masks and Faces*, must employ transparently improbable devices to put money into Triplet's pocket. She believes that if Triplet knew what she was doing he would reject it; and while in the ethical context of the play the rejection would hang upon the hook of dignity, it is in fact a necessary device to make the play accord with the harsher conditions of reality. *Angels* do not intervene every day, and so the conditions in which it can be allowed to happen must be made to accord more with the audience's perception of the daily struggle. It is made less improbable by surrounding it with difficulty; but it is a disguise, for though moral problems might have moral solutions, material problems want material remedies.

Mabel Vane's problem, the desertion of her husband, therefore could be solved, for it wanted only a correction of vision. Triplet's poverty needed an authorial magic wand. Twentieth-century hindsight makes the difficulty easier to grapple with because it is now identified, but Reade's generation was only in the process of becoming aware of it. While he was an agent in his own play, by authorial manipulation he could overcome material problems. But he felt the need for material solutions if he could discover them, for he himself was being swept along by materialist thought. His collection of scrapbooks, his search for facts, his collation of empirical data as we would now say, represent an ambition to come to grips with the material universe. He wanted a real treadmill on stage in *It Is Never Too Late to Mend*; he wanted a credible sinking in *The Scuttled Ship*; he wanted Henry Neville to forge a real knife on stage; and all of these things he took a keen personal interest in arranging, just as he arrived at the theatre one day with a carriageful of livestock to furnish the farm scene.

This kind of approach was better suited to the three-volume novel where there was time and space enough to travel as many continents as were necessary to happen upon a resolution to his plot. It was more difficult in the theatre where his plays were often criticized for excessive length, and for his *realism*. That *realism*, of course, might be rejected for its shocking brutality rather than its truth, but essentially it was found difficult to accept because it jarred with the theatre's own cultural dynamic. The *thought* of a treadmill might have its place in the drama and could be manipulated within the continuum of the play. A *real* treadmill was symbolically intractable; it stood there large as life, but inert, and ultimately meaningless. It must distract from the thread of the narrative unless it was made the occasion of vigorous action, which itself has a subversive tendency to become meaningless if it is not invested with symbolic gesture and ritual.

Realism, however, whatever its dramatic deficiencies, did show the poverty and brutality which were the actual conditions of many of the people, and which were the product not only of fate, but of capitalism and the industrial revolution. Suffering enjoined by fate could, perhaps, only be borne, though it was apparent that material development and the empirical sciences would alleviate some of it if they could be applied. While, however, industry and the law appeared to treat some brutally for the benefit of others, it must be seen as a man-made evil, not the workings of fate, and capable of man-made remedy. *Realism* was not, therefore, merely a literary fashion, but, with all its inherent difficulties, it seemed a powerful instrument for the exposure of vice, and of new kinds of vice at that. The moralist faded into the background together with seemingly impotent religion, which was later to be stigmatized as an opiate by Marx, and the reformist came to the fore armed with facts. The question of whether there could be moral solutions to material problems was shelved while the possibility of material solutions seemed to exist.

The question, of course, if it was not answered long ago and the answer forgotten, is yet to be solved. And it is probable that Reade adopted *realism* because it was there to be used, and suited his purposes and his method of working, rather than for a conscious, theoretical reason. In his literary work he wished to be to the fore, and to be modern, not least because it was something he could do, and it sold books. He may have learned to use *realism* just as he had learned to adapt plays for managers and actors, at least to the extent that he was consciously able to direct his work, and, too, because he was a child of his age. He might describe the author starving in his garret, but *he* didn't live in one, nor did he starve.

If the *realism* better suited the novel than the stage, Reade did not let it so far obtrude into his dramatic work as to vitiate it. He began his author's career by writing plays and he continued to supply the theatre throughout his life, re-adapting his pieces to suit new requirements right up to the last. If he was not an out-and-out playwright in some pure and dedicated sense, adhering to the unities, or tradition, or to some theoretical conception of the drama, he nevertheless could not stay out of the theatre. His plays met with varying measures of success: *Masks and Faces, The Courier of Lyons*, and *It Is Never Too Late to Mend* were immensely popular both with actors and with audiences, and, with the various versions of *Nance Oldfield*, were kept in repertoires, and revived over and over again. His adaptation of Zola, *Drink*, enjoyed a sensational popularity for a period, but then dropped from view, while many pieces sank quickly, and without trace. His essays in management were similarly either greatly successful, or spontaneously disastrous. Despite his choleric treatment of publishers, and his acrimonious relations with them, he could better produce for the literary market than for the theatre. and did so more regularly and more often, but always he returned to the theatre, using the proceeds of his novels to finance new dramatic ventures.

Moreover, Mrs Seymour, if she was a substitute for Mrs Stirling in the first place, and an actress who might fill his central role, became his lifelong companion. It was, certainly, a convention of the time that a leading woman should take a key role in the drama: a convention that Reade did not invent, but merely followed. But he took the role to be axiomatic, a *sine qua non* of his dramatic style which lived, also, in his novels. The principle achieved its highest professional expression when he managed Ellen Terry's return to the stage to play his major female roles, culminating in a Peg Woffington for the Bancrofts.

It was clearly an important convention to the theatre, but particularly so to Reade. It is made more complex by the fact that Woffington is not only the key conscience through whose moral evolutions the drama is satisfactorily resolved, but she is also an actress. In *The Courier of Lyons* Julie represents a pure and untrammelled moral conscience in whose suffering the potential tragedy of the plot is articulated, but in Reade's ending she is also the agent of the happy dénouement because she rescues Jeanne. Jeanne herself is the visible index of the consequence of Dubosc's personal depravity for, though loyal and honest to the last, she is ultimately the cause of Dubosc's unmasking. Susan Merton, in *It Is Never Too Late to Mend*, is through an innate and essential goodness, both the cause of Fielding's problems, and the object of Meadows's base stratagems, while she is also the holy grail whose quest sustains Fielding through his tribulations.

Julie is a rather sketchy character, and Jeanne not much more, though she is fleshed out a little with the realities of poverty. Peg Woffington and Susan

Merton, however, are not presented without bad traits of character. They both contain selfishness and aggression in as great measure as the other characters, and so they are not idealized. They are at other moments presented as weak or deluded, but so are the other characters, and they are not presented as without the power of initiative; indeed, they exhibit it with great force and consequence at key moments in the plot. They are both prepared to step outside the constraints of conventional propriety, if need be, to secure a morally good end. So, too, is Mabel Vane; and we might imagine it of Julie and Jeanne if they had greater parts in the play. It is true that Reade allows of evil only in men, but this is to some extent a distraction, for Reade is not primarily interested in women as women, but because of important qualities which could be expressed more easily through them than through men.

Reade's women invariably possess an unshakeable high moral sense; they exhibit a great power of sympathy; they possess a subtlety of thought which allows them to perceive solutions where the men cannot; and they possess a flexibility of behaviour which enables then to avoid the pitfalls of over-rigorous convention and pomp. They are all actresses without playing a false part. Thus they are better equipped for survival in rigid social and economic situations, and possess a confidence of purpose which is unwavering. They are not represented as morally perfect, indeed they can be suspected of falling short of perfection in sexual matters, but Reade allows them no great vice, and attributes to them a constant practicality in the long run. None of his women are incompetent, while some of his men are.

What is clearly noticeable is that, though Reade's women are the medium through which the play's deepest anguish or tragedy is expressed, and through whose actions or existence a satisfactory end is resolved, their plane of operation is moral rather than material. Peg Woffington's relief of Triplet's distress in the short term is achieved through material means, but it is a much less important matter in the scheme of the play than her renunciation of Vane, and the rehabilitation of his marriage with Mabel. It is made abundantly clear in *It Is Never Too Late to Mend* that Susan Merton is wealthy enough to solve George Fielding's economic problems, but that it is inadmissible. Reade's leading women may act, therefore, and act forcefully, so as to control the plot and to articulate the values proposed and tested in the play, but they belong principally to a moral universe, not a material one.

The women's role in Reade's drama is therefore crucial, for he cannot solve material problems except by moral intervention. His world picture is that of Isaac Levi: one of endless suffering, in which the women suffer as a condition of existence, but are also the source of assuagement and renewal. But they are more than that, for the pleasure that they bring, both within the plays, and as actresses, is a joy in life which is eternal, in contradistinction to the material gain with which most of his characters are preoccupied.

It is the women who resonate with anguish at the evolutions of the plot. Reade is skilled at heaping the threat of unimaginable disaster upon the threat of unimaginable disaster. As he turns the dramatic screw it is evidently a principle that the worst thing that can go wrong in a given situation will go wrong. His skill is to be measured in the degree to which he can prevent this device from becoming mechanically apparent. He does so with deftness and economy; indeed, so successfully that it prompts the question, why could not the whole scheme of his plays be organized with such skill? Why could not his characters have a similar complexity? Why are his moral dilemmas so comparatively simple, when clearly he is capable of subtlety and complexity?

The answer lies in the nature of the theatre for which he wrote, and his approach to writing for it. With a great number of competing theatres, the managers relied upon consistency of reputation to commend them, and consistency of production qualities to give them an illusory security. It seemed better to say that a play was an Adelphi play, or suited to an Adelphi audience than to try to describe its individual characteristics. 'By the author of *It Is Never Too Late to Mend*' served to identify Reade and to characterize his play. The managers might advertise novelty in effects, but conservatism in the play and its authorship seemed the best policy.

Reade possessed a melodramatic sense of drama, and a novelist's eye for detail and panorama. The theatre of his time wanted both, and he could supply them. He could add his personal moralizing and reformist zeal which, while quite genuine, possessed the advantage of attracting attention. Reade possessed these qualities without having too hard to study them. The acquisition of facts was his greatest task, and in this, with success, he could employ people to assist him in the Bodleian and the British Museum. His maintenance of notebooks and scrapbooks together with personally conducted research supplied his material. The theatre and the publishing industry themselves supplied the form, and Reade made no effort to change it, though he would use it for his own crusades.

His moralizing was conventional, and inherited. It is by and large Christian and sympathetic, rather then retributive or vengeful. The aboriginal, Jacky, in *It Is Never Too Late to Mend*, is illustrative. Jacky is presented as a noble savage, having a virtuous simplicity and instinct, but with a capacity to learn from the white man. What he chooses to adopt from the white man, however, is consistent with his primitive nobility; he discards the white man's vices as Reade perceived them. But Jacky's simple concept of justice is expressed in his being made to feel so *uncomfortable* by immoral behaviour that he must take direct action. Consistent with his *savage* circumstances and ethic, he wishes to wreak a violent retribution on men like Abner who behave badly and transgress honourable relations between men. He sets off to do so with club and spear in a way which is calculated to produce shudders of alarm in the Christian and civilized white man, but, importantly, even though it seems that he must brutally have killed Abner, it turns out that he only stuns him. Reade's authorial intervention, like a just Fate, prevents Jacky's lapse into a degrading immorality. Fielding and Robinson may therefore approve of him in a way that is quite respectful and genuine, if it is to the twentieth-century reader a patronizing and paternalistic moral approval. Similarly, the oppressive prison governor, Hawes, is not killed by Robinson, as it seems at one time that he must be, he is only dismissed from the service; and when Isaac Levi, according to an ancient formula, pronounces a curse upon Meadows who has wronged him, its force is only to turn the latter's every hopeful aspiration into ashes.

Reade's reformism is similar in character. He is clearly concerned with the penal system, with the abuse of mental asylums, with the over-hasty or merciless execution of the law and the risk of accidental injustice, and with the economic causes of degradation and of poverty. He saw man and his institutions as merciless and unkind, while he believed them to be capable of kindness and mercy. Reade could envisage how to produce his desired end in the narrow and limited scale of legal reform, but to the larger problems he saw no answer. He accepted that there were evil men, and evil traits in humanity. He proposed that many might be remedied, given the right circumstances; none the less, evil as an absolute still remained, just as poverty might be alleviated in the individual case, but in the general case was an unalterable condition.

In this, perhaps, he was a realist, thinking great reforms in his society impossible. Perhaps to have gone further would have left his books unpublished, and his plays unstaged. His most strident demands were pursued in journalism, letters, and pamphlets outside his literary and dramatic work. Indeed, the evidence of proposed revisions in the text of *It Is Never Too Late to Mend* suggests that he was alert to the possibility of going beyond critical or public tolerance. It was Reade's commercial skill to be able to remain on that knife-edge, to his profit.

There may, therefore, have been limitations of practicability to his reformism, yet there were philosophic limits too. Throughout his work for the theatre the character of the actress represented the character of woman. Woman on the stage, and in life, was engaged in a play not of her own making, ever disguising her deepest ambitions within the subtleties of her role. Yet it is not the woman that is important to Reade; it is the set of characteristics, the subtlety, the compassion, the adeptness at disguise and role transformation, and the sympathetic emotional power which was employed to win over the audience, and to persuade the plot to a satisfying conclusion. That it is the characteristics not the gender which were important to him is shown by the fact that they occur in Reade's most sympathetic male characters too. Triplet, Fielding, Eden, Robinson, Josephs and Joliquet (these last two actually played by women) all contain those characteristics of which Peg Woffington is a masterly exponent. Lesurques possesses some, but not enough of them, and so cannot save himself; Dubosc possesses none at all, and so must perish. Those characteristics represent immaterial powers, ancient and spiritual, usable only for moral ends, and ultimately more powerful than any material cause or physical force. If these sympathetic powers are abstracted from Reade's characters, then only crude stereotypes remain, and they stand out the more starkly and uncomfortably against Reade's own material *realism*.

Charles Reade himself wore the disguise of his times so well that he fades almost completely into the background of the theatre and literature of the period. And yet in both he was successful and respected. The mirror which he held up to his world was so perfect as to be almost invisible.

BIOGRAPHICAL NOTES

1814   Born at Ipsden House, Oxfordshire, 8 June.
1822   At school under the Rev. John Slatter, Rose Hill, Iffley.
1827   At school under Mr Hearn at Staines.
1829   Studies with a 'crammer'.
1831   Matriculates at Oxford University, as a 'demy' at Magdalen College.
1835   Graduates with a third class degree in 'Greats', and later admitted as a probationary Fellow at Magdalen. Entered at Lincoln's Inn.
1838   Takes M.A. degree.
1839   Tours France and Switzerland.
1841   Becomes Junior Dean of Arts at Magdalen.
1842   Called to the Bar. Elected Vinerian Fellow at Magdalen.
1844   Bursar at Magdalen.
1846   At Edinburgh.
1847   Becomes D.C.L. at Oxford. Sells violins at Birkenhead.
1848   Visits the continent as a buyer of violins.
1849   Bursar at Magdalen.
1850   Offers the play, *Christie Johnstone*, to Mrs Stirling.
1851   Publishes *Peregrine Pickle* at his own expense. Vice-President at Magdalen. Visits Paris. Writes *The Ladies' Battle*, his first acted play. Commences *Masks and Faces* with Tom Taylor.
1852   In Paris. First venture in theatrical management at the Strand Theatre.
1852   At Malvern. At Durham; finishes *Peg Woffington*, and begins *Gold*. Finishes *Gold* at Oxford. *Masks and Faces* produced. *Peg Woffington* published. *Christie Johnstone* begun.
1853   *Gold* produced. Finishes *Christie Johnstone*, and begins *It Is Never Too Late to Mend*. Goes to live in chambers in Piccadilly, and begins writing short stories.
1854   Season at St James's theatre in joint management with Mrs Seymour, beginning in October and going on to April of following year.
1855   Working on *It Is Never Too Late to Mend*, and *The First Printer*, his fourth and last collaboration with Tom Taylor.
1856   *It Is Never Too Late to Mend* published. In Paris. Goes to live with Mrs Seymour in Mayfair. Writes *Poverty and Pride*.
1857   Writing *White Lies* (serialized in *London Journal*), then published in three volumes. Litigation over *Poverty and Pride*.
1858   Writing *Love Me Little, Love Me Long*, published in two volumes

38

in the following year. Begins *The Eighth Commandment*, published in 1860.

1859   Writing *A Good Fight* (serialized in *Once a Week*). Visits Bulwer-Lytton at Knebworth.

1860   Whole year occupied with *The Cloister and the Hearth*. Receives offer from Dickens for a story in *All the Year Round*.

1861   *The Cloister and the Hearth* published.

1862   Contracts with Dickens for a serial in *All the Year Round*. Writing *Hard Cash*.

1863   Finishes *Hard Cash* (serial in *All the Year Round*), later published in three volumes.

1864   Dramatizing *It Is Never Too Late to Mend*, which is produced the following year.

1865   Writing *Griffith Gaunt*, which is first published as a serial, and then in three volumes in 1866.

1866   Defends attacks against *Griffith Gaunt*, and starts proceedings against the *Round Table*.

1867   Works on plays: *Dora*, *Griffith Gaunt*, and *The Double Marriage*. Commences collaboration with Dion Boucicault. *Griffith Gaunt* produced at Newcastle.

1868   Finishes *Foul Play* (as a serial in *Once A Week*), which is then produced in a dramatic version by Boucicault. Contracts with George Smith for a novel. Commences *Put Yourself in His Place*.

1869   *Put Yourself in His Place* serialized in the *Cornhill Magazine* and then published in three volumes in following year. Moves to house in Knightsbridge.

1870   Dramatizes *Put Yourself in His Place* as *Free Labour*. Engaged in management of the Adelphi Theatre. Contracts for a novel with Cassell's. *A Terrible Temptation* published first as serial and then in three volumes in following year.

1871   Defends Tom Taylor against the *Athenaeum*. Controversy over *A Terrible Temptation*. Goes to Oxford and begins *A Simpleton*.

1872   Much occupied with journalism. Produces *Shilly-shally*, and quarrels with Trollope. *A Simpleton* serialized in *London Society*; writes *The Wandering Heir*, which was published in the *Graphic*. Begins libel actions against *Morning Advertiser*.

1873   Dispute with Mortimer Collins. Dramatizes *The Wandering Heir*, and engages Mrs John Wood for a provincial tour. *The Wandering Heir* afterwards produced in London.

1874   Brings Ellen Terry out of retirement. Writes letters on the Tichbourne case. Stars Ellen Terry and Forbes Robertson at Astley's. Takes Ellen Terry on provincial tour. Publishes *A Hero and a Martyr* in *Pall Mall Gazette*.

1875   Occupied with the Lambert affair, and writing *The Rights and Wrongs of Authors*. The Bancrofts revive *Masks and Faces*. Confined to his house with bronchitis.

1876   Publishes *Good Stories of Man and Other Animals* in *Belgravia*. Opens negotiations for a serial with Blackwood's, and begins *A Woman-hater* (serialized in 1876/7 and published as novel in 1877). To Oxford, then to Scotland, concluding the Lambert affair, and conducting an action against the *Glasgow Herald*. Finishes *A Woman-hater*.

1877   Revises *Foul Play* drama as *The Scuttled Ship*, and *The Courier of Lyons* as *The Lyons Mail*. At Margate. Writes *Hang in Haste: Repent at Leisure*, and secures reprieve of the Penge murderers.

1878   Agitates against demolition of Albert Terrace (where he lived), c.f. *Private Bills and Public Wrongs* and *The History of an Acre*. Published a pamphlet defending his adaptation of Tennyson's *Dora*. Adapts Sardou's *Andrée* as *Jealousy*. Produces *Joan* at Liverpool and takes it on provincial tour.

1879   Adapts Zola's *L'Assommoir* as *Drink*, and finances a provincial tour of it. Dispute with E. Romaine Callender over rights of *Drink*. Mrs Seymour dies. Meets the Rev. Charles Graham.

1880   Visits his brother William at Margate. Makes an effort to resume his work.

1881   Writes *Singleheart and Doubleface*.

1882   Collaborates with Henry Pettitt in *Love and Money*. Last venture in theatrical management.

1883   Almost fatally ill. Visits the continent. Last visit to a theatre. Finishes *A Perilous Secret*, and writes *Bible Characters*. Goes to Cannes for the winter.

1884   Returns to London, and dies on 11 April.

MASKS AND FACES: or, BEFORE AND BEHIND THE CURTAIN

Masks and Faces; or, Before and Behind the Curtain was written in collaboration with Tom Taylor, and first produced at the Haymarket Theatre on 20 November 1852, with the following cast:

SIR CHARLES POMANDER	Mr Leigh Murray
MR ERNEST VANE	Mr Parselle
COLLEY CIBBER	Mr Lambert
QUIN	Mr James Bland
TRIPLET	Mr Benjamin Webster
LYSIMACHUS TRIPLET (his son)	Master Caulfield
MR SNARL	Mr Stuart
MR SOAPER	Mr Braid
JAMES BURDOCK	Mr Rogers
COLANDER	Mr Clark
HUNDSDON	Mr Coe
CALL BOY	Mr Edwards
POMPEY	Master C. J. Smith
MRS VANE	Miss Rosa Bennett
PEG WOFFINGTON	Mrs Stirling
KITTY CLIVE	Miss Maskell
MRS TRIPLET	Mrs Leigh Murray
ROXALANA (her daughter)	Miss Caulfield
MAID	Miss E. Woulds

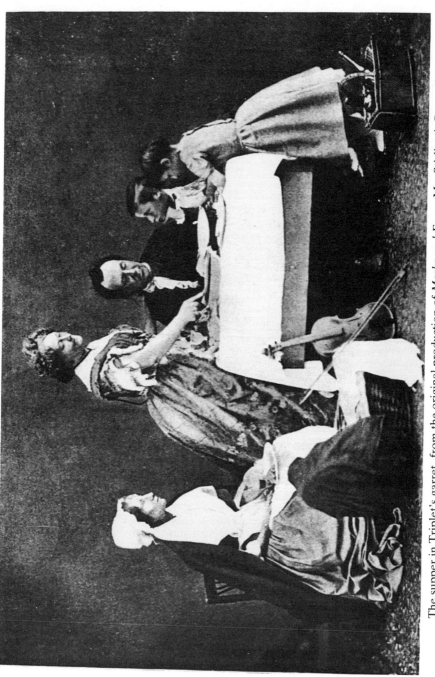

The supper in Triplet's garret, from the original production of *Masks and Faces*. Mrs Stirling is Peg and Ben Webster is Triplet

ACT I

SCENE 1. *The green room of the Theatre Royal, Covent Garden. In the centre, a large fire-place, with a looking glass above it.* MR QUIN, *and* MRS CLIVE *are seated at either side of the fire-place.*

CLIVE: Who dines with Mr Vane besides ourselves?

QUIN: His inamorata, Mrs Woffington, of this theatre.

CLIVE: Of course. But who else?

QUIN: Sir Charles Pomander. The critics, Snarl and Soaper, are invited, I believe.

CLIVE: Then I shall eat no dinner.

QUIN: Pooh! There is to be a haunch that will counterpoise in one hour a century of censure. Let them talk! The mouth will revenge the ears of Falstaff; besides, Snarl is the only ill-natured one, Soaper praises people, don't he?

CLIVE: Don't be silly, Quin! Soaper's praise is only a pin for his brother executioner to hang abuse on: by this means Snarl, who could not invent even ill-nature, is never at a loss. Snarl is his own weight in wormwood; but Soaper is – hush! – hold your tongue.
               (*Enter* SNARL *and* SOAPER. QUIN *and* CLIVE *rise.*)

CLIVE: (*with engaging sweetness*) Ah, Mr Snarl! Mr Soaper! We were talking of you.

SNARL: I am sorry for that, madam.

QUIN: We hear you dine with us at Mr Vane's.

SOAP: We have been invited, and are here to accept. I was told Mr Vane was here.

QUIN: No, but he is on the stage.

SNARL: Come, then, Soaper. (*They move towards door.*)

SOAP: (*aside*) Snarl!

SNARL: Yes. (*with a look of secret intelligence*)

SOAP: (*crossing slowly to Clive*) My dear Mrs Clive, there was I going away without telling you how charmed I was with your Flippanta; all that sweetness and womanly grace, with which you invested that character, was....

SNARL: Misplaced. Flippanta is a vixen, or she is nothing at all.

SOAP: Your Sir John Brute, sir, was a fine performance: you never forgot the gentleman even in your cups.

SNARL: Which, as Sir John Brute is the exact opposite of a gentleman, he ought to have forgotten. (*Exit.*)

SOAP: But you must excuse me now: I will resume your praise at dinner-time. (*Exit, with bows.*)

CLIVE: (*walks in a rage*) We are the most unfortunate of all artists. Nobody regards our feelings.
               (QUIN *shakes his head as, enter* CALL-BOY.)

CALL-BOY: Mr Quin and Mrs Clive!
               (*Exit* CALL-BOY.)

QUIN: I shall cut my part in this play.

CLIVE: (*yawns*) Cut it as deep as you like, there will be enough left; and so I shall tell the author if he is there. (*Exeunt* QUIN *and* CLIVE.)
               (*Enter* MR VANE *and* SIR CHARLES POMANDER.)

POM: All this eloquence might be compressed into one word – you love Mrs Margaret Woffington.

VANE: I glory in it.

POM: Why not, if it amuses you? We all love an actress once in our lives, and none of us twice.

VANE: You are the slave of a word, Sir Charles Pomander. Would you confound black and white because both are colours? Actress! Can you not see that she is a being like her fellows in nothing but a name? Her voice is truth, told by music: theirs are jingling instruments of falsehood.

POM: No – they are all instruments; but hers is more skilfully tuned and played upon.

VANE: She is a fountain of true feeling.

POM: No – a pipe that conveys it, without spilling or retaining a drop.

VANE: She has a heart alive to every emotion.

POM: And influenced by none.

VANE: She is a divinity to worship.

POM: And a woman to fight shy of. No – no – we all know Peg Woffington; she is a decent actress on the boards, and a great actress off them. But I will tell you how to add a novel charm to her. Make her blush – ask her for the list of your predecessors.

VANE: (*with a mortified air*) Sir Charles Pomander! But you yourself profess to admire her.

POM: And so I do, hugely. Notwithstanding the charms of the mysterious Hebe I told you of, whose antediluvial coach I extricated from the Slough of Despond, near Barnet, on my way to town yesterday, I gave La Woffington a proof of my devotion only two hours ago.

VANE: How?

POM: By offering her three hundred a year – house – coach – pin-money – my heart – and the etceteras.

VANE: You? But she has refused.

POM: My dear Arcadian, I am here to receive her answer. You had better wait for it before making your avowal.

VANE: That avowal is made already; but I will wait, if but to see what a lesson the calumniated actress can read to the fine gentleman.

(*Exit* VANE.)

---

the mysterious Hebe: Hebe was the personification of the Greek word for youth; she was said to be the daughter of Zeus and Hera. Here the term clearly means an attractive young lady. Classical names are used throughout the play as part of an *artistic* vocabulary, with some satirical effect perhaps both upon aestheticists and neo-classicism, but with little symbolic meaning.

Slough of Despond: an infelicitous pun upon a place name.

La Woffington: the French definite article serves to enlarge the actress's persona, and to remind us of the influence of the Parisian theatre. French terms are frequently used as a matter of style, invoking French authority and mystique.

My dear Arcadian: Arcadia was the idealized home of pastoral poetry and song, where nymphs, satyrs, shepherds and their loves lived an idyllic life of innocence and simplicity.

POM: The lesson will be set by me – Woffington will learn it immediately. It is so simple, only three words, £.s.d. (*Exit* POMANDER.)

TRIP: (*off stage*) Mr Rich not in the theatre? Well, my engagements will allow of my waiting for a few minutes.

> (*Enter* TRIPLET *and* CALL-BOY. TRIPLET *carries an unframed picture wrapped in baize.*)

TRIP: And if you will just let me know when Mr Rich arrives … (*He winks, and touches his pocket.*) Heaven forgive me for raising groundless expectations!

CALL-BOY: What name, sir?

TRIP: Mr Triplet.

CALL-BOY: Triplet! There is something left for you in the hall, sir.

> (*Exit* CALL-BOY.)

TRIP: I knew it. I sent him three tragedies. They are accepted; and he has left me a note in the hall, to fix the reading – at last. I felt it must come, soon or late; and it has come – late. Master of three arts, painting, writing, and acting, by each of which men grow fat, how was it possible I should go on perpetually starving. But that is all over now. My tragedies will be acted, the town will have an intellectual treat, and my wife and children will stab my heart no more with their hungry looks.

> (*Enter* CALL-BOY *with parcel.*)

CALL-BOY: Here is the parcel for you, sir. (*Exit* CALL-BOY.)

TRIP: (*weighs parcel in his hand*) Why, how is this? Oh, I see; he returns them for some trifling alterations. Well, if they are judicious, I shall certainly adopt them, for (*opening the parcel*) managers are practical men. My tragedies! – Eh? Here are but two! One is accepted! No! They are all here (*sighs*). Well, (*spitefully*) it is a thousand pounds out of Mr Rich's pocket, poor man! I pity him; and my hungry mouths at home. Heaven knows where I am to find bread for them tomorrow! Everything that will raise a shilling I have sold or pawned. Even my poor picture here, the portrait of Mrs Woffington from memory – I tried to sell that this morning in every dealer's at Long Acre – and not one would make me an offer.

> (*Enter* WOFFINGTON, *reciting from a part.*)

WOFF: 'Now by the joys
> Which my soul still has uncontroll'd pursued,
> I would not turn aside from my least pleasure,
> Though all thy force were armed to bar my way.

TRIP: (*aside*) Mrs Woffington, the great original of my picture!

WOFF: 'But like the birds, great nature's happy commoners
> Rifle the sweets' – I beg your pardon, sir!

TRIP: Nay, madam, pray continue; happy the hearer, and still happier the author of verses so spoken.

WOFF: Yes, if you could persuade the authors how much they owe us, and how hard it is to find good music for indifferent words. Are you an author, sir?

£:s:d: a system of British coinage. He means *money*.

TRIP: In a small way, madam. I have here three tragedies.

WOFF: (*looking down at them with comical horror*) Fifteen acts, mercy on us!

TRIP: Which if I could submit to Mrs Woffington's judgement ...

WOFF: (*recoiling*) I am no judge of such things, sir.

TRIP: No more is the manager of this theatre.

WOFF: What! Has he accepted them?

TRIP: No, madam! He has had them six months, and returned them without a word.

WOFF: Patience, my good sir, patience! Authors of tragedy should learn that virtue of their audiences. Do you know I called on Mr Rich fifteen times before I could see him?

TRIP: You, madam, impossible!

WOFF: Oh, it was some years ago – and he has had to pay a hundred pounds for each of those little visits – let me see – fifteen times ... you must write twelve more tragedies – sixty acts – and then he will read one, and give you his judgement at last, and when you have got it – it won't be worth a farthing. (*She turns away, reading her part.*)

TRIP: (*aside*) One word from this laughing lady, and all my plays would be read – but I dare not ask her; she is up in the world, I am down. She is great; I am nobody. Besides, they say she is all brains, and no heart. (*He moves sorrowfully towards the door, taking his picture.*)

WOFF: He looks like the fifth act of a domestic tragedy. Stop, surely I know that doleful face – sir!

TRIP: Madam!

WOFF: (*beckons*) We have met before – don't speak – yours is a face that has been kind to me, and I never forget those faces.

TRIP: Me, madam! I know better what is due to you than to be kind to you.

WOFF: To be sure! It is Mr Triplet, good Mr Triplet of Goodman's Fields Theatre.

TRIP: It is, madam (*opening his eyes with astonishment*); but we don't call him Mr, nor even good.

WOFF: Yes, it is Mr Triplet. (*She shakes both his hands warmly. He timidly drops a tragedy or two.*)

WOFF: Don't you remember a little orange girl at Goodman's Fields you used sometimes to pat on the head and give sixpence to, some seven years ago, Mr Triplet?

TRIP: Ha! Ha! I do remember one, with such a merry laugh and bright eye; and the broadest brogue of the whole sisterhood.

WOFF: Get along with your blarney then, Mr Triplet, an' is it the comether ye'd be puttin' on poor little Peggy?

TRIP: Oh! Oh! Gracious goodness! Oh!

WOFF: Yes, that friendless orange girl was Margaret Woffington! Well, old friend, you see time has treated me well. I hope he has been as kind to you; tell me, Mr Triplet.

TRIP: (*aside*) I must put the best face on it with her. Yes, madam, he has blessed me with an excellent wife and three charming children. Mrs Triplet was Mrs Chatterton of Goodman's Fields – great in the juvenile parts – you remember her?

WOFF: (*very drily*) Yes, I remember her; where is she acting?

TRIP: Why, the cares of our family ... and then her health ... (*sighs*). She has not acted these eight months..

WOFF: Ah! And are you still painting scenes?

TRIP: With the pen, madam, not the brush! As the wags said, I have transferred the distemper from my canvas to my imagination. Ha! Ha!

WOFF: (*aside*) This man is acting gaiety. And have your pieces been successful?

TRIP: Eminently so ... in the closet. The managers have yet excluded them from the stage.

WOFF: Ah! Now if those things were comedies, I would offer to act in one of them, and then the stage door would fly open at the sight of the author.

TRIP: I'll go home and write a comedy. (*He moves to go.*)

WOFF: On second thoughts, perhaps you had better leave the tragedies with me.

TRIP: My dear madam! And you will read them?

WOFF: Ahem! I will make poor Rich read them.

TRIP: But he has rejected them.

WOFF: That is the first step. Reading comes after, when it comes at all.

TRIP: (*aside*) I must fly home and tell my wife.

WOFF: (*aside*) In the mean time I can put five guineas into his pocket. Mr Triplet, do you write congratulatory verses – odes – and that sort of thing?

TRIP: Anything, madam, from an acrostic to an epic.

WOFF: Good, then I have a commission for you; I dine today at Mr Vane's, in Bloomsbury Square. We shall want some verses. Will you oblige us with a copy?

TRIP: (*aside*) A guinea in my way, at least. Oh, madam, do but give me a subject.

WOFF: Let's see – myself, if you can write on such a theme.

TRIP: 'Tis the one I would have chosen out of all the heathen mythology; the praises of Venus and the Graces. I will set about it at once. (*He takes up the portrait.*)

WOFF: (*seeing the picture*) But what have you there? Not another tragedy?

TRIP: (*blushing*) A poor thing, madam, a portrait – my own painting, from memory.

WOFF: Oh! Oh! I'm a judge of painted faces; let me see it.

TRIP: Nay, madam!

WOFF: I insist! (*She takes off the baize.*) My own portrait, as I live! And a good likeness too, or my glass flatters me like the rest of them. And this you painted from memory?

TRIP: Yes, madam; I have a free admission to every part of the theatre before the curtain. I have so enjoyed your acting, that I have carried your face home with me every night, forgive my presumption, and tried to fix in the studio the impression of the stage.

WOFF: Do you know your portrait has merit? I will give you a sitting for the last touches.

---

transferred the distemper: a pun. Distemper was both a kind of paint and a poor humour.
five guineas: a quite large sum of money in terms of personal expenditure.
in Bloomsbury Square: an elevated and artistic part of nineteenth-century London.
a judge of painted faces: a pun. The paint refers to stage make-up as well as to the artist's medium.
my glass flatters: a looking-glass, a mirror.
a free admission: a professional privilege, much argued over.

TRIP: Oh, madam!

WOFF: And bring all the critics – there, no thanks or I'll stay away. Stay, I must have your address.

TRIP: (*returning*) On the fly leaf of each work, madam, you will find the address of James Triplet, painter, actor, and dramatic author, and Mrs Woffington's humble and devoted servant. (*He bows ridiculously low, moves away, but returns with an attempt at a jaunty manner.*) Madam, you have inspired a son of Thespis with dreams of eloquence; you have tuned to a higher key a poet's lyre; you have tinged a painter's existence with brighter colours; and – and – (*he gazes on her and tries in vain to speak*) God in heaven bless you, Mrs Woffington. (*Exit* TRIPLET, *hastily.*)

WOFF: So! I must look into this!

(*Enter* SIR CHARLES POMANDER.)

POM: Ah, Mrs Woffington, I have just parted with an adorer of yours.

WOFF: I wish I could part with them all.

POM: Nay, this is a most original admirer, Ernest Vane, that pastoral youth who means to win La Woffington by agricultural courtship, who wants to take the star from its firmament, and stick it in a cottage.

WOFF: And what does the man think I am to do without this (*she imitates applause*) from my dear public's thousand hands.

POM: You are to have that from a single mouth instead (*he mimics a kiss*).

WOFF: Go on, tell me what more he says.

POM: Why, he –

WOFF: No, you are not to invent; I should detect your work in a minute, and you would only spoil this man.

POM: He proposes to be your friend, rather than your lover; to fight for your reputation instead of adding to your éclat.

WOFF: Oh! And is Mr Vane your friend?

POM: He is!

WOFF: (*with significance*) Why don't you tell him my real character, and send him into the country again!

POM: I do, but he snaps his fingers at me and common sense and the world: there is no getting rid of him except in one way. I had this morning the honour, madam, of laying certain propositions at your feet.

WOFF: Oh, yes, your letter, Sir Charles (*she takes it out of her pocket*). I ran my eye down it as I came along. Let me see, (*she reads*) a coach, a country house, pin-money. Heigh ho! And I am *so* tired of houses, and coaches, and pins. Oh, yes, here *is* something. What is this you offer me, up in this corner?

(*They examine the letter together.*)

POM: That – my heart!

WOFF: And you can't even write it; it looks just like 'earth'. There is your letter, Sir Charles. (*She curtseys and returns it; he takes it and bows.*)

POM: Favour me with your answer.

---

son of Thespis: Thespis was a poet of the sixth century B.C., traditionally the inventor of ancient Greek drama.
take the star from its firmament: a pun; 'star' refers also to a celebrated actor.

WOFF: You have it.

POM: (*laughing*) Tell me, do you really refuse?

WOFF: (*inspecting him*) Acting surprise? No, genuine! My good soul, are you so ignorant of the stage and the world, as not to know that I refuse such offers as yours every week of my life? I have refused so many of them, that I assure you I have begun to forget they are insults.

POM: Insults, madam! They are the highest compliment you have left it in our power to pay you.

WOFF: Indeed! Oh, I take your meaning. To be your mistress would be but a temporary disgrace; to be your wife might be a lasting discredit. Now, sir, having played your rival's game . . .

POM: Ah!

WOFF: And exposed your own hand, do something to recover the reputation of a man of the world. Leave the field before Mr Vane can enjoy your discomfiture, for here he comes.

POM: I leave you, madam, but remember, my discomfiture is neither your triumph nor your swain's. (*Exit.*)

WOFF: I do enjoy putting down these irresistibles.
       (*Enter* VANE.)

WOFF: At last! I have been here so long.

VANE: Alone?

WOFF: In company and solitude. What has annoyed you?

VANE: Nothing.

WOFF: Never try to conceal anything from me. I know the map of your face. These fourteen days you have been subject to some adverse influence; and today I have discovered whose it is.

VANE: No influence can ever shake yours.

WOFF: Dear friend, for your own sake, not mine; trust your own heart, eyes, and judgement.

VANE: I do. I love you; your face is the shrine of sincerity, truth, and candour. I alone know you: your flatterers do not, your detractors – oh, curse them!

WOFF: You see what men are! Have I done ill to hide the riches of my heart from the heartless, and keep them all for one honest man, who will be my friend, I hope, as well as my lover?

VANE: Ah, that is my ambition.

WOFF: We actresses make good the old proverb, 'Many lovers, but few friends'. And, oh, it is we who need a friend. Will you be mine?

VANE: I will. Then tell me the way for me, unequal in wit and address to many of your admirers, to win your esteem.

WOFF: I will tell you a sure way; never act in my presence, never try to be very clever or eloquent. Remember! I am the goddess of tricks; I can only love my superior. Be honest and frank as the day, and you will be my superior; and I shall love you, and bless the hour you shone on my artficial life.

VANE: Oh, thanks, thanks, for this, I trust, is in my power!

WOFF: Mind – it is no easy task: to be my friend is to respect me, that I may respect myself the more; to be my friend is to come between me and the temptations of an unprotected life – the recklessness of a vacant heart.

VANE: I will place all that is good about me at your feet. I will sympathize with you when you are sad; I will rejoice when you are gay.

WOFF: Will you scold me when I do wrong?

VANE: Scold you?

WOFF: Nobody scolds me now – a sure sign nobody loves me. Will you scold me?

VANE: (*tenderly*) I will try! And I will be loyal and frank. You will not hate me for a confession I make myself (*agitated*)?

WOFF: I shall like you better – oh, so much better!

VANE: Then I will own to you –

WOFF: Oh, do not tell me you have loved others before me; I could not bear to hear it.

VANE: No – no – I never *loved* till now.

WOFF: Let me hear that only. I am jealous even of the past. Say you never loved but me, never mind whether it is true, say so; but it is true, for you do not yet know love. Ernest, shall I make you love me, as none of your sex ever loved? With heart, and brain, and breath, and life, and soul?

VANE: Teach me so to love, and I am yours for ever. (*Pauses.*) And now you will keep your promise, to make me happy with your presence this morning at the little festival I had arranged with Cibber and some of our friends of the theatre.

WOFF: I shall have so much pleasure; but, apropos, you must include Snarl and Soaper in your list.

VANE: What! The redoubtable Aristarchuses of the pit?

WOFF: Yes. Oh, you don't know the consequences of loving an actress. You will have to espouse my quarrels, manage my managers, and invite my critics to dinner.

VANE: They shall be invited, never fear.

WOFF: And I've a trust for you; poor Triplet's three tragedies. If they are as heavy in the hearing as the carrying ... But here comes your rival, poor Pomander.
(*Enter* SIR CHARLES.)

WOFF: You will join our party at Mr Vane's, Sir Charles? You promised, you know.

POM: (*coldly*) Désolé to forfeit such felicity; but I have business.

VANE: By-the-bye, Pomander, that answer to your letter to Mrs Woffington?

WOFF: He has received it. N'est-ce pas, Sir Charles? You see how radiant it has made him! Ha! Ha! (*Exeunt* WOFFINGTON *and* VANE.)

POM: Laughing devil! If you had wit to read beneath men's surface, you would know it is no jest to make an enemy of Sir Charles Pomander.
(*Enter* HUNDSDON.)

HUNDS: Servant, Sir Charles.

POM: Ah, my yeoman pricker, with news of the mysterious Hebe of my Barnet rencontre. Well, sirrah, you stayed by the coach as I bade you?

HUNDS: Yes, Sir Charles.

Aristarchuses of the pit: Aristarchus was an ancient grammarian and critic, celebrated for his severity.

my yeoman pricker: a pricker was a light-horseman.

POM: And pumped the servants?

HUNDS: Yes, Sir Charles, till they swore they'd pump on me.

POM: My good fellow, contrive to answer my questions without punning, will you?

HUNDS: Yes, Sir Charles.

POM: What did you learn from them? Who is the lady, their mistress?

HUNDS: She is on her way to town to join her husband. They have only been married a twelvemonth; and he has been absent from her half the time.

POM: Good. Her name?

HUNDS: Vane.

POM: Vane!

HUNDS: Wife of Mr Ernest Vane, a gentleman of good estate, Willoughby Manor, Huntingdonshire.

POM: What! – What! – His wife, by heavens! Oh, here is a rare revenge! Ride back, sirrah, and follow the coach to its destination.

HUNDS: They took master for a highwayman. If they knew him as well as I do, they wouldn't do the road such an injustice. (*Exit.*)

POM: (*with energy*) I'll after them; and if I can but manage that Vane shall remain ignorant of her arrival, I may confront Hebe with Thalia; introduce the wife to the mistress under the husband's roof. Aha! My Arcadian pair, there may be a guest at your banquet you little expect, besides Sir Charles Pomander! (*Exit.*)

SCENE 2. *A spacious and elegant apartment in the house of Mr Vane, opening into a formally planted garden with statues etc. A table set for a collation with fruit, flowers, wine, and plate. A central door communicates with the entrance hall, and there are other doors to left and right. There are settees and high backed chairs.* COLANDER *is discovered arranging the table.*

COL: So! Malmsey, fruit, tea, coffee. Yes, all is ready against their leaving the dining-room!

(*Enter* BURDOCK, *a salver with letters in his hand.*)

BUR: Post letters, Master Colander.

COL: Put 'em on the salver. You may go, honest Burdock. (BURDOCK *fidgets, turning the letters on the salver.*) When I say you *may* go – that means you *must*; the stable is your place when the family is not in Huntingdonshire, and at present the family is in London.

BUR: And I wish it was in Huntingdonshire, with the best part of it, and that's the mistress. Poor thing! A twelvemonth married, and six months of it as good as a widow.

COL: We write to her, James, and receive her replies.

BUR: Aye! But we don't read 'em it seems.

COL: We intend to do so at our leisure – meanwhile we make ourselves happy among the wits and the players.

---

pumped the servants: extracted information by prolonged interrogation

pump on me: a pun. A suitable discouragement for bailiffs and the like was to drench them with water.

confront Hebe with Thalia: Thalia was one of the Muses who presided over festivals together with pastoral and comic poetry.

BUR: And she do make others happy among the poor and the suffering.

COL: James Burdock, property has its duties, as well as its rights. Master enjoys the rights in town, and mistress discharges the duties in the country; 'tis the division of labour – and now vanish, honest James, the company will be here directly, and you know master cannot abide the smell of the stable.

BUR: But, Master Colander, do let him have this letter from missus. (*He holds out a letter he has taken from the salver.*)

COL: James Burdock, you are incorrigible. Have I not given it to him once already? And didn't he fling it in my face and call me a puppy? I respect Mistress Vane, James; but I must remember what's due to myself – I shan't take it. (*Exit* COLANDER.)

BUR: Then I will – there! Poor dear lady! I can't abear that her letters, with her heart in 'em, I'll be sworn, should lie unopened. Barnet post mark! Why, how can that be? Well, it's not my business. (*He puts the salver on a table.*) Master shall have it though. (*A hurried knocking is heard.*) There goes that door. Ah, I thought it wouldn't be quiet long! What a rake-helly place this London is!

> (*Exit* BURDOCK. *He re-enters with* MRS VANE *in a hood and travelling dress.*)

BUR: Stop! Stop! I don't think master can see you, young woman.

MABEL: Why, James Burdock, have you forgotten your mistress? (*She removes her hood.*)

BUR: Mistress! Why, Miss Mabel – I ask your pardon, miss – I mean, madam. Bless your sweet face! Here, John, Thomas!

MABEL: Hush!

BUR: Lord, lord, come at last! Oh, how woundy glad I am, to be sure. Oh, lord, lord, my old head's all of a muddle with joy to see your kind face again.

MABEL: But Ernest – Mr Vane, James, is he well – and happy – and (*seeing his change of face*) – Eh! He is well, James?

BUR: Yes, yes, quite well, and main happy.

MABEL: And is he very impatient to see me?

BUR: (*aside*) Lord help her!

MABEL: But mind, James, not a word; he doesn't expect me till six, and 'tis now scarce four. Oh, I shall startle him so!

BUR: Yes, yes, madam; you'll startle him woundily.

MABEL: Oh, it will be so delightful to pop out upon him unawares – will it not, James?

BUR: Yes, Miss Mabel – that is, madam; but hadn't I better prepare him like?

MABEL: Not for the world. You know, James, when one is wishing for anyone very much, the last hour's waiting is always the most intolerable, so when he is most longing to see me, and counting the minutes to six, I'll just open the door, and steal behind him, and fling my arms round his neck, and – but I shall be caught if I stay prattling here, and I must brush the dust from my hair, and smooth my dress, or I shall not be fit to be seen; so not a word to anybody, James, I insist,

---

how woundy glad: 'woundy' meant 'excessively'.

or I shall be angry. Where is my room? (*She opens the door on the right.*) Oh, here!

BUR: Your room, Miss Mabel; no! no! That is Mr Vane's room, ma'am.

MABEL: Well, Mr Vane's room is my room, I suppose (*pausing at the door*). He is not there, is he?

BUR: No, ma'am, he is in the dining-room. (*There is a knock.*) Anon! Anon!

MABEL: I fear my trunks will not be here in time for me to dress; but Ernest will not mind. He will see my heart in my face, and forgive my travelling sacque. (*Exit.*)

BUR: Poor thing! Poor thing! (*A knocking.*) There goes that door again – darn me if I go till I've seen Colander. Anon – Miss Mabel! (*He goes to the door.*)

(*Enter* HUNDSDON.)

HUNDS: (*aside, and looking at* BURDOCK) For all the world the twin brother to those bumpkins behind Hebe's coach. Well, my honest fellow!

BUR: Well, my jack-a-dandy!

HUNDS: Can'st bring me Sir Charles Pomander hither, my honest fellow?

BUR: Here he's a bringing himself, my jack-a-dandy. (*Exit.*)

HUNDS: For so pretty a creature, she hath an establishment of the veriest brutes. Ah, here comes my master!

(*Enter* SIR CHARLES POMANDER.)

POM: Well! Is she arrived?

HUNDS: (*aside to* POMANDER) I've marked her down, sir. She is here – in that room.

POM: Is her arrival known?

HUNDS: But to a rustic savage of a servant.

POM: Good! Take thy sheep's face out of sight, incontinently.

HUNDS: Yes, Sir Charles.

POM: Hold! I have kept thee sober for two days. Here's for thee to make a beast of thyself.

HUNDS: Nay, I'll disappoint him, and profit by sobriety. (*Exit.*)

POM: So, the train is laid, and I hold the match in my hand.

(COLANDER *returns with servants who bring tea, coffee, etcetera.* Enter VANE, WOFFINGTON, QUIN, CLIVE, CIBBER, SNARL, and SOAPER, *as from the dining-room, laughing.*)

QUIN: I hate this detestable innovation of outlandish drawing-room drinks – your tea and coffee – pshaw!

VANE: But you forget the ladies, Mr Quin, and in the presence of Mr Cibber too, whom I cannot thank enough for the honour of this visit.

CIBBER: Nay, sir, I bring my wit in exchange for your wine; we barter our respective superfluities.

---

jack-a-dandy: a little fop; an insignificant fellow. An unfavourable contrast with the country bumpkin is being made.
marked her down: the terminology of the hunt is used to indicate that he had tracked her to her location. Several hunting terms follow, their meanings obvious.
train is laid: a line of gunpowder to act as a fuse.

QUIN: Good wine is no superfluity, Mr Cibber; 'tis a necessary of life, just as much as good victuals.

SOAP: I vow Mr Cibber is as lively as ever, and doesn't look a day older: does he, Mr Snarl?

SNARL: 'Tis that there's no room on Mr Cibber's face for another wrinkle.

CIBBER: (*taking snuff*) Puppies!

QUIN: Really this is too bad, the coffee is getting cold.

CLIVE: So, no wonder Quin is getting warm (*gives him coffee*) – Here, bear! (WOFFINGTON *presides over tea.*)

CIBBER: You have a charming house here, Mr Vane, I knew it in poor dear Lord Loungeville's time. You may just remember him, Sir Charles?

POM: I never read ancient history.

CIBBER: An unrivalled gallant, Peggy. Oh, the *petits soupers* we have had here! Loungeville was a great creature, Sir Charles. I wish you may ever be like him.

POM: I sincerely trust not. I do not feel at all anxious to figure in the museum of town antiquities labelled 'Old Beau, very curious'.

CIBBER: (*aside*) Coxcomb! Let me tell you your old beaux were the only ones worthy of winging the shafts from Cupid's quiver.

SNARL: Witness Mr Cibber.

WOFF: Oh, Colley is like old port – the more ancient he grows the more exquisite his perfume becomes.

SOAP: Capital! She alludes to Mr Cibber's pulvilio.

SNARL: And the crustier he gets.

SOAP: Delicious! He alludes to Mr Cibber's little irritability.

CIBBER: Ah, laugh at us old fellows, young people; but I have known Loungeville entertain a fine lady in this very saloon, whilst a rival was fretting and fuming on the other side of that door. Ha, ha! (*He sighs.*) It is all over now.

POM: Nay, Mr Cibber, why assume that the house has lost its virtue in our friend's hands?

CIBBER: Because, young gentleman, you all want *savoir faire*; the fellows of the day are all either unprincipled heathens like you, or cold blooded Amadisses like our host. The true *Preux des Dames*, (*regretfully*) went out with the full periwig, stap my vitals!

QUIN: A bit of toast, Mr Cibber?

CIBBER: Jemmy, you are a brute.

QUIN: You refuse, sir?

CIBBER: (*with dignity*) No, sir, I accept. (QUIN *places a plate of toast on the table.*)

POM: You Antediluvians must not flatter yourselves you have monopolized iniquity, or that the deluge washed away intrigue, and that a rake is a fossil. We are still as vicious as you could desire, Mr Cibber. What if I bet a cool hundred pound

---

shafts from Cupid's quiver: Cupid, the Roman god of love, hit those he inspired with love with arrows.

Mr Cibber's pulvilio: pulvilio is a cushion or an architectural convexity. The physical effects of Cibber's good living are indicated.

cold blooded Amadisses: an ancient warrior.

Preux des Dames: a gallant.

that Vane has a petticoat in the next room, and Mrs Woffington shall bring her out.

VANE: Pomander! (*He checks himself.*) But we all know Pomander.

POM: Not yet, *but you shall.* Now don't look so abominably innocent, my dear fellow, I ran her to earth in this house not ten minutes ago.

CIBBER: Have her out, Peggy! I know the run – there's the cover – hark forward! Yoicks! Ha, ha, ha! (*coughing*) Ho, ho!

VANE: Mr Cibber, age and infirmity are privileged; but for you, Sir Charles Pomander –

WOFF: Don't be angry. Do you not see it is a jest, and, as might be expected, a sorry one?

VANE: A jest; it must go no farther, or by heaven!

(WOFFINGTON *places her hand on his shoulder.* MABEL *appears.*)

MABEL: Ernest, dear Ernest! (WOFFINGTON *removes her hand quickly.*)

VANE: Mabel!

POM: I win (*a pause of silent amazement*).

(VANE *looks round on the reverse side from* WOFFINGTON.)

WOFF: (*aside to* VANE) Who is this?

VANE: My – my wife!

(*All rise and bow.* COLANDER *places chair for* MRS VANE.)

CIBBER: 'Fore Gad, he is stronger than Loungeville!

MABEL: You are not angry with me for this silly trick? After all, I am but two hours before my time. You know, dearest, I said six in my letter.

VANE: Yes – yes!

MABEL: And you have had three days to prepare you, for I wrote like a good wife to ask leave before starting, ladies and gentlemen; but he never so much as answered my letter, madam (*to* WOFFINGTON, *who winces*).

VANE: Why, you c – c – couldn't doubt, Mabel?

MABEL: No, silence gives consent; but I beg your pardon, ladies (*looking to* WOFFINGTON), for being so glad to see my husband.

SNARL: 'Tis a failing, madam, you will soon get over in town (*laugh*).

MABEL: Nay, sir, I hope not; but I warrant me you did not look for me so soon.

WOFF: Some of us did not look for you at all.

MABEL: What! Ernest did not tell you he expected me?

WOFF: No; he told us the entertainment was in honour of a lady's first visit to his house; but he did *not* tell us that lady was his wife.

VANE: (*aside to* WOFFINGTON) Spare her!

WOFF: (*aside to* VANE) Have you spared me?

POM: No doubt he wished to procure us that agreeable surprise, which you have procured him.

SNARL: And which he evidently enjoys so much.

SOAP: Oh, evidently.

(CIBBER, SOAPER, *and* SNARL *laugh, aside.*)

VANE: You had better retire, Mabel, and change your travelling dress.

MABEL: Nay, you forget, I am a stranger to your friends. Will you not introduce me to them first?

VANE: No, no; it is not usual to introduce in the polite world.

WOFF: We always introduce ourselves (*she rises*).
        (*All come down except* VANE *and* QUIN.)
VANE: (*aside to* WOFFINGTON) Madam, for pity's sake!
WOFF: So, if you will permit me.
POM: (*aside*) Now for the explosion!
VANE: (*aside*) She will show me no mercy.
WOFF: (*introducing* CLIVE) Lady Lurewell!
CLIVE: Madam! (*She curtsies.*) If she had made me a commoner, I'd have exposed
    her on the spot.
WOFF: (*introducing* QUIN) Sir John Brute!
QUIN: (*coming forward, aside to* WOFFINGTON) Hang it! Falstaff!
WOFF: Sir John Brute Falstaff! We call him for brevity, Brute.
POM: (*aside*) Missed fire! Confound her ready wit.
VANE: (*aside*) I breathe again.
WOFF: That is Lord Foppington (*crossing to* CIBBER), a butterfly of long standing
    and a little gouty. Sir Charles Pomander!
POM: Who will spare you the trouble of a description (*crossing to* MABEL), as he
    has already had the honour of avowing himself Mrs Vane's most humble
    servant.
VANE: How?
MABEL: The good gentleman who helped my coach out of the slough yesterday.
VANE: Ah!
WOFF: Mr Soaper and Mr Snarl – gentlemen who would butter and cut up their own
    fathers!
MABEL: Bless me; cannibals!
WOFF: (*with a sweet smile*) No, critics.
MABEL: But yourself, madam?
WOFF: (*curtseying*) I am Lady Betty Modish, at your service.
CLIVE: (*aside to* QUIN) And anybody else's.
MABEL: Oh, dear, so many lords and ladies!
VANE: Pray go, and change your dress, Mabel.
MABEL: What! Before you hear the news of dear Willoughby, Ernest? Lady Betty,
    I had so many things to tell him, and he sends me away.
CIBBER: Nay, really, 'tis too cruel.
WOFF: Pray, madam, your budget of country news: clotted cream so seldom comes
    to London quite fresh.
MABEL: There you see Ernest. First, then, Grey Gillian is turned out for a brood
    mare, so old George won't let me ride her.
WOFF: The barbarian!
MABEL: Old servants are such hard masters, my lady; and my Barbary hen has laid
    two eggs, Ernest. Heaven knows the trouble we have had to bring her to it.
    And dame Best (that's his old nurse, Lady Lurewell) has had soup and
    pudding from the hall every day.
QUIN: Soup and pudding! That's what I call true charity.
MABEL: Yes, and once she went so far as to say, 'It wasn't altogether a bad
    pudding.' I made it with these hands.
CIBBER: Happy pudding!

VANE: Is this mockery, sir?

CIBBER: No, sir, it is gallantry; an exercise that died before you were born. Madam, shall I have the honour of kissing one of the fair hands that made that most favoured of puddings?

MABEL: Oh, my Lord, you may, because you are so old; but I don't say so for a young gentleman, unless it was Ernest himself, and he doesn't ask me.

VANE: (*angrily*) My dear Mabel, pray remember we are not at Willoughby.

CLIVE: Now, bear, where's your paw?

QUIN: All I regret is, that I go without having helped Mrs Vane to buttered toast.

CLIVE: Poor Quin, first to quit his bottle half finished, and now, to leave the run of the table for a walk in the garden! (*Exeunt.*)

VANE: Let me show you to your apartment (*rings bell and leads her to door on the right*).

(*Enter* SERVANT.)

VANE: Bid the musicians play. (*Exit* SERVANT. VANE *offers his arm to* WOFFINGTON.) Let me conduct you to the garden. (*Music plays.* WOFFINGTON *gives her hand to* VANE, *and as they leave, she looks back.*)

WOFF: (*aside*) Yes; there are triumphs out of the theatre. (*Exit.*)

CIBBER: (*to* MABEL) Mr Vane's garden will lack its fairest flower, madam, if you desert us.

MABEL: Nay, my Lord, there are fairer here than I.

POM: Jealous, I see, already. Shall I tell her all? I will let the green-eyed monster breach the fortress, and then I shall walk in without a contest.

CIBBER: (*meeting* POMANDER) Your arm, Sir Charles.

POM: At your service, Mr Cibber. (*Exeunt* POMANDER *and* CIBBER.)

SNARL: A pleasant party, Mr Soaper.

SOAP: Remarkably. Such a delightful meeting of husband and wife, Mr Snarl. (*Exeunt. The music stops.*)

MABEL: How kind they all are to me, except him whose kindness alone I value, and he must take Lady Betty's hand instead of mine; but that is good breeding I suppose. I wish there was no such thing as good breeding in London, any more than in Huntingdonshire.

COL: (*offstage, and angrily*) I tell you Mr Vane is not at home.

MABEL: What is the matter?

(TRIPLET *attempts to force his way in.* COLANDER *bars his entrance.* TRIPLET *carries a portfolio, two volumes, and a roll of manuscript.*)

COL: I tell you he is not at home, sir.

MABEL: How can you say so, when you know he is in the garden.

COL: Ugh! (*aside*) the simpleton.

MABEL: Show the gentleman in.

COL: Gentleman!

TRIP: A thousand thanks, madam, for this condescension; I will wait Mr Vane's leisure in the hall.

---

green-eyed monster: jealousy.

MABEL: Nay, sir, not in the hall, 'tis cold there. Tell Mr Vane the gentleman waits. Will you go, sirrah?

COL: I am gone, madam. (*aside*) Porter to players! And now usher to an author! Curse me if I stand it. (*Exit*.)

TRIP: A thousand apologies, madam, for the trouble I put you to. I – madam – you overwhelm me with confusion.

MABEL: Nay, nay, be seated.

TRIP: Madam, you are too condescending. (*aside*) Who can she be? (*He bows repeatedly*.)

MABEL: Nay, sit down and rest you. (TRIPLET *bows, and sits on the edge of a chair, astonished*.) You look sadly adust and tired.

TRIP: Why, yes, madam; it is a long way from Lambeth; and the heat is surpassing. (*He mops his brow with his handkerchief, which he returns hastily to his pocket*.) I beg your pardon, I forgot myself.

MABEL: (*aside*) Poor man, he looks sadly lean and hungry. And I'll be bound you came in such a hurry, you forgot – you mustn't be angry with me – to have your dinner first.

TRIP: How strange! Madam, you have guessed it. I did forget – he, he! – I have such a head – not that I need have forgotten it – but being used to forget it, I did not remember not to forget it today. (*He smiles absurdly*.)

MABEL: (*pouring wine*) A glass of wine, sir?

TRIP: (*rising and bowing*) Nay, madam. (*He eyes the wine, and drinks*.) Nectar, as I am a man. (MABEL *helps* TRIPLET *to refreshments*.)

MABEL: Take a biscuit, sir?

TRIP: Madam, as I said before, you overwhelm me. Walking certainly makes one hungry. Oh, yes, it certainly does. (MABEL *helps him to more*.) And though I do not usually eat at this time of the day . . . (MABEL *helps him again*.)

MABEL: I am sorry Mr Vane keeps you waiting.

TRIP: By no means, madam, it is very fortunate (*eats*) – I mean it procures me the pleasure of (*eats*) your society. Besides, the servants of the Muse are used to waiting. What we are not used to is (*she fills his glass*) being waited on by Hebe and the Twelve Graces, whose health I have the honour! . . . Falernian, as I'm a poet!

MABEL: A poet! (*clapping her hands*). Oh, I am so glad! I never thought to see a living poet; I do so love poetry!

TRIP: Ha! It is in your face, madam. I should be proud to have your opinion of this trifle composed by me for Mr Vane, in honour of the lady he expected this morning.

MABEL: (*aside*) Dear Ernest! How ungrateful I was. Nay, sir, I think I know the lady; and it would be hardly proper for me to hear them.

TRIP: (*laying his MS by the side of his plate, with another plate to keep it open, his hand on his heart*) Oh, strictly correct, madam. James Triplet never stooped to the loose taste of the town, even in trifles of this sort. (*He reads*.) 'When first from Albion's isle – '

MABEL: Take another glass of wine first.

---

a long way from Lambeth: a poor quarter of London.
Falernian, as I'm a poet: a celebrated wine from ancient Campania.

TRIP: Madam, I will. (*He drinks.*) I thank you infinitely. (*He reads.*) 'When first from Albion's isle – '

MABEL: Another biscuit.

TRIP: Madam (*eating a mouthful*), you do me infinite honour. (*He reads.*) 'When first from Albion's isle – '

MABEL: No – no – no! (*She stops her ears.*) Mr Vane intended them for a surprise, and it would spoil his pleasure were I to hear them from you.

TRIP: (*sighing*) As you please, madam! But you would have liked them, for the theme inspired me. The kindest, the most generous and gifted of women! Don't you agree with me, madam?

MABEL: (*laughing*) No, indeed!

TRIP: Ah, if you knew her as I do.

MABEL: I ought to know her better, sir.

TRIP: Her kindness to me, for instance: a poor devil like me, if I may be allowed the expression.

MABEL: Nay, you exaggerate her trifling act of civility.

TRIP: (*reproachfully*) Act of civility, madam! Why she has saved me from despair – from starvation perhaps.

MABEL: (*aside*) Poor thing! How hungry he must have been.

TRIP: And she's to sit to me for her portrait, too.

MABEL: Her portrait! (*Aside*) Oh, another attention of Ernest's – but I thought you were a poet, sir?

TRIP: So I am, madam, from an epitaph to an epic. Let me convince you. (*He reads.*) 'When first from Albion's isle – '

MABEL: But you spoke just now of painting. Are you a painter too?

TRIP: From a scene to a sign-board; from a house-front to an historical composition.

MABEL: Oh, what a clever man! And so Ernest commissioned you to paint this portrait?

TRIP: No; for that I am indebted to the lady herself.

MABEL: The lady? (*She rises.*)

TRIP: I expected to find her here. Perhaps you can inform me whether she has arrived?

MABEL: (*aside*) Not my portrait after all. Who?

TRIP: Mrs Woffington.

MABEL: Woffington? No, there was no such name among the guests Mr Vane received today.

TRIP: That is strange! She was to be here; and therefore I expedited the verses in her honour.

MABEL: (*ruefully*) In *her* honour?

TRIP: Yes, madam: the subject is 'Genius Trampling on Envy'. It begins: 'When first from Albion's Isle – '

MABEL: Nay, I do not care to hear them, for I do not know the lady.

TRIP: Few really know her; but at least you have seen her act.

MABEL: Act! Is she an actress?

TRIP: *An* actress, madam! *The* actress! And you have never seen her! Madam, you have a great pleasure before you; to see her act is a privilege, but to act with her, as I once did, though she doesn't remember it – I was hissed, madam, owing to circumstances which for the credit of our common nature I suppress.

MABEL: An actor too!

TRIP: And it was in a farce of my own too, madam, which was damned – accidentally.

MABEL: And a play-writer?

TRIP: Plays, madam! I have written a library of them; but the madmen who manage the patent houses won't act them and make their fortunes. You see in me a dramatic gold mine, lost because no company will work me.

MABEL: Yes, yes; but tell me, this actress – Mr Vane admires her?

TRIP: Mr Vane is a gentleman of taste, madam.

MABEL: And she was to have been here? There were none but persons of quality – ah, the news of my intended arrival, no doubt . . . Well, Mr –

TRIP: Triplet, madam! James Triplet, 10, Hercules Buildings, Lambeth: occasional verses, odes, epithalamia, elegies, dedications, translations, and every species of literary composition executed with spirit, punctuality, and secrecy. Portraits painted, and lessons given in declamation and the dramatic art. The card, madam (*presents card*), of him who, to all these qualifications adds a prouder still – that of being your humble, devoted, and truly grateful servant – James Triplet. (*He bows, and moves off, but returns.*) The fact is, madam, it may appear strange to you, but a kind hand has not so often been held out to me, that I should forget it, especially when that hand is so fair and gracious as yours. May I be permitted, madam? (*He puts her hand to his lips.*) You will impute it to gratitude rather than audacity – madam, I am gone. I flatter myself James Triplet, throughout this charming interview, has conducted himself like what he may not appear to be – a gentleman. Madam, I take my final leave. (*Exit.*)

MABEL: Invite an actress to his house! But Ernest is so warm-hearted and generous; no doubt 'tis as Mr Triplet says; he has admired her acting and wished to mark his sense of her merit by presenting her these verses and a dinner. (*Music plays.*) These poor actors and actresses! I have seen some of them down in Huntingdonshire, and I know what a kindness it is to give them a good meal.

(*Enter* SIR CHARLES POMANDER.)

POM: What, madam, all alone, here as in Huntingdonshire! Force of habit. A husband with a wife in Huntingdonshire is so like a bachelor.

MABEL: Sir!

POM: And our excellent Ernest is such a favourite.

MABEL: No wonder.

POM: There are not many who can so pass in six months from the larva state of bumpkin to the butterfly existence of beau. (*The music ceases.*)

MABEL: Yes; (*sadly*) I find him changed.

POM: Changed? Transformed! He is now the prop of the cocoa-tree, the star of Ranelagh, the Lauzun of the green room.

MABEL: The green room?

POM: Ah, I forgot! You are fresh from Eden; the green room, my dear madam, is the bower where fairies put off their wings and goddesses become dowdies –

where Lady Macbeth weeps over her lap-dog's indigestion, and Belvidera groans over the amount of her last milliner's bill. In a word, the green room is the place where actors and actresses become mere men and women, and the name is no doubt derived from the general character of its unprofessional visitors.

MABEL: And is it possible that Ernest, Mr Vane, frequents such places?

POM: He has earned in six months a reputation that many a fine gentleman would give his ears for – not a scandalous journal he has not figured in – not an actress of reputation or no reputation, but gossip has given him for a conquest.

MABEL: You forget, sir, you are speaking to his wife.

POM: On the contrary, madam; but you would be sure to learn this, and it is best you should learn it at once and from a friend.

MABEL: It is the office of a friend to calumniate the husband to the wife?

POM: When he admires the wife, he reprobates the husband's ill-taste in neglecting her.

MABEL: Do you suppose I did not know of his having invited Mrs Woffington to his house today?

POM: What! You found her out? You detected the actress-of-all-work under the airs of Lady Betty Modish.

MABEL: Lady Betty Modish!

POM: Yes; that was La Woffington.

MABEL: Whom he had invited hither to present her with a copy of verses.

POM: Et cetera.

MABEL: And who in an actress's sudden frolic, gave herself and her companions those titles without my husband's connivance.

POM: Vane could not have explained it half so well. These women are incredibles.

MABEL: Had the visit been in any other character, do you think he would have chosen it for the day of my arrival?

POM: Certainly not, if he knew you were coming.

MABEL: And he did know; why here (*seeing letters on the table*) are my letters announcing my intention to start – my progress on the road – the last written from Barnet, only yesterday.

> (*While speaking she has gone to the salver, and hastily taken the letters, which she offers to* POMANDER *with triumph. He takes them with an uncertain air, looks at them, gives them back to her.*)

POM: (*after a pause, coolly*) The seals have not been broken, madam.

MABEL: (*bursting into tears*) Unopened! It is too true! Flung aside unread. And I have learned by heart every word he ever wrote to me. Sir, you have struck down the hope and trust of my life without remorse. May heaven forgive you!

POM: Madam! Let me, who have learned to adore you –

MABEL: I may no longer hold a place in my husband's heart, but I am still mistress of his house – leave it, sir!

POM: Your wishes are my law (*going*). But here they come. Use the right of a wife, watch them unseen, and you will soon learn whether I am mistaken, or you misinformed.

---

the green room is the place: a pun on 'green', meaning 'inexperienced', like Ernest Vane.

MABEL: No (*violently*). I will not dog my husband's steps at the bidding of his treacherous friend. (*She watches* POMANDER *out.*)

POM: (*aside*) She will watch them. (*Exit.*)

        (*After a moment's irresolution,* MABEL *crouches behind a chair.*
        Enter VANE *and* WOFFINGTON, *without observing her.*)

VANE: But one word – I can explain all. Let me accompany you to this painter's. I am ready to renounce credit – character – wife – all for you!

WOFF: I go alone, sir. Call Mrs Woffington's coach. (*Exit* WOFFINGTON, *followed by* VANE.)

MABEL: (*starting up from behind her chair*) Oh! No, no! You cannot use me so. Ernest! Husband! (*She rushes towards the door, but swoons.* VANE *returns.*)

VANE: Who called me? Mabel – my wife! (*He stamps.*) Help, here! What have I done? (*He raises her in his arms.*)

ACT II

SCENE – *A large, roughly furnished garret. There is an easel with* WOFFINGTON's *picture on it, half concealed by a green baize drapery.* MRS TRIPLET *is reclining in a large chair, wrapped like an invalid. There is a violin hanging on the wall.* TRIPLET *is seated, writing, at a small table. There are two children. The* BOY *is rocking a cradle, and singing.*

TRIP: Do keep those children quiet, Jane.

MRS T: Hush, my dears, let your father write his comedy. Comedy seems so troublesome to write.

TRIP: Yes! Somehow sorrow comes more natural to me. (*Pauses.*) I've got a bright thought; you see, Jane, they are all at a sumptuous banquet: all the dramatis personae except the poet (*he writes*), music – sparkling wine – massive plate – soups – fish – shall I have three dishes of fish? Venison – game – pickles and provocatives in the centre, then up jumps one of the guests, and says he –

BOY: Oh, dear! I am so hungry!

GIRL: And so am I.

TRIP: That is an absurd remark, Lysimachus, not four hours after breakfast.

BOY: But father – there wasn't any breakfast for breakfast!

TRIP: Now I ask you, Mrs Triplet, how am I to write comic scenes, if you let Lysimachus and Roxalana there put the heavy business in every five minutes?

MRS T: Forgive them, the poor things are hungry!

TRIP: Then they must learn to be hungry in another room. They shan't cling round my pen and paralyze it, just when it is going to make all our fortunes (*he rises*); but you women have no consideration – send 'em all to bed, every man Jack of 'em (*the children raise a doleful cry*). Hungry! Hungry! Is that a proper expression to use before a father who is sitting down (*he seats himself*), all gaiety, and hilarity, to write a com– a com– (*he chokes*)? Where's the youngest – where's Cleopatra? (MRS TRIPLET *takes the child to him, and he takes her on his knee.*)

GIRL: Father, I'm not so very hungry!

BOY: (*who has come to* TRIPLET) And I'm not hungry at all – I had a piece of bread and butter yesterday!

TRIP: Wife; they'll drive me mad!

BOY: (*sotto voce*) Mother; father made us hungry out of his book.

GIRL: Is it a cookery book, father?

TRIP: Ha, ha! Is my comedy a cookery book? The young rogues say more good
things than I do – that is the worst of it. Wife, I took that sermon I wrote –

MRS T: And beautiful it was, James.

TRIP: I took it to the reverend gentleman, and he would not have it, he said it was
too hard upon sin for the present day (*dashes at the paper*). Ah! If my friend
Mrs Woffington would but leave this stupid comedy and take to tragedy, things
would smile again.

MRS T: Oh, James, how can you expect anything from that woman? You won't
believe what all the world says – you measure folk by your own good heart.

TRIP: I haven't a good heart, I spoke like a brute to you just now.

MRS T: Never mind, James, I wonder how you put up with me at all, a sick, useless
creature! I often wish to die for your sake – I know you would do better – I am
such a weight round your neck.

> (TRIPLET *takes* MRS TRIPLET *back to her chair, and returns with
> energy to his comedy. The* BOY *brings the violin.*)

BOY: Play us a tune on the fiddle, father!

MRS T: Ay do, husband. That often helps you in your writing. (TRIPLET *plays a
merry tune dolefully.*)

TRIP: It won't do, music must be in the heart, or it will never come out of the
fingers. (*He puts the fiddle down. The* BOY *takes it and puts it in the cradle.*)
No! Let us be serious and finish the comedy. Perhaps it hitches because I
forgot to invoke Thalia, the Muse of Comedy, Mrs Triplet. She must be a
black hearted jade if she won't lend a broad grin to a poor devil starving in the
middle of his hungry little ones.

MRS T: Heathen goddesses can't help us. We had better pray to heaven to look
down on us and our children.

TRIP: (*suddenly*) You forget, Mrs Triplet, that our street is very narrow, and the
opposite houses are very high.

MRS T: James!

TRIP: How can heaven see an honest man and his family in such an out-of-the-way
place as this.

MRS T: Oh, what words are these?

TRIP: Have we given honesty a fair trial? Yes or no! (*He walks about in great
agitation.*)

MRS T: No, not till we die as we have lived.

TRIP: I *suppose* heaven is just, I can't know it, till it sends me an angel to take my
children's part; they cry to me for bread, I have nothing to give them but hard
words. God knows it has taken a great deal to break my heart, but it is broken
at last, broken – broken – (*he sobs with his head in his hands on the table*).

> (*Enter* WOFFINGTON, *speaking.*)

WOFF: Wasn't somebody inquiring after an angel? Here I am!

TRIP: Mrs Woffington! (*Seeing* TRIPLET's *distress,* MRS WOFFINGTON *retreats,
but presently returns.*)

WOFF: See (*she shows him a letter*). 'Madam, you are an angel' from a gentleman, a perfect stranger to me, so I must be correct. (*Enter* POMPEY *with a basket.*) Ah! Here is another angel. There are two sorts, you know, angels of light, and angels of darkness (*she takes the basket from* POMPEY). Lucifer, avaunt (*in a terrible tone*), and wait outside the door (*in a familiar tone*).

    (*Exit* POMPEY.)

WOFF: (*aside*) They are in sore distress, poor things. I am sorry you are ill, Mrs Triplet. I have brought you some physic – black draught from Burgundy. (MRS TRIPLET *attempts to rise, but sinks back again.*) Don't move, I insist!

TRIP: Oh, Mrs Woffington, had I dreamed you would deign to come here –

WOFF: You would have taken care to be out. (*aside*) Their faces look pinched. I know what that means. Mrs Triplet, I have come to give your husband a sitting for my portrait, will you allow me to eat my little luncheon in your room? I am so hungry. Pompey! (POMPEY *runs in.*) Run to the corner and buy me that pie I took such a fancy to as we came along. (*She gives money to* POMPEY. *Exit* POMPEY.)

BOY: Mother, will the lady give me a bit of her pie?

MRS T: Hush, you rude boy!

WOFF: She is not much of a lady if she doesn't! Now children, we'll first look at father's comedy. Nineteen dramatis personae – cut out seven. Don't bring your armies into *our* drawing-rooms, Mr Dagger and Bowl: can you marshal battalions on a Turkey carpet, and make gentlefolks witty in platoons? What's here in the first act? A duel! And both wounded – you butcher!

TRIP: (*deprecatingly*) They are not to die, they shan't die, upon my honour!

WOFF: Do you think I'll trust their lives with you? I'll show you how to run people through the body. (*She takes the pen and writes.*) Business, 'Araminta looks out of garret window, the combatants drop their swords, put their hands to their hearts, and stagger off, O.P. and P.S.' Now children! Who helps me lay the cloth?

CHILD: I, and I. (*They run to the dresser.*)

MRS T: (*half rising*) Madam, I can't think of allowing you.

WOFF: Sit down, ma'am, or I must use brute force (*in* MRS TRIPLET's *ear*), shake hands with distress, for it shall never enter your door again. (MRS TRIPLET *clasps her hands.* MRS WOFFINGTON *meets the children with the tablecloth, which she lays.*) Twelve plates, quick! Twenty-four knives, quickest!

    (*Enter* POMPEY, *who sets the pie on the table, and exit, looking wistfully at it.*)

WOFF: Mr Triplet, your coat if you please – and carve.

TRIP: My coat, madam?

WOFF: Yes; off with it, there's a hole in it. (TRIPLET *with signs of astonishment, gives her his coat, then he carves the pie, and they eat.* WOFFINGTON *seats herself.*) Be pleased to cast your eye on that, ma'am. (*The* BOY *passes a*

Don't bring your armies: a reference to a change in theatrical fashion from melodrama to a more refined style suitable to the drawing-room.

O.P. and P.S.: the prompter's side of the stage (to the actor's left), and the opposite side to it. Theatrical terminology.

to the dresser: a kitchen cupboard with open shelving above for the storage of plates, etc.

housewife to MRS TRIPLET.) Woffington's housewife, made by herself, homely to the eye, but holds everything in the world, and has a small space left for everything else; to be returned by the bearer. Thank you, sir! (WOFFINGTON *stitches away very rapidly*.) Eat away; children, when once I begin the pie will soon end; (*the* GIRL *takes a plate to her mother*). I do everything so quick.

GIRL: The lady sews faster than you, mother.

WOFF: Bless the child, don't come near my sword-arm, the needle will go into your eye, and out at the back of your head. (*The* CHILDREN *laugh*.) The needle will be lost, the child will be no more, enter undertaker, house turned topsyturvy, father shows Woffington the door, off she goes, with face as long and as dull as papa's comedy, crying, 'Fine Chaney o-ran-ges!' (*The* CHILDREN *laugh heartily*.)

GIRL: Mother, the lady is very funny!

WOFF: You'll be as funny when you're as well paid for it.

(TRIPLET *chokes with laughing, and lays down knife and fork*.)

MRS T: James, take care!

WOFF: There's the man's coat, (*aside*) with a ten pound note in it. (*The* GIRL *takes it to* TRIPLET.)

TRIP: My wife is a good woman, ma'am, but deficient in an important particular.

MRS T: Oh, James!

TRIP: Yes, my dear, I regret to say you have *no sense of humour*: no more than a cat, Jane.

WOFF: What! Because the poor thing can't laugh at your comedy?

TRIP: No, ma'am, but she laughs at nothing.

WOFF: Try her with one of your tragedies!

MRS T: I am sure, James, if I don't laugh, it is not for the want of the will. (*dolefully*) I used to be a very hearty laugher; but I haven't laughed this two years. (WOFFINGTON *leads* MRS TRIPLET *to a chair*.)

WOFF: Oh, you haven't, haven't you? Then the next two years you shall do nothing else.

TRIP: Oh, madam, that passes the talent even of the great comedian.

BOY: *She* is not a comedy lady.

WOFF: Hallo!

BOY: You don't ever cry, pretty lady.

WOFF: (*ironically*) Of course not.

BOY: (*confidentially*) Comedy is crying. Father cries all the time he writes his comedy.

WOFF: Oh!

TRIP: Hold your tongue. They were tears of laughter, you know, ma'am. Wife, our children talk too much; they thrust their noses into everything, and criticise their own father.

WOFF: Unnatural offspring!

---

passes a housewife: a folded cloth or wallet containing needles, thread, etc. for sewing repairs.
Fine Chaney o-ran-ges: she would be compelled to return to her former occupation as an orange seller. Chaney means Chinese.

TRIP: And when they fake up a notion, the devil himself couldn't convince them to the contrary; for instance, all this morning they thought fit to assume that they were starving.

BOY: So we were till the angel came, and the devil went for the pie.

TRIP: There, there, there, there! Now, you mark my words, Jane, we shall never get that idea out of their heads –

WOFF: Till we (*she cuts a large piece of pie and puts it onto a child's plate*) put a different idea into their stomachs. Come, *trinquons*, as they do in France! (*She fills glasses, and touches hers with those of the children, who crowd round her with delight.*) Were you ever in France, Triplet?

TRIP: No, madam, I am thoroughly original.

WOFF: That's true. Well, I went there once to learn tragedy of the great Dumesnil (*she recites several lines of French tragedy*). But Peg Woffington was never meant to walk the stage on stilts; no, let Mrs Pritchard pledge Melpomene in her own poison-bowl, I'll give you Thalia in a bumper of Burgundy. Come, drink to your new mistress, Triplet (*fills her glass*). Mrs Triplet (*she rises, bottle and glass in hand*), I must prescribe for you too. A wine glass full of this *elixir* six times a day until further notice. Success to your husband's comedy! What's this? (*She sees the fiddle in the cradle.*) A fiddle, as I'm an ex-orange wench! (*giving it to* TRIPLET) Here, Triplet, a jig – a jig. (TRIPLET *takes the fiddle.*) Peggy has not forgotten how to cover the buckle. Come, young ones. (TRIPLET *plays. She dances a jig with the children.*) More power to your elbow, man – shake it, ye sowl! Hurroo! (*She dances up to* TRIPLET *who, in his excitement, rises and joins in the jig, while* MRS TRIPLET *follows their movements with her body.*) But come, Mr Triplet, you really shan't make me play the fool any longer. Business! My picture is to be finished. Mrs Triplet, we must clear the studio; take your cherubs into the bed-room.

MRS T: Oh, madam, (*seizing her hand*) may the blessings of a mother watch over you in life and after it, and the blessings of these innocents too!

WOFF: Pooh, pooh! Let me kiss the brats, (*aside*) poor things!

BOY: I shall pray for you after father and mother.

GIRL: I shall pray for you after daily bread, because we were so hungry till you came.

WOFF: (*putting them off*) There, there. Exeunt mother and cherubs. Music for the exit, Trippy – the merriest you can extort from that veteran Stradivarius of yours. (*aside*) Heaven knows I've as much need of merry music as the saddest of them. (*seeing* TRIPLET *overcome*) Why, how now? If there isn't this kind-hearted, soft-headed, old booby of a Triplet making a picture of himself in water colours. (*She goes up to him, and taps him on the arm.*) Come, to work – to work, and with a will, for I have invited Cibber, and Quin, and

---

the devil went for the pie: Pompey was of negroid origin.
walk the stage on stilts: a reference, perhaps, to the built-up shoes of classical Greek actors.
let Mrs Pritchard pledge Melpomene: Mrs Pritchard was a celebrated eighteenth-century tragedienne. Melpomene was the Muse who presided over tragedy.
a picture of himself in water colours: a pun on a kind of painting and on Triplet's tears.

Clive, and Snarl, Soaper and all, to see the portrait, which is to make your fortune and hand me down to posterity not half as handsome as nature made me. There (*she sits*), I must put on my most bewitching smile of course. (*aside*) Oh, dear! How it belies my poor aching heart. (TRIPLET *has set to work.*) Well, are you satisfied with it?

TRIP: Anything but, madam (*he paints*).

WOFF: Cheerful soul! Then I presume it is like.

TRIP: Not a bit. (WOFFINGTON *stretches.*) You must not yawn, ma'am – you must not yawn just now!

WOFF: Oh, yes, I must, if you will be so stupid.

TRIP: I was just about to catch the turn of the lip.

WOFF: Well, catch it, it won't run away.

TRIP: A pleasant half-hour it will be for me, when all your friends come here, like cits at a shilling ordinary, each for his cut. Head a little more that way. (*sadly*) I suppose you can't sit quiet, madam: then never mind. Look on this picture and on that!

WOFF: Meaning, that I am painted as well as my picture.

TRIP: Oh, no, no, no! But to turn from your face, on which the lighting of expression plays continually, to this stony, detestable, head daub: I could (*seizes palette-knife*) – miserable mockery, vile caricature of life and beauty, take that! (*He stabs the knife through the picture.*)

WOFF: Oh, right through my pet dimple! Hark! I hear the sound of coaches. The hour of critique approaches!

TRIP: Two coach-loads of criticism, and the picture ruined!

WOFF: (*reflecting*) I'll give you a lesson – your palette-knife. (*She cuts away the face of the picture.*)

TRIP: There will be Mr Cibber with his sneering snuff-box; Mr Quin with his humorous bludgeon; Mrs Clive with her tongue, Mr Snarl with his abuse; and Mr Soaper with his praise – but I deserve it all!

WOFF: That green baize – (*she gets behind the easel*) – fling it over the easel – so; and now (*showing her face through the picture*) you shall criticise criticism, and learn the true weight of goose's feathers.

> (TRIPLET *throws the baize over the picture. Enter* CIBBER, CLIVE, QUIN, SNARL, *and* SOAPER. TRIPLET *bows humbly. They return his salute carelessly.*)

CIBBER: Ough! Four pair of stairs!

QUIN: Well, where's the picture?

> (*They take up positions to look at it.*)

TRIP: Mrs Woffington, gentlemen! (*He removes the baize, and suppresses a start.*)

SOAP: Ah!

SNARL: Umph!

CLIVE: Eh?

---

cits at a shilling ordinary: 'cits' is a derogatory abbreviation of citizens, and 'shilling ordinary' indicates a cheap entertainment.

CIBBER: Ah!

QUIN: Whose portrait did you say?

CLIVE: He, he! Peg Woffington's – it's a pretty head enough, and not a bit like Woffington.

QUIN: Nay – compare paint with paint, Kitty – who ever saw Woffington's real face?

SOAP: Now, I call it beautiful; so smooth, polished, and uniform.

SNARL: Whereas nature delights in irregular and finely graduated surfaces. Your brush is not destitute of a certain crude talent, Mr Triplet, but, you are deficient in the great principles of Art; the first of which is a loyal adherence to truth; beauty itself is but one of the forms of truth, and nature is our finite exponent of infinite truth.

SOAP: What wonderful criticism! One quite loses oneself among such grand words!

CIBBER: Yes, yes! Proceed, Mr Snarl, I am of your mind.

SNARL: Now in nature, a woman's face at this distance, has a softness of outline (*he draws back and makes a lorgnette of his two hands, the others do the same*), whereas your work is hard and tea-boardy.

SOAP: Well it is a *leettle teaboardy*, perhaps. But the light and shade, Mr Snarl! The – what-d'ye-call – the – um – you know – eh?

SNARL: Ah, you mean the chiaroscuro.

SOAP: Exactly!

SNARL: The chiaroscuro is all wrong. In nature, the nose, intercepting the light on one side of the face, throws a shadow under the eye. Caravaggio, the Venetians, and the Bolognese, do particular justice to this – no such shade appears in your portrait.

CIBBER: 'Tis so, stap my vitals!

(*All express assent except* SOAPER.)

SOAP: But, my dear Mr Snarl, if there are no shades, there are lights – loads of lights.

SNARL: There are, only they are impossible (*superciliously*). You have, however, succeeded tolerably in the mechanical parts – the dress, for example; but your Woffington is not a woman, sir – nor nature!

(*All shake their heads in assent.*)

WOFF: Woman! For she has tricked four men. Nature! For a fluent dunce does not know her when he sees her!

CIBBER: Why – what the deuce?

CLIVE: Woffington!

QUIN: Pheugh!

WOFF: (*stepping out of the picture*) A pretty face, and not like Woffington! I owe you two, Kitty Clive. (CLIVE *bridles. Then to* QUIN) Who ever saw Peggy's real face? Look at it now if you can without blushing.

ALL: Ha, ha! (*Except* SNARL.)

SNARL: For all this, I maintain on the unalterable rules of art –

ALL: Ha, ha, ha!

SNARL: (*fiercely*) Goths! Good morning, ladies and gentlemen!

CIBBER: Good morning, Mr Snarl!

SNARL: I have a criticism to write of last night's performance. I shall sit on your pictures one day, Mr Brush.

TRIP: Pictures are not eggs, sir – they are not meant to be sat upon.

SNARL: Come, Soaper. (*Exit.*)

SOAP: You shall always have my good word, Mr Triplet.

TRIP: I will try and not deserve it, Mr Soaper.

SOAP: At your service, Mr Snarl! (*Exit.*)

CIBBER: Serve 'em right – a couple of serpents, or rather one boa-constrictor! Soaper slavers, for Snarl to crush. But we were all too hard on poor Trip; and if he will accept my apology –

TRIP: Thank you! 'Colley Cibber's Apology' can be got at any book-stall.

CIBBER: Confound his impertinence! Come along, Jemmy!

QUIN: If ever you paint my portrait –

TRIP: The bear from Hockley hole shall sit for the head.

QUIN: Curse his impudence! Have with you, Mr Cibber. (*Exeunt* CIBBER *and* QUIN.)

CLIVE: I did intend to have my face painted, sir, but after this –

TRIP: You will continue to do it yourself!

CLIVE: Brute! (*Exit in a rage.*)

TRIP: Did I show a spirit, or did I not, ma'am?

WOFF: Tremendous!

TRIP: Did you mark the shot I fired into each as he sheered off?

WOFF: Terrific!

TRIP: I defy them, the coxcombs! As for real criticism, I invite it. Yours for instance, or that sweet lady I met at Mr Vane's, or anybody that appreciates one's beauties. By-the-bye, you were not at Mr Vane's yesterday?

WOFF: Yes, I was!

TRIP: No! I came with my verses, but she said you were not there.

WOFF: Who said so?

TRIP: The charming young lady who helped me with her own hand to nectar and ambrosia.

WOFF: A young lady?

TRIP: About twenty-two.

WOFF: In a travelling dress?

TRIP: Yes – brown hair – blue eyes! I poured out all to her: that I expected to find you; that Mr Vane admired you; and that you were sitting to me for your portrait; that I lived at 10, Hercules Buildings, and should be proud to show her the picture for her judgement.

WOFF: You told her all this?

TRIP: I did. Do you know her?

WOFF: Yes.

TRIP: Who is she?

WOFF: Mrs Vane.

TRIP: Mrs Vane! Mr Vane's mother? No, no, that can't be!

---

sit on your pictures: to sit in judgement, and also to crush. A pun is to follow.
nectar and ambrosia: food and drink to the classical gods.

WOFF: Mr Vane's wife!

TRIP: Wife?

WOFF: Yes.

TRIP: Then she wasn't to know you were there?

WOFF: No.

TRIP: Then I let the cat out of the bag?

WOFF: Yes.

TRIP: And played the devil with their married happiness?

WOFF: Probably. (*She turns her back to him.*)

TRIP: Just my luck! Oh, Lord, Lord! To see what these fine gentlemen are! To have a lawful wife at home, and then to come and fall in love with you! *I* do it for ever in my plays, it is all right there! But in real life it is abominable!

WOFF: You forget, sir, that I am an actress! A plaything for every profligate who can find the open sesame of the stage-door. Fool! To think there was an honest man in the world, and that he had shone on me!

TRIP: Mrs Woffington!

WOFF: But what have we to do (*she walks agitatedly*) with homes and hearth, and firesides? Have we not the theatre, its triumphs, and full-handed thunders of applause? Who looks for hearts beneath the masks we wear? These men applaud us, cajole us, swear to us, lie to us, and yet, forsooth, we would have them respect us too.

TRIP: (*fiercely*) They shall respect you before James Triplet. A great genius like you, so high above them all! My benefactress . . . (*He whimpers.*)

WOFF: (*taking his hand*) I thought this man truer than the rest. I did not feel his passion an insult. Oh, Triplet! I could have loved this man – really loved him!

TRIP: Then you don't love him?

WOFF: Love him! I hate him, and her, and all the world!

TRIP: You will break with him, then?

WOFF: Break with him! I will feed his passion to the full – tempt him – torture him – play with him as the anger plays the fish upon his hook! He shall rue the hour he trifled with a heart and brain like mine!

TRIP: But his poor wife?

WOFF: His wife! And are wives' hearts the only hearts that throb, and feel, and break? His wife must take care of herself, it is not from me that mercy can come to her.

TRIP: But, madam – (*he is interrupted by a knock at the door*). Who's this at such a moment? (*He goes to the window.*) 'Tis a lady! Eh! Cloaked and hooded. Who can she be? Perhaps a sitter? My new profession has transpired!

> (*There is a tap at the room door. Enter a slatternly* SERVANT, *who hands a paper.*)

SERV: From a lady who waits below.

TRIP: (*reads and drops the paper*) 'Mabel Vane'!

WOFF: His wife here! (*to* SERVANT) Show the lady upstairs. (*Exit* SERVANT.) What does she come for?

TRIP: I don't know, and I wish to heaven she had stayed away! You will retire, of course you will retire?

WOFF: No, sir! I will know why she comes to you. (*She reflects, then enters the picture again.*) Keep it from me if you can!

    (TRIPLET *sinks into a chair, the picture of consternation.*)

TRIP: (*with a ghastly smile, going slowly towards the door*) I am going to be in the company of the two loveliest women in England; I would rather be between a lion and a unicorn – like the royal arms. (*A tap at the door.*)

    (*Enter* MABEL VANE *in hood and cloak, a mask in her hand.*)

TRIP: Madam!

MABEL: See first that I am not followed; that man who pursued me from my husband's house – look out.

TRIP: (*looking through the window*) Sir Charles Pomander! He examines the house – his hand is on the knocker – no! He retires! (TRIPLET *rids* MABEL *of her hood, mantle, mask et cetera.*)

MABEL: (*hastily*) I breathe again. Mr Triplet, you said I might command your services. (TRIPLET *bows.*) You know this actress you spoke of today, Mrs Woffington?

TRIP: (*aside*) Curse it! I am honoured by her acquaintance, madam!

MABEL: You will take me to her, to the theatre where she acts?

TRIP: But consider, madam!

MABEL: You must not refuse me.

TRIP: But what can be the use of it?

MABEL: I am sure you are true and honest – I will trust you. (TRIPLET *bows.*) When you saw me yesterday, I was the happiest woman in the world, for I love my husband; and I thought then he loved me as he used to do. Two days ago I left our country home – I yearned to be by my husband's side; I counted the hours of the journey, the miles, the yards of the road – I reached his house at last – to find that the heart, on which I had so longed to rest my head, was mine no longer.

TRIP: Poor thing! Poor thing!

MABEL: And she who held my place, was the woman – the actress you so praised to me; and now you pity me, do you not; and will not refuse my request?

TRIP: But be advised; do not think of seeking Mrs Woffington; she has a good heart, but a fiery temper; besides, good heavens, you two ladies are rivals! Have you read 'The Rival Queens', madam?

MABEL: I will cry to her for justice and mercy; I never saw a kinder face than this lady's; she must be good and noble!

TRIP: She is! I know a family she saved from starvation and despair.

MABEL: (*seeing the picture, and approaching it*) Ah, she is there! See! See!

TRIP: (*interposing*) Oh, my portrait! You must not go near that, the colours are wet!

MABEL: Oh, that she were here as this wonderful portrait is; and then how I would plead to her for my husband's heart! (*to the picture*) Oh, give him back to me! What is one more heart to you? You are so rich, and I am so poor, that without his love I have nothing; but must sit me down and cry till my heart breaks – give him back to me, beautiful, terrible woman; for with all your gifts you cannot love him as his poor Mabel does. Oh, give him back to me – and I will love you and kiss your feet, and pray for you till my dying day. (MABEL

kneels before the picture, and sobs.) Ah! A tear! It is alive! (*She runs to* TRIPLET, *and hides her head.*) I am frightened! I am frightened!
> (WOFFINGTON *steps out of the frame and stands with one hand on her brow, in a half-despairing attitude. She waves her hand to* TRIPLET *to retire.* MABEL *stands trembling.*)

WOFF: We would be alone.

TRIP: (*in consternation*) But, Mrs Woffington, but ladies!

WOFF: Leave us!

TRIP: I will retire into my sleeping apartment. (*He does so, putting out his head.*) Be composed, ladies. Neither of you could help it.

WOFF: Leave us, I say! (TRIPLET *vanishes suddenly. There is a long, uneasy pause. Then, with forced coldness*) At least, madam, do me the justice to believe I did not know Mr Vane was married.

MABEL: I am sure of it – I feel you are as good as you are gifted.

WOFF: Mrs Vane, I am not – you deceive yourself.

MABEL: Then heaven have mercy on me! But you are, I see it in your face! Ah, you know you pity me!

WOFF: I do, madam, and I could consent never more to see your – Mr Vane.

MABEL: Ah, but you will give me back his heart? What will his presence be to me if his love remain behind?

WOFF: But how, madam?

MABEL: The magnet can repel as well as attract. You who can enchant – can you not break your own spell?

WOFF: You ask much of me!

MABEL: Alas, I do!

WOFF: But I could do even this.

MABEL: You could!

WOFF: And perhaps if you, who have not only touched my heart, but won my respect, say to me, 'Do so', I shall do it. (MABEL *clasps her hands.*) There is only one way – I have only to make him (*with a trembling lip*) believe me worse than I am, and he will return to you, and love you better, far better, for having known, admired, and despised, Peg Woffington.

MABEL: Oh, I shall bless you every hour of my life (*pause*). But rob you of your good name! Bid a woman soil her forehead so for me! (*She sighs, and there is a long pause.*) With heaven's help I do refuse your offer; it is better I should die with my heart crushed, but my conscience unstained; for so my humble life has passed till now.

WOFF: Humble! Such as you are the diamonds of the world!!! Angel of truth and goodness, you have conquered! The poor heart we both overrate shall be yours again. In my hands, 'tis painted glass at best, but set in the lustre of your love, it may become a priceless jewel. Can you trust me?

MABEL: With my life!

WOFF: And will you let me call you friend?

MABEL: Friend! No – not friend!

WOFF: Alas!

MABEL: Let me call you sister? I have no sister! (*timidly, and pleadingly*).

WOFF: Sister! Oh, yes, call me sister! (*They embrace.*) You do not know what it is to me, whom the proud ones of the world pass by with averted looks, to hear that sacred name from lips as pure as yours. Let me hold you in my arms – so – a little while – if you knew the good it does me to feel your heart beating close to mine (*pause*). And now to bring back this truant – how this heart flutters – you must compose yourself. (*She goes to the door leading to the inner room, and opens it.*) And I have need to be alone awhile. (WOFFINGTON *passes* MABEL *into the inner room, then sits a moment with her hands pressed over her forehead.*) 'Twas a terrible wrench, but 'tis over; and now 'about my brains' as Hamlet says – to bring back the husband to his duty. What a strange office for a woman like me! How little the world knows about us after all (*she sighs and sobs convulsively*). I ought to feel very happy – pshaw! On with the mask and spangles, Peggy, and away with the fumes of this pleasant day-dream. How to bring Pomander hither? Let me see – this paper (*she takes the paper which* MABEL *had sent up*) signed in her hand, Mabel Vane. What if, by its aid . . . I have it – pen – ink – one never can find writing materials in an author's room. Triplet! (*Enter* TRIPLET.) Pens, and ink – quick!

TRIP: (*looking at her*) Here, madam – and paper?

WOFF: No, I have that here. (*She writes, and he watches her.*)

TRIP: Her eyes are red – and Mrs Vane all of a flutter inside. There's been a storm – but they haven't torn each other in pieces, that's one comfort. But has she relented, I wonder?

WOFF: Triplet! This note to Sir Charles Pomander.

TRIP: Madam. What is it, I wonder? However 'tis not my business. (*He pauses.*) But it is my business. I'm not a postman; if I carry letters, I ought to know the contents. Madam –

WOFF: Well?

TRIP: Madam – I – I –

WOFF: I see. You wish to know the contents of that letter. Hear them: 'Follow the bearer.'

TRIP: Madam!

WOFF: (*reading*) I am here without my husband's knowledge.

TRIP: Mrs Woffington!

WOFF: (*reading*) Alone and unprotected – signed Mabel Vane.

TRIP: Her own signature too! Mrs Woffington – you are a great actress – you have been cruelly wronged – you have saved me from despair, and my children from starvation; but before I carry that letter, I will have my hands hacked off at the wrists.

WOFF: (*aside*) What a good creature this is. Then you refuse to obey my orders.

TRIP: No, no! Ask me to jump out of that window, to burn my favourite tragedy, to forswear pen and ink for ever – anything but carry that letter – and I will do it.

WOFF: Well, leave the letter. (TRIPLET *runs for his hat.*) Where are you going?

TRIP: To bring the husband to his wife's feet, and so to save one angel – that's the lady in the other room – from despair; and another angel, that's you, from a great crime. Trust poor Jemmy Triplet for once to bring this domestic drama to a happy denouement! (*Exit* TRIPLET.)

WOFF: How innocently he helps my plot! I must have all the puppets under my hand. If I know Sir Charles, he is still on the watch. (*She goes to the window.*)

Yes! (*She goes to the inner door.*) Here, your eldest boy, Mrs Triplet; I want him. (*Enter* LYSIMACHUS.) Lysimachus, you see that gentleman, run down – give him this letter – and then show him up here (*Exit* LYSIMACHUS.) And now Mrs Vane's mantle, the hood well forward, so, we are nearly of a height – he does not knov I am here – if I can but imitate her voice and rustic shyness – *allons*, Peggy, 'tis seldom you acted in so good a cause (*assuming the air of Mrs Vane*).

> (*Enter* POMANDER *behind.* WOFFINGTON *appears sunk in grief. He comes forward. She starts, and gives a little shriek.*)

POM: My dear Mrs Vane (*she shrinks*). Do not be alarmed. Loveliness neglected, and simplicity deceived, give irresistible claims to respect as well as adoration. Had fate given me this hand (*he takes her hand*) –

WOFF: Oh, please sir!

POM: Would I have abandoned it for that of a Woffington, as artificial and hollow a jade as ever winked at a side- box. Oh, had I been your husband, madam, how would I have revelled in the pastoral pleasures you so sweetly recalled yesterday – the Barbary mare –

WOFF: (*timidly*) Hen!

POM: Ah, yes, the Barbary hen; and old dame – dame –

WOFF: Best, please, sir!

POM: Yes, Best – that happy though elderly female for whom you have condescended to make puddings.

WOFF: Alas, sir!

POM: You sigh! It is not yet too late to convert me. Upon this white hand I swear to become your pupil, as I am your adorer (*he kisses it*); let me thus fetter it with a worthy manacle. (*aside*) What will innocence say to my five hundred guinea diamond?

WOFF: La, sir, how pretty!

POM: Let me show how poor its lustre is to that of your eyes. (*He tries to draw back her hood. She suddenly starts away, and listens in an attitude of alarm.*)

WOFF: Oh, sir, hark!

POM: Ah! (*There is a noise without.*) Footsteps on the stairs! (*He goes to the door, opens it, and listens.*)

VANE: (*off*) Another flight!

POM: Ha! Vane's voice, by all that's mal-à-propos. (WOFFINGTON *screams and rushes into the inner apartment.*) And now for Monsieur le mari. (TRIPLET *appears at the door leading to the staircase, his back to the stage, and speaking off.*)

TRIP: Have a care, sir! There is a hiatus in the fourth step. And now for the friend who waits to forget grief and suspicion in your arms. That friend is –

> (*Enter* VANE. TRIPLET *turns round and recognizes* POMANDER.)

TRIP: The Devil!

POM: You flatter me!

VANE: So this is the mysterious rencontre. Pray, Sir Charles, what is it you want to forget in my arms?

POM: In your arms! (*aside*) Confounds himself with his wife. Perhaps you had better explain, my friend?

TRIP: Nay, sir – be yours the pleasing duty!

VANE: In one word, Sir Charles Pomander, why are you here? And for what
purpose am I sent for?

POM: In two words, my dear fellow, I don't choose to tell you why I am here – and
'twas not I who sent for you.

VANE: (*to* TRIPLET) Speak, sirrah – your riddling message!

TRIP: There's nothing for it but the truth. Then, sir, the friend I expected you would
find here was Mrs –

POM: (*to* TRIPLET) Stop, my deplorable-looking friend: (*to* VANE) when the
answer to such a question begins with a mistress, I think you had better not
enquire further. (*To* TRIPLET) Don't complete the name.

VANE: I command you to complete it, or –

TRIP: Gentlemen, gentlemen, how am I to satisfy both of you?

POM: My dear Vane, remember it is a lady's secret – the only thing in the world one
is bound to keep, except one's temper, which, by-the-bye, you're losing
rapidly.

VANE: (*aside*) He spoke of griefs and suspicions to be forgiven and forgotten.
Mabel has left my house. Sir Charles Pomander, I insist on knowing who this
lady is. If it is as I fear, I have the best right to ask.

POM: But the worst right to be answered.

VANE: How am I to construe this tone, sir?

POM: Do as we did at school with a troublesome passage: don't construe it at all.

VANE: Sir Charles Pomander, you are impertinent.

POM: My dear Vane, you are in a passion.

VANE: By heaven, sir –

TRIP: Gentlemen, gentlemen, I give you my word, Mr Vane, she does not know of
Sir Charles Pomander's presence here.

VANE: She? 'S death, who?

TRIP: Mrs Vane!

VANE: My wife here, and with him?

TRIP: No, not with *him*!

POM: I regret to contradict you, my dilapidated friend, or to hurt you, my dear
Vane; but really in self-defence – you know this signature (*offers paper written
by* WOFFINGTON).

VANE: Mabel's hand!

POM: Yes. What my attentions began, your little peccadilloes finished. Cause and
effect, my dear fellow. Pure cause and effect.

VANE: Coxcomb and slanderer! Draw and defend yourself. (*He draws.*)

POM: If you will have it! (*He draws.*)

TRIP: (*throwing himself between them*) Hold! Hold!

> (WOFFINGTON *suddenly opens the inner room door, and presents
> herself at the threshold. Her hood is drawn over her face.*)

TRIP: Mrs Vane!

VANE: Mabel! Wife! Say that this is not true – that you were lured by stratagem.

---

don't construe it at all: to construe a passage of an ancient language was to translate and
interpret it. A pun is intended.

Oh, speak! Belie this coxcomb! You know how bitterly I repented the
infatuation that brought me to the feet of another.

    (WOFFINGTON *bursts into a laugh, and throws back the hood.*)

POM: Woffington!

VANE: She here!

WOFF: There, Sir Charles, did I not wager he would confess he was heartily
ashamed of himself?

TRIP: (*aside*) I have a glimmer of comprehension.

WOFF: Yes, we have had our laugh – and Mr Vane his lesson. As for Mrs Vane –
this way, madam, and satisfy yourself.

    (*Enter* MABEL.)

MABEL: Ernest – dear Ernest!

VANE: (*sternly*) Mabel, how came you here?

WOFF: In such very questionable company as a town rake and a profane
stage-player? Mrs Vane might have asked the same question yesterday. Why
Mrs Vane somehow fancied you had mislaid your heart in Covent Garden
green room, and that I had feloniously appropriated it: she came here in
search of stolen goods. Would you could rummage here, madam, and satisfy
yourself if you still want proof, that I have no such thing as a heart about me –
not even one of my own.

TRIP: I deny that! A better heart than Mrs Woffington's –

WOFF: What on earth do you know about it, man?

VANE: (*to* MABEL) But this letter?

WOFF: Was written by me on a paper which by accident bore Mrs Vane's signature.
The fact is I had a wager with Sir Charles here – his diamond ring against my
left-hand glove – that I could bewitch a certain country gentleman's
imagination, though his heart all the while belonged to its rightful owner, and I
have won (*she sighs*).

VANE: What a dupe I have been. Am I enough humiliated?

POM: Ha, ha, ha! My poor fellow, you had better return to Huntingdonshire, and
leave town and the players to us, who know how to deal with them.

WOFF: And are quite safe against being taken in, eh, Sir Charles? (*She points to the
ring on her finger.*)

POM: Oh, perfectly. We know each other's cards. Retain that ring as a mark of my –
    (WOFFINGTON *holds up her finger.*)

POM: Respect!

WOFF: No, no! I accept your ring, but I shall always hate you.

POM: I welcome the sentiment – I can endure anything but your indifference.

VANE: And you, Mabel, will you forgive my infatuation?

MABEL: I forgive all, Ernest. (*aside to* WOFFINGTON) What do we not owe you,
sister?

WOFF: Nothing that word does not pay for. (*aside*) Alas! And so ends the game.
You and I have the tricks, I think, Sir Charles – Mrs Vane the honours.
Mr Vane will quit hazard and the clubs for Willoughby Manor and the
double dummy of a matrimonial rubber. As for me, I revoke my lead of
hearts.

POM: After taking my ace of diamonds!

TRIP: And poor Jemmy Triplet, I suppose, must once again take up his solitary hand of patience.

WOFF: Unless manager Rich is fool enough to accept my judgement for gospel, and then – but whom have we here?

(*Enter* CIBBER, QUIN, MRS CLIVE, SNARL *and* SOAPER.)

CIBBER: Ah, Mrs Vane, Mr Vane, Sir Charles, Peggy – Bonjour Mesdames et Messieurs – Mr Triplet, I congratulate you, stap my vitals!

TRIP: Congratulate me!

CLIVE: Yes, Quin here, who's a good natured bear, declares we behaved shamefully to you today, and so as Mr Rich has just told us of your good fortune –

TRIP: My good fortune! There must be some mistake. You've come to the wrong house.

QUIN: No; you have a prospect henceforward of dining every day of your life. 'Tis a great comfort, and I wish you appetite to enjoy it, Mr Triplet.

TRIP: Am I awake? Pinch me, somebody. (WOFFINGTON *pinches him.*) Thank you – I am awake.

CIBBER: Manager Rich, thanks to Peggy's influence here, and a good word or two from one who shall be nameless, has accepted one of your tragedies.

TRIP: Oh, Lord!

SOAP: He, he! I give you joy, Mr Triplet; Mr Snarl and I are so glad, for as Mr Snarl said to me, as we left your studio this morning, 'I do so wish they'd play one of Mr Triplet's tragedies.'

SNARL: That I might have the pleasure of criticising it. Mr Rich did me the honour to ask which of the three he should accept. I told him, the shortest.

CLIVE: You'll be pleased to hear, Mrs Woffington, there's a capital part for *me*. (*aside*) Now she could knock me down, I know.

TRIP: One of my tragedies accepted at last! Oh, gracious goodness! Break it gently to my wife – I know I'm dreaming, but, prithee, don't anybody wake me. Oh, Mrs Woffington, my guardian angel, my preserver! (*He seizes her hand.*)

WOFF: No, no! We had better wait and see on which act of your tragedy the curtain falls.

TRIP: Ah, I forgot that.

MABEL: I need not wait to express my gratitude – say in what way can I ever thank you?

WOFF: Dear sister, when hereafter in your home of peace you hear harsh sentence passed on us, whose lot is admiration, but rarely love, triumph but never tranquillity – think sometimes of poor Peg Woffington, and say, stage masks may cover honest faces, and hearts beat true beneath a tinselled robe –

    Nor ours the sole gay masks that hide a face
    Where care and tears have left their withering trace,
    On the world's stage, as in our mimic art,
    We oft confound the actor with the part.

POM: Distrust appearances – an obvious moral –
    With which, however, I've no time to quarrel;
    Though for my part, I've found, the winning riders
    In the world's race are often the outsiders.

VANE:	So I have played at love, witched from my will.
MABEL:	My love was always, Ernest, and is still.
CIBBER:	Pshaw! Stap my vitals! 'Manners make the man',
	They have made *me*!
SNARL:	'Tis about all they can!
SOAP:	Yes; Mr Cibber's epitaph shall be,
	He played Lord Foppington at seventy-three.
CLIVE:	I'm for plain speaking – let the truth be shown –
SNARL:	Truth's in a well – best leave that well alone –
QUIN:	Its bitter waters why should *you* uncork?
	No; play like me – an honest knife and fork.
TRIP:	That part would be well played by many a poet,
	Had he the practice one must have to know it,
	But 'tis the verdict by the public past,
	Must sentence scribblers or to feast or fast.
	Be kind tonight: in triplet tone I sue,
	As actor, manager, and author too.
POM:	Mind that for sentence when they call the cause on,
	You've at least one Peg here to hang applause on.
WOFF:	Yes; sure those kind eyes and bright smiles one traces,
	Are not deceptive *masks* – but honest *faces*.
	I'd swear it – but if your hands make it certain,
	Then all is right on both sides of the curtain.
	(*Curtain*)

THE COURIER OF LYONS

First performed at the Princess's Theatre on 26 June 1854, with the following cast:

DAUBENTON (a magistrate)	Mr J. Vining
JEROME LESURQUES (innkeeper)	Mr Graham
JOSEPH LESURQUES (his son) }	Mr C. Kean
DUBOSC (a celebrated criminal) }	
DIDIER (a young citizen)	Mr J. F. Cathcart
JOLIQUET (Lesurques's garçon)	Miss Kate Terry
GUERNEAU (friends of Joseph Lesurques)	Mr Terry
LAMBERT	Mr Raymond
DUMONT (Courier of Lyons)	Mr J. Collet
MAGLOIRE (the postilion)	Mr Stoakes
CHOPPARD (a horse dealer, called 'The Irresistible')	Mr Addison
COURRIOL ('The Dandy')	Mr D. Fisher
FOUINARD ('The Chicken')	Mr H. Saker
POSTMASTER	Mr J. Chester
HIS GARÇON	Mr Collis
WAITER	
JULIE LESURQUES (daughter of Joseph)	Miss C. Leclerq
JEANNE (an outcast)	Miss Heath
POSTMASTER'S DAUGHTER	Miss S. Ternan
TRAVELLER	
GENDARMES	
AGENTS DE POLICE	
MOB	

ACT I

SCENE 1. *A public room in an old fashioned hotel.* CHOPPARD *and* FOUINARD *are discovered sitting at a table with a* WAITER *in attendance.*
WAIT: Citizens, will you take anything, while waiting for your friends?
CHOP: No!
FOU: No!
WAIT: Please yourselves, citizens, please yourselves. Should you alter your minds, you will be pleased to call. (*Exit.*)
CHOP: Well, Fouinard, this waste of time is too bad. He does not come, this Courriol – he that is to show himself and change into louis d'ors the sous – that we have not.
FOU: I believe that he will bring some great idea, but what will this idea be, Choppard? I have a presentiment that it will be the clothing of the armies of the Republic – pretty pickings sometimes found that way, Choppard! I have nothing, I am only a philosopher – but you could patriotically assist your countrymen; you are a lender of horses, at twenty sous the hour, you must supply them.
CHOP: If the Cavaliers of the Republic give chase to the Prussians with the horses I lend it we shan't take many prisoners, Fouinard. But not yet, not yet, you see – what can detain him!
FOU: Are you quite sure that this was the appointed place of meeting?
CHOP: Quite! Here is the note: 'Fouinard and you be at the house of Hardouin, traiteur, No 17, Rue du Bac, on the eighth of May, at ten o'clock in the morning. I shall be there. Be punctual – I shall explain all.'
FOU: It is the writing of Courriol!
CHOP: This is the eighth of May?
FOU: Yes.
CHOP: And this house is No 17 in the Rue du Bac. And do you think that it is ten o'clock yet? (*A clock strikes twelve.*)
FOU: Hark! That is twelve striking.
CHOP: (*rising*) I am not going to remain here any longer. Do you see, Fouinard, I like independence. I should be sorry to serve under this Courriol – who does the dandy – like the Citizen Director Barras – who makes us wait here counting our fingers. What is he more than we? Excepting indeed he has been to college, and has fine white hands – one who has two sides to everything.
FOU: Come, be patient.
CHOP: I can't; I am too hungry. I shall go!
FOU: Hush! If the garçon hears you . . .!
CHOP: Bah! What does it signify? Here have I danced attendance for two hours. I shall decamp. Adieu, Fouinard!
FOU: If you go, I shall go.
> (*They begin to leave, but stop at the voice of the* WAITER *who enters.*)
WAIT: This way, citizen; there is room here.
FOU: (*to* CHOPPARD) Stop! Here comes Courriol!
> (*Enter* COURRIOL.)

COUR: Ah, good-day! What going?

CHOP: We have been waiting here these two hours and –

COUR: And you find the time long? Excuse me, but coming here I perceived some figures that rather excited my observation, and thought it would be polite and prudent to avoid encountering individuals whose enquiries and attentions might be prolonged and unsatisfactory. I therefore took a circuitous route, and arrived safely.

CHOP: The explanation is satisfactory. We may be quiet enough here.

COUR: Yes; for I know no-one in this quarter.

WAIT: (*advancing*) These gentlemen will take breakfast?

FOU: Yes, citizen. (*Exit* WAITER.)

COUR: You have read my letter?

CHOP: You have promised to explain this affair.

COUR: At present I am as much in the dark as yourselves.

CHOP: Why do we meet here?

COUR: I am expecting our chief – as yet unknown – he that will give the idea and means of executing it.

CHOP: Who is he?

COUR: I have never seen him.

CHOP: You appear remarkably well informed! What's his name?

COUR: That I don't know.

CHOP: How are we to recognize him?

COUR: By a signal. A man will come here at two o'clock; he will place himself at one of the tables, and call for a bottle of brandy, which is his favourite drink, and finish it at a sitting, for that is his custom. That is the description. Recognize him who can.

CHOP: I know one man of that description, but he will not be here today.

FOU: And why not?

CHOP: Because those persons to whom the Republic has delegated the honour of watching and tending his health object to his appearance on the outside of the gates of his residence.

FOU: Of whom do you speak?

CHOP: Dubosc!

COUR: The famous Dubosc! Who has been confined these two years in the Chateau Trompette, at Bordeaux.

CHOP: Ah, if it is Dubosc, I shall have confidence. When in his sober senses he has ideas! But unhappily he is not always so. He is sometimes drunk – I may say, he is very often drunk, and then –

   (*Enter* WAITER *with breakfast on a tray.*)

WAIT: Citizens, your refreshments.

   (*Enter* GUERNEAU *and* LAMBERT.)

GUER: Garçon!

WAIT: Sir!

GUER: We shall do very well here, Lambert, I think?

LAM: Yes, Guerneau, very well. Some wine. (*They sit. Exit* WAITER.)

COUR: (*turning round*) Ah, mon dieu – what a fatality – those men will recognize me!

CHOP: Who are they?

COUR: Two old college chums. If they see me with you it may compromise us all.

CHOP: Compromise – bah! They're no chums of mine – they've not been to college with me. And so Fouinard and I will breakfast.

GUER: Courriol! Is it you, Courriol?

COUR: I am recognized.

LAM: Yes, it is he! How do you do, Courriol?

COUR: (*turns*) Ha! What Lambert! Guerneau! By what chance – (*He crosses to them.*)

GUER: We are expecting Lesurques, who arrived this morning from Douai. You remember the excellent and respected citizen Lesurques?

COUR: Yes, I remember him well!

LAM: He intends remaining at Paris, to marry his daughter; and we have appointed to meet him here, as being the most convenient rendezvous near his notary's.

GUER: But you – what do you do here with these queer looking gentlemen?

COUR: I! Oh, I was sitting down to breakfast and being alone, joined their table for company's sake.

CHOP: He denies us – the dandy!

FOU: Hush! Be prudent!

CHOP: (*striking the table*) What does he mean?

COUR: Eh! He means to call the garçon and pay the bill.

CHOP: (*rising*) That is good!

COUR: I believe they are going to pay at the bar, for they seem pressed for time. (COURRIOL *makes signs to them to go.*)

FOU: Let's be off!

CHOP: Nom d'un tonnerre! It is humiliating.

FOU: I see nothing humiliating in having a good breakfast and not paying for it. Come along! Garçon – a toothpick!

LAM: Come join us at table.

COUR: (*aside to* FOUINARD *and* CHOPPARD) Go! I will remain and watch the grain; and at three o'clock you return here.
(*Exeunt* FOUINARD *and* CHOPPARD *murmuring. The* GARÇON *enters with wine which he places on the table.*)

COUR: (*to* GARÇON) Those gentlemen have left: bring here what I ordered – (*aside*) and silence. (*He gives the* WAITER *money.*)

LAM: A quarter past twelve! Lesurques is late!
(*Enter* LESURQUES, JULIE, *and* DIDIER.)

GUER: Ha, he is here!

LES: Come in, my children, come in! Good day, my friends! How are you, Guerneau – Lambert? (*They shake hands.*) Allow me to introduce my daughter, Julie, and her betrothed.

DIDIER: What, Courriol!

COUR: How are you, Lesurques? It is an age since we met.

LES: We were at the college of Louis le Grand!

GUER: Mon dieu, Lesurques! That sweet girl your daughter? Ah, Monsieur Didier, you have done well to be first in the field; one feels inclined to dispute the point with you!

DIDIER: It is necessary to prove first of all, monsieur that they love Mademoiselle more than I, or I will not yield her. (*He places a chair for Julie to sit.*)
LES: (*sitting*) It is a glorious thing to be happy, is it not?
COUR: You are happy, Lesurques?
LES: Yes, I am happy! You need not ask it – you see it! All my life is a link of prosperity – good parents, good health, an honourable service in the army (when soldier in the regiment of Auvergne), a small fortune that I have amassed from my own labour – and then, a daughter, such as I have; and a son-in-law, such as I am going to have – with all this, still a little youthfulness left, and good friends – oh, I feel a happy man! Yes, heaven never made a happier man than I!
COUR: I am astonished to hear you say so much!
LES: Is it then so rare a thing, this happiness? But you rise, Julie.
JULIE: It is one o'clock, papa.
DIDIER: And you know we have many purchases to make.
LES: Yes, my children. Go, yes, go!
JULIE: What, must we leave you Father? When shall we see you? At five o'clock?
LES: Yes, that is to say, no; do not wait for me.
DIDIER: What! Will you not return home to dine with us?
LES: Oh, I shall not be hungry before tomorrow.
DIDIER: Well, then, we will call here for you as we return.
LES: No, no. I shall come to the house. You may expect me. Adieu, adieu – go, my children, go.
JULIE: ⎫
DIDIER: ⎭ Messieurs!

(COURRIOL, GUERNEAU, *and* LAMBERT *bow.* JULIE *kisses her father, and exit with* DIDIER.)
GUER: You have quite grieved your children.
LAM: Mademoiselle Julie is quite uneasy.
COUR: Why not tell them your plans?
LES: You ask me why I will not tell them what I am going to do – I will tell you. It is a little secret – however, it turns upon the subject that I before alluded to, and however perfectly happy one may be, there is always some little annoyance, from here, or from there. I have two sorrows – first, the remembrance of my poor wife that I have lost; secondly, my father.
GUER: Your father!
LES: He has not had the good fortune in life that I have had – the Revolution ruined him; but he is proud, and will not receive any assistance from me, his son, who owes him all, and two years since, he quitted Douai, in spite of all our prayers.
GUER: What has become of him?
LES: With his last resources, he has opened an auberge, a cabaret – I know not what: in the environs of Paris. It is very humble, but there is no honest trade humiliating for men of honour. Even there, misfortune still pursues him – and now, to satisfy his creditors, he is compelled to sell his establishment; but as no purchaser has presented himself, they will expel him.
GUER: And he does not address himself to you?
LES: Ah, you know him not – he would rather die of hunger! An old soldier – a man

who has been in the possession of fortune – lost it, but never sacrificed either probity or honour!

GUER: And what do you intend to do?

LES: If possible, induce him to return with us, in spite of this exaggerated delicacy. It is a surprise that I intend for my dear Julie. Didier and Julie love him, as they love and respect me. Didier is a merchant, and a thriving man – if my father rebels, they will find him employment in attending to the books, or watching over the clerks. It will spare his scruples, and he shall, in spite of himself, eat the cake with us, instead of nibbling his own hard crust.

LAM: Brave Lesurques, go! Heaven will recompense you.

COUR: I think he has already been recompensed. Rich – flourishing – joyous – look at him! He gives one the wish to be an honest man!

GUER: How?

COUR: That is – if one was not so already.

LES: (*to* GUERNEAU) I believe you have a horse, Guerneau?

GUER: Yes, but they have taken it for the Government requisition.

LES: I would have borrowed it.

LAM: Nothing – merely a ride.

COUR: Hire one.

LES: I know not where.

COUR: (*aside*) It will put a few sous in the pocket of one that will not be sorry to receive it. There is Choppard!

LES: Where does he reside?

COUR: Rue Saint-Honoré, No. 213.

LES: Good horses?

COUR: Yes, and not dear.

LES: Rue Saint-Honoré, 213. Good! Thank you! (*He rises.*)

GUER: You are going to leave us?

LES: I confess that I am rather in a hurry – but I shall see you tomorrow – it is tomorrow that I sign the contract with Julie and Didier. I have good apartments, newly furnished. I expect my friend, Daubenton, he is justice of the peace of the division of Pont-Neuf. You will come, Guerneau, and you also, Lambert? As to you, Courriol, as an old college friend, you will not refuse to sign the contract of Julie?

COUR: Thank you! Your address?

LES: Rue Montmartre, No. 118.

COUR: At what hour?

LES: (*rising*) At four o'clock to dinner. My friends, I will say, adieu! Remember tomorrow!

GUER: We shall not remain here as you are leaving, we will go together.

LAM: We will pay the bill and go.

LES: (*looking at his watch*) A quarter to three! Diable, the time has passed quickly with you, I shall be off, for I am rather in a hurry. (*Exit.*)

COUR: (*aside*) In a quarter of an hour the stranger will be here! If I remain it will not look well. I must accompany them and hurry back to my appointment.

GUER: Courriol, we will accompany Lesurques as far as the Tuileries. Garçon, my hat and cane! (*The* WAITER *brings them.*)

COUR: (*taking his hat*) I am ready!

LES: (*off*) Come, Courriol – I am in a hurry. (*Exeunt, followed by the* WAITER.
  Enter DUBOSC.)

DUBOSC: (*looking about him*) Good – no one!
    (*Enter* WAITER.)

WAIT: Can I bring you anything? (*The* WAITER *removes a table, and exit.*)

DUBOSC: Presently! This is the house – this is the room – but there is no one here.
  Hark! someone comes! (*He sits at a table.*)
    (*Enter* JEANNE *from door. She looks around her, sees DUBOSC,
    and speaks in a low voice.*)

JEANNE: It is he, Dubosc!

DUBOSC: (*starting*) My name?

JEANNE: Dubosc, Dubosc, do not fear –

DUBOSC: (*aside*) That voice, Jeanne!

JEANNE: Dubosc, it is I, Jeanne –

DUBOSC: Pardon, madame, were you speaking to me?

JEANNE: You do not know me! Well then, I will aid your memory. I am the poor
  girl who believed you an honest man, and who loved you – now do you know
  me?

DUBOSC: My good madame, you really mistake me for someone else.

JEANNE: I have been mistaken in you, but am not so now! – She that you robbed
  of her honour, she that you robbed of her gold, she that you abandoned when
  she was a mother, abandoned with her little helpless child, now stands by your
  side! Do you not know her?

DUBOSC: No.

JEANNE: She that has no longer parents (for shame and misery have killed them);
  she who soon will have no longer any child (for he will die of hunger); she who
  has no longer any shelter – not even bread; she that has no refuge from vice,
  but suicide or starvation, starvation with her child – Dubosc, do you know her
  now?

DUBOSC: This cursed woman will mar all.

JEANNE: You do not speak. Will you do nothing to soften your crime? It is charity
  I ask, but not for myself – no, no, no! Were it not for my child I should call for
  death with cries of despair! You have escaped from the prison at Bordeaux!
  Dubosc, I have followed you! I came on foot, counting every step! I have
  found you! I supplicate you to give me money to take me to Alsace, there I
  shall find charitable people who will assist me if I work – will help to nourish
  my child – and I shall have time to reconcile myself with heaven. Will you? ...
  Will you?

DUBOSC: (*seated*) I repeat, I have not the honour of knowing you.

JEANNE: If you will grant it, I will pardon you all the ill that you have done me – if
  you will listen to my prayer, never shall you hear of me – never – I swear by
  the memory of my poor parents! I swear by the life of my poor child! (*She
  kneels.*)

DUBOSC: I have no money.

JEANNE: For my child – for my child!

DUBOSC: Here comes the garçon, if you do not go, I will.

JEANNE: Dubosc, I will leave you until tomorrow to reflect. If tomorrow you do not give me that I ask, to support my child and aid me to hide my shame –
DUBOSC: Well?
JEANNE: Well! Tomorrow I shall be desperate – and you will learn what it is for a mother to be in despair, Dubosc!
DUBOSC: Tomorrow – be it so, tomorrow! I shall be far away from here tonight.
JEANNE: Adieu, Dubosc! I feel the cravings of hunger, but I must wait until tomorrow. (*Exit.*)
DUBOSC: Well, there was one advantage in being imprisoned, I was free from such absurd and intolerable intrusions., Ah, footsteps! (*He sits, and a clock strikes three.*)
      (*Enter* CHOPPARD, *and* FOUINARD.)
DUBOSC: It strikes three. Ah, here is someone.
CHOP: (*pushing* FOUINARD) Go on!
FOU: But suppose it shouldn't be –
DUBOSC: Garçon!
      (*Enter* WAITER.)
DUBOSC: Some brandy.
CHOP: Eh!
FOU: Oh!
WAIT: A small glass?
DUBOSC: A bottle, and a large glass.
      (*Exit* WAITER, *who returns with a bottle and a tumbler, which he places on the table, before going off.*)
CHOP: (*to* FOUINARD) Do you see! (DUBOSC *pours a glass, and drinks.*)
FOU: (*singing to himself joyfully*) Oh, la, la, la!
CHOP: It must be he.
DUBOSC: (*regarding them*) All right I think. (*He pours out a second glass, and drinks it rapidly, they gazing upon him with admiration.*)
CHOP: Citizen, in the manner in which you have rinsed down those two tumblers of brandy, I believe I can perceive –
DUBOSC: That I shall soon finish the bottle. (*He drinks.*)
FOU: I am sure it is he.
CHOP: It is Dubosc. (*They bow with reverence. He extends his hands, which they shake with respect and fervour.*)
DUBOSC: You know me – how is that?
CHOP: All the army know their general; but the general knows not all his soldiers.
DUBOSC: You reason well, thank you – it is flattering, but long, and we have no time to lose.
CHOP: Come, let us have something to drink.
DUBOSC: Yes, I am thirsty. Garçon, some brandy!
      (*Entre* WAITER, *who takes bottle and glasses, and exit. They sit.*)
DUBOSC: Which of you is a lender of horses?
CHOP: I, Pierre Choppard, the jockey, generally known and appreciated as the amiable.
DUBOSC: And this imbecile is Fouinard, whom they call the philosopher.
FOU: (*flattered*) He knows me – the great thief knows me – oh, citizen! (*He bows.*)

DUBOSC: We want a third.

CHOP: We want Courriol, who is never to his time.

DUBOSC: I cannot wait for him – I have business – here! (DUBOSC *signs to* FOUINARD *to come near, pours out a glass, and they touch glasses and drink. Then to* CHOPPARD) You have four horses?

CHOP: Yes.

DUBOSC: They will be ready! –

CHOP: In an hour.

DUBOSC: At the barrier of Charenton!

CHOP: Good.

FOU: (*timidly*) And – the object – for which we shall employ these quadrupeds?

DUBOSC: Fifty-seven thousand livres in gold; thirty for me, forty-five you three.

FOU: Oh, oh! (*He sings and dances.*)

DUBOSC: You shall know more when we are on horseback and upon our road. You will let Courriol know? (*going*)

(*Enter* COURRIOL.)

COUR: Here I am! Here I am!

CHOP: Ah, Monsieur Courriol, always behind time!

COUR: It was not my fault. (*He sees* DUBOSC.) Ah! (*in amazement*).

DUBOSC: Explain it all to him, I am going to the bar. Adieu, my chickens, adieu! (*Exit.*)

FOU: What is the matter?

COUR: Who is this man?

FOU: The famous Dubosc – the Man and the Brandy!

COUR: Dubosc! Is it Dubosc? – If I had not left Lesurques on horseback this very minute, I could swear – what a resemblance!

CHOP: Come, come, we have but one hour, come!

FOU: Seventy-five thousand livres – oh! (*He sings and dances in delight.* CHOPPARD *pushes him, and exeunt.*)

SCENE 2. *The front of Lesurques's cabaret at Lieursaint, with its sign, set upon the high road from Paris to Lyons. It is five o'clock in the afternoon. The cabaret, which is open to the audience's view, is raised by three steps above the ground. Tables, stools, buffet, bottles, and candles are visible. There is a door to an inner room at the back, and traps to the cellar at the front. There is a table outside, and trees extend to the back of the stage where the high road lies.* JEROME *comes out of the house, and sits at the table.*

JEROME: No travellers! No visitors! This, the last day of my residence here, will be as the preceding. No one! The house is cursed! 'Tis well that I am compelled to quit it. I must go to Lieursaint, and give my consent that the auberge be sold, that my creditors, having all, may have nothing more to claim from me – and tomorrow – well tomorrow, I shall be without shelter, without resources – but at least my honour will remain.

(*Enter* JOLIQUET *from the road.*)

JOLI: Master! Master!

JEROME: Well, Joliquet?

JOLI: What will you give me for what I am going to give you?

JEROME: Is it good or is it bad?

JOLI: It comes from Douai, therefore it must be good. (*He gives* JEROME *a letter, and goes behind the house to the road.*)

JEROME: From Douai! From my son Joseph! Ah, thank heaven! I was despairing and you have sent me consolation. (*He reads.*) 'Dear father, I shall arrive at Paris tomorrow with my daughter Julie; we are residing Rue Montmartre, No. 118; I shall marry Julie to a noble fellow, who will make her happy. Come and see us as soon as you receive this note. We sign the contract tomorrow after dinner – from your affectionate son, Joseph Lesurques.' Tomorrow! (*with sadness*) Yes I shall be able to visit you tomorrow – I shall be free – for tomorrow I shall have no business, no home. But my son shall not know my misery, nor the unhappiness that surrounds me: poor fellow! He who has laboured so hard and so well, why grieve him with my misfortunes. Tomorrow, I will put on my Sunday suit, and an air of contentment; I will not carry a gloom to the betrothal of my dear grandchild: and afterwards – we shall see. Joliquet!

JOLI: (*advancing from the road*) Master!

JEROME: I am going out – take care of the house.

JOLI: Ah, that will not be difficult, for there is very little for anyone to run away with.

JEROME: True! But there is some wine and brandy; and it is necessary someone should be here when the courier of Lyons passes. We always take care that the courier shall be well served.

JOLI: Do not fear, master – a small glass of the hard for the postilion, a half bottle of the old for the courier – but where are you going, if I may ask, master?

JEROME: I am going to Lieursaint, Joliquet.

JOLI: And what to do, master?

JEROME: Sell the house and find you a better master.

JOLI: Sell the house! And me with it!

JEROME: Yes, you with it.

JOLI: Well, whoever buys us will have a bargain with me, whatever he may have with the inn, not that that would be a bad speculation if we ever had customers – but you're not going to Lieursaint tonight?

JEROME: Yes, I must, but you will not stir from here. (*with a sigh*) Now, Joliquet – my hat! (*Hat and stick are fetched.*) Yes, the house must be sold – it is a sacrifice, but it must be made. (*Exit.*)

JOLI: Good-bye, master, and may you find a good customer for the house! Well, this is not a very bad place, that's a fact; I don't tire myself in waiting on the guests; the perquisites will never burn a hole in my pocket. It is funny, but I like to be left alone because I am frightened; and when I am frightened, I go to the top of the hill to the cabaret of our neighbour – there they laugh and talk. It is not a hermitage like this. He is gone! Yes, I'll go too; the house can take care of itself, and I'll be back before eight o'clock to receive the courier. It is not likely that anyone will come while I'm away, when for days we do not see a

---

glass of the hard: a glass of the hard stuff; a spiritous liquor.

single person. Hollo! Who is this, I wonder! A traveller! What's he looking at? Why does he stop? It looks very suspicious that a traveller should come to our inn – I feel very nervous – if I hide myself, I shall see what he is after.

> (*Music.* JOLIQUET *enters the house, and hides behind the door. Darkness comes on gradually. There is complete darkness during the attack on the mail. Enter* LESURQUES, *enveloped in a cloak.*)

LES: Yes, it was my father I saw in the distance. Oh, yes, I could not mistake him.He looked sad and bowed down with grief. Thank heaven! Now his troubles will cease. What solitude! And what misery! No one to receive travellers. I did well to leave my horse down in the little wood. I will go in and see if there is anyone in the house. (*One of his spurs drags on the ground. He knocks on the door.*)

JOLI: (*within, in a tremulous voice*) Who's there? (*He calls.*) A thief! A thief!

LES: Eh! – a thief. Which is he - you or I?

JOLI: I don't know. What do you want?

LES: Refreshment.

JOLI: You must go somewhere else, we don't sell it.

LES: Then what means this sign here? Open, I say! Give me one of your best bottles of wine and here is a crown for you.

JOLI: A crown! (*He opens the door a little, and peers out.*) Yes, it looks like a crown – he must be an honest man. (JOLIQUET *emerges.*) You wish for some wine, citizen?

LES: Yes.

JOLI: Why did you not come earlier? Will you have white or red? You will lose your spur, the chain is broken.

LES: True. Give me a little thread, I will join the links; as to the wine, which you like. Where is the cellar? (*They enter the house.* JOLIQUET *lights two candles, and gives to* LESURQUES *some thread.*) Thank you. One can go there? (*He points to the door of the inner chamber.*)

JOLI: There? No, not there. That is the master's chamber.

LES: (*mending the spur*) That is his chamber, eh? Good! My wine, garçon, and let it be fresh.

JOLI: I will fetch it from the cellar. (*He opens the trap, and disappears with a candle, but the light is seen through a small grating in front.*)

LES: (*producing from under his cloak a small bag of money*) With this money, my poor father, you can pay all your debts, and be under no obligation to anyone – not even to me. I have fixed upon the bag a label, which will put you at your ease in accepting it, 'Restitution'. My poor father has been often robbed, and, believing in the remorse of the robbers, he will think it is his own property restored. Now then, to place the bag. (*He enters the inner chamber, and returns immediately.* JOLIQUET *sings while in the cellar.*) I have nothing more to do here. My dear child expects me, and I would not make her uneasy. (*Six o'clock strikes.*) Oh! Six o'clock! I shall be in Paris before seven. (*Exit.*)

JOLI: (*returned, singing*) There, you'll like this, it's only disturbed once a day, that's every night, for the courier, who passes at eight o'clock. There! Do not break the glass, that is so unlucky and costs two sous. Shall I pour it out for you? Where are you? (*He looks about, and then goes outside.*)

(*Enter* DUBOSC *wearing a dark mantle like* LESURQUES, *together with* FOUINARD, COURRIOL, *and* CHOPPARD, *who remain at the back.*)

DUBOSC: Wait while I knock.

JOLI: (*seeing him*) Ah, there you are! Drink that – and give me your opinion. I like the white myself, but everyone to his taste. (*He offers* DUBOSC *the glass.*)

DUBOSC: What do you mean? Who is this animal?

JOLI: (*placing the bottle upon the table*) Animal?

DUBOSC: You are alone here?

JOLI: No, I'm not.

DUBOSC: Eh?

JOLI: Not if you call yourself anybody.

DUBOSC: Give us something to drink.

JOLI: (*pointing to the bottle*) There's your bottle.

DUBOSC: Is one bottle sufficient for four persons?

JOLI: Four! You're not four. (*He sees the others.*) Ah, those heads!

DUBOSC: Where is the cellar?

JOLI: (*trembling*) You know very well – you asked me once before.

DUBOSC: (*menacing*) Well, will you bring it?

JOLI: (*trembling*) I am going. (*He enters the house and descends into the cellar.*)

DUBOSC: Advance, comrades. You have seen this fellow who is in the cellar?

COUR: Yes.

CHOP: The rascal. Well?

DUBOSC: We must begin by stopping his mouth.

FOU: Poor little devil.

COUR: What do you gain by killing him?

DUBOSC: This much, that he will not see what we are going to do.

COUR: Well, then, I will prevent his seeing – Garçon!

(JOLIQUET *comes from the cellar.*)

COUR: How many bottles have you brought, my man?

JOLI: (*placing the bottles upon the table*) Two, sir. (*aside*) I like the looks of this one.

COUR: We must have two more, go fetch them. (*Gives him money.*) Here!

JOLI: It rains money today – I am going, sir! (*He goes down into the cellar.*)

COUR: (*to* CHOPPARD, *and* FOUINARD, *who enter the house*) Now assist me in placing the buffet upon the trap – then this table – there, if he comes up now it will surprise me.

CHOP: I believe we are quite alone, now we can drink.

DUBOSC: Is that the wind? (*He drinks, goes out of the house, and listens.*) Nothing yet – what is that?

COUR: What do you hear?

DUBOSC: What is the time?

COUR: A quarter to eight.

JOLI: (*from the cellar*) Ah, they have locked me in! Let me out! Open the trap!

DUBOSC: (*enters the house and speaks at the trap*) If you speak another word, I will open it, and then that word shall be your last! Do you hear? Silence, or death!

CHOP: (*to* DUBOSC) Come, let us know your plans and intentions.

DUBOSC: (*makes sign for them to listen*) At eight o'clock you will hear the noise of
    horses, and the tinkling of the bells upon the horses –
ALL: Well?
DUBOSC: It is the courier of Lyons coming this way, before mounting the hill side,
    he will stop here to take a glass with the postilion.
ALL: Well?
DUBOSC: This courier has in charge, a coach, and in this coach there is a chest; and
    in this chest, there is at this moment the seventy-five thousand livres that
    I spoke about this morning – this is the speculation.
FOU: But the mail courier always carries pistols.
DUBOSC: (*producing his*) So do I.
FOU: And the postilion carries a hunting knife.
CHOP: And I a table knife (*showing one*).
COUR: There is generally a traveller who accompanies the courier – that makes
    three men.
DUBOSC: I have foreseen that; do not make yourselves uneasy. You have perfectly
    understood me?
FOU: Perfectly.
DUBOSC: Fifteen thousand livres for each of you, and thirty for me.
COUR: Be it so.
DUBOSC: Now this is the plan of the attack. When the courier arrives here,
    Courriol will follow the coach; I will pour out the wine; Fouinard must watch
    the road; Choppard must look to the postilion, and I will take the courier for
    myself.
        (*Eight o'clock strikes.*)
DUBOSC: Now let me see, are your hearts strong?
CHOP: Yes.
DUBOSC: (*regarding* FOUINARD) Master Fouinard looks pale.
FOU: It's my courage!
DUBOSC: But, Monsieur Courriol!
FOU: Oh, the coward!
CHOP: With his white hands!
COUR: (*calmly, while removing his gloves*) Monsieur Dubosc, when I am in want of
    money, nothing stops me, not even the soiling of my hands.
        (*The stage has become quite dark. The group in the inn are illuminated
        by a red glare from the fireplace.*)
DUBOSC: Hush! (*The distant noise of whip and bells increases as the coach arrives.*)
CHOP: There!
DUBOSC: Yes! Come, Fouinard, before; Courriol, behind the trees; Choppard, in
    the ditch; I remain here. (*They retire to their positions.*) This brute of a garçon
    remains still – he is quite alone here! Let me see! (*He enters the chamber with a
    candle, and brings out the bag of money.*) What is this – money! 'Restitution!'
    Come, that's delicate! Good, I accept the restitution. (*He puts it in his pocket.
    The noise of the coach comes closer.*) They come! (*The coach appears at the
    back of the stage, and the* POSTILION *alights.*)
POST: Hollo there, father Jerome! House!
JOLI: (*from the cellar*) Here! Here!

DUBOSC: The rascal! (*Concealing the voice of* JOLIQUET) Here! Here! (*He comes out of the house with brandy.*)

POST: It is not Joliquet.

DUBOSC: (*offering wine*) No, I have taken his place – but here is your glass.
>   (*The* COURIER *and a* TRAVELLER *come from within the coach to take refreshment.*)

POST: Your health, citizen! (*He drinks.*) I will go to my horses. (*He goes off behind the house.*)

COURIER: (*advancing*) It is not Joliquet.

DUBOSC: (*offering wine*) All the same, citizen, your wine.

COURIER: The same wine?

DUBOSC: Taste.

TRAV: Drink, courier, drink.

COURIER: Your health, sir. (*They drink. There are cries from the back of the stage.*) What is that?

POST: (*killed at the back by* CHOPPARD) Ah, they have killed me! Help! (*He staggers in, and falls.*)

COURIER: My postilion assassinated! Murder! (*He points a pistol towards* CHOPPARD, *and* DUBOSC *shoots him*) Wounded! Ah, brigands! There are two, but I have a companion! (*To* TRAVELLER) Assist me! Defend me! You have a sword!

TRAV: Yes, I have a sword. (*He stabs the* COURIER, *who falls.*)

DUBOSC: Well done, Durochat! Now, quick, break open the chest.
>   (FOUINARD *is upon the coach, throwing down all the papers and packets that he finds. They hand down the box, and break it open.*)

DUBOSC: Durochat, here is your part; jump upon the postilion's horse, and fly! (*The* TRAVELLER *runs away.*) Choppard, here is yours; you, Courriol; and you, Fouinard – now save yourselves! (*They go off.*) I must look after the courier's purse.

JOLI: (*from the trap*) Ah, he's here at last! Master! Master! Murder! Murder!
>   (*Enter* JEROME.)

JEROME: Ah, what is this? (*He seizes* DUBOSC.) Wretch! You shall not escape me!

DUBOSC: (*struggling with him*) Fool! Let me go – or die! (*He draws a pistol, and shoots* JEROME.)

JEROME: (*seeing his features by the light of the flash*) Ah! Great heavens! My son! My son! (*He totters and falls.* DUBOSC *escapes.*)

ACT II

SCENE – *An elegant apartment in the house of* LESURQUES *at Paris. There are doors to each side, and in the centre, opening into another room. There is a small table, with books and writing materials upon it; a sofa, another table, and chairs.*
DIDIER *and* JULIE *are discovered.*

DIDIER: (*a list in his hand*) I have counted and recounted; we shall be thirteen at table.

JULIE: (*seated on the sofa*) How unlucky! Thirteen at table on the day for signing our marriage contract.

DIDIER: A day commenced by so good an action, my dear Julie!

JULIE: What! You call it a good action, Didier, to succour a poor woman in misery? It should be but natural!

DIDIER: You might have done as many of the rich – turn the head, and pass on!

JULIE: Poor creature! She was dying with despair and famine; she had not eaten for three days. She would have expired with her child!

(*Enter* LESURQUES.)

LES: (*who has listened*) Yes, but heaven had seen this misery, has had pity, and sent to the poor mother one of its angels – my dear Julie.

JULIE: You there – and listening, fie! We shall be thirteen at table, dear papa.

LES: We shall be fourteen, my child, and he who makes the fourteenth you will not be sorry to see. Adieu, my children, I am going to the notary.

JULIE: Are you going to leave us again? Not as yesterday, I hope, going no one knows where, and breaking your spurs!

LES: (*laughing*) Ah, true, true!

DIDIER: And mending it with thread!

LES: I will escape now by running away. Au revoir, my dear children, au revoir.

(*Exit by the centre door, which remains open.*)

JULIE: Dear, good father.

DIDIER: He has an excellent heart! Can I be of any service to you before I leave, Julie? (*He takes his hat.*)

JULIE: No – I will excuse your absence knowing that you have affairs to attend to.

DIDIER: Thanks, dearest – but who comes here?

(JEANNE *appears at the back.*)

JULIE: Ah, it is the poor woman that I succoured.

DIDIER: And comes to thank you – I will leave you. (*To* JEANNE) Come in.

JULIE: Yes, (*to* DIDIER) you will return soon. (*Exit* DIDIER.)

JEANNE: (*near to the door*) You have saved me, madame, and saved my child! Heaven bless you!

JULIE: (*sitting*) Do not tremble thus, come nearer to me – you are better, are you not?

JEANNE: (*approaching*) Thank you, yes!

JULIE: I have given orders that your wants shall be attended to; but how is it you have suffered so much, and without making your misery known?

JEANNE: I have made it known.

JULIE: To whom?

JEANNE: Oh, not to hearts like yours, madame!

JULIE: You have a child – but – your husband? Perhaps you are a widow?

JEANNE: (*with hesitation*) Yes, madame – I am – a widow.

JULIE: You have parents, or friends?

JEANNE: No one. This morning I expected a little money that had been promised me, to take me to Alsace with my son –

JULIE: Well?

JEANNE: Well! The person that promised me the money, this morning, I have not been able to find.

JULIE: (*rising*) You conceal part of your misfortune – you have not confidence in me – you are wrong – what can I do for you? Speak!

JEANNE: Nothing! Nothing! You have already done too much – but why hesitate? I shall never have such another benefactress – so compassionate – so good. Madame, will you save me? (*She goes up to* JULIE.)

JULIE: In what way?

JEANNE: They tell me you are going to be married; you are rich, will require someone to attend upon you – I offer myself with all the ardour of deep-felt gratitude; I will not quit you, or give you time to form a wish; day and night I will devote myself to you; you may command my life! Only promise me that my poor child shall be cared for.

JULIE: I consent; you shall remain with us, but I am not yet at liberty to act according to the impulse of my heart. I must consult my husband tomorrow; today, my father; but he is so kind, so good –

JEANNE: Oh, madame, heaven will bless you for all the good you have done me!
    (*Enter* DIDIER *and* COURRIOL.)

DIDIER: Not here, Monsieur Courriol, not here.

COUR: No one yet – I am very happy to be the first to arrive. (*saluting her*) Mademoiselle – I should say, madame.

JULIE: (*curtseys*) You are welcome, sir. (*to* JEANNE *who is leaving*) Stay! Here comes my father.
    (*Enter* LESURQUES, GUERNEAU, *and* LAMBERT.)

LES: Enter, my dear friends. We are punctual to our time. Ah, Courriol, how are you? (GUERNEAU *and* LAMBERT *pay their respects to* JULIE, *then sit and talk.*)

JULIE: (*in a low voice*) Father, here is the poor woman.

LES: Ah, well?

JULIE: To assist without humiliating her, I would take her into our service.

LES: Very well. What is her name?

JEANNE: Jeanne, sir. (*She raises her eyes towards* LESURQUES.) Ah!

LES: Why this emotion?

JEANNE: Pardon me, monsieur – a resemblance.

LES: You are now one of our household, Jeanne; we receive you willingly –
    (DIDIER *goes towards* JULIE, *who has remained sitting*) try to do your duty, and we will do all in our power to render your labour agreeable, and your life happy.

JEANNE: I thank you, sir, with all my heart! (*aside*) So good – when the other –

LES: Come, my friends, and see my little gallery in the dining-room.

GUER: (*to* JULIE) Mademoiselle, allow me to offer my arm?

DIDIER: Pardon, sir, but –

GUER: I am sorry – pardon me, sir.
    (GUERNEAU *bows;* JULIE *takes* DIDIER's *arm, and exeunt.*)

COUR: Of what resemblance were you speaking, my good woman?

JEANNE: (*hesitating*) I! Sir –

COUR: (*aside*) She hesitates! Can she have seen Dubosc? Impossible! (*aloud*) You do not reply?

JEANNE: (*aside*) Why does he ask me that question?

(*Enter* DAUBENTON.)

DAUB: (*to* JEANNE) Monsieur Lesurques?

JEANNE: Yes, here, sir.

DAUB: Announce Monsieur Daubenton, judge of the division of Pont-Neuf.

COUR: A judge – oh! (*Salutes him.*)

JEANNE: (*going to the door*) Monsieur Daubenton, madame!
(*Enter* JULIE.)

JULIE: Monsieur Daubenton! Ah, my father will be very delighted to welcome you.
(*Exit* JEANNE.)

DAUB: And how are you, my dear little friend? You have returned – returned for ever?

JULIE: For ever – yes, sir. But excuse me, I will inform my father of your arrival – he is showing his pictures to his friends.

DAUB: (*retaining* JULIE) Do not disturb him, for I have not a moment to spare. A crime has been committed near to Paris. The affair has been confided to me, and I have witnesses to examine.

COUR: A crime? Where, sir?

DAUB: Sir, at Lieursaint.

COUR: (*aside*) At Lieursaint, Diable!

DAUB: (*to* JULIE) Who is this gentleman?

JULIE: Monsieur Courriol, a college friend of my father's, who dined yesterday with him. But what crime were you speaking of, Monsieur Daubenton?

DAUB: A frightful one! A terrible mystery!

COUR: (*aside*) A mystery – good! (*aloud*) Ah, a mystery?

DAUB: But we have some indication. I have sent off agents to collect witnesses. There is a certain innkeeper, named Jerome, that they have not yet found – but –
(*Enter* JEANNE.)

JEANNE: (*announcing*) Monsieur Jerome Lesurques!
(*Enter* JEROME.)

JULIE: My dear grandfather!

JEROME: My dear Julie! (*Exit* JEANNE.)

JULIE: This is the surprise – the fourteenth guest that he expected! But sit down, grandfather. (*She conducts him to the couch.*)

COUR: (*aside*) I think I know that figure! I have heard that voice!
(*Enter* DIDIER.)

JULIE: Monsieur Didier, dear grandfather, my future husband; who will be a good son to you.

DIDIER: Truly I will, sir.

JEROME: (*presses the hand of* DIDIER, *and embraces* JULIE) Is your father here?

JULIE: Yes, grandfather, he is with some friends – I will call him –

JEROME: No, no!

DIDIER: Permit me to go. (*Exit.*)

JULIE: You look pale, grandfather – you are fatigued?

COUR: Do you come far, sir? Perhaps from the country?

JEROME: Lieursaint, sir.

DAUB: From Lieursaint, sir! Do you know a person of the name of Jerome?

JEROME: (*rising*) It is I, sir!

COUR: (*aside*) I thought so.

DAUB: (*to* JEROME) You, sir! You the father of Monsieur Lesurques, established at Lieursaint?

JEROME: His father – yes! Is it astonishing that I am his father? ... That I come from Lieursaint?

JULIE: Dear grandfather, this is Monsieur Daubenton, a magistrate, who has been relating to Monsieur Courriol that a terrible crime has been committed this night at Lieursaint.

    (LESURQUES, GUERNEAU, *and* LAMBERT *appear at the door.*)

LES: Ah, my father! Dear and excellent father! You have arrived, then?

JEROME: (*trembling, and pushing him from him*) Oh, it is he!

LES: My father, are you not well?

JEROME: Well? Yes! (LESURQUES *takes his hand.*)

JEROME: (*again repulsing him*) Ah, you hurt me!

LES: }
JULIE: } What mean you?

JEROME: (*with pain*) A slight wound in the shoulder.

LES: (*with emotion*) A wound!

JEROME: (*quickly*) It is nothing.

DAUB: But, sir, you are from Lieursaint – you inhabit the place where the crime was committed! Saw you the horrible scene? Speak, Monsieur Jerome, I have sent agents to seek you for your deposition! Give me the details (*he sits, ready to write*).

LES: Ah, yes, speak, my father!

JEROME: You wish me to speak, Lesurques – be it so – the courier of Lyons has been assassinated with his postilion before my door!

    (COURRIOL *wipes his forehead with his handkerchief.*)

LES: (*with surprise*) Before your door! Yesterday evening! At what hour?

JEROME: (*equally astonished*) What audacity!

DAUB: (*writing*) Yes, at what hour?

JEROME: (*with calmness*) The courier passed regularly at eight o'clock.

DAUB: (*continues to write*) And you saw –

JEROME: I was absent at the time of the murder.

DAUB: You have a servant, I believe!

LES: Yes.

JEROME: (*quickly*) You know that? This lad, the assassins locked in the cellar, and there –

COUR: (*with emotion*) And there?

JEROME: From there he could see nothing. (COURRIOL *breathes again.*)

DAUB: They say you arrived at the time when the courier was shot.

JEROME: It is true.

DAUB: And you were wounded by one of the assassins?

JEROME: By one of the assassins.

DAUB: Then you saw him?

JEROME: As clearly as I see my son.

LES: You could recognize him then. A crime thus odious must not remain unpunished; give the description clearly, Father – say all that you know.

DAUB: (*to* JEROME, *rising*) It is your duty, Monsieur Jerome, and I now resume the character of magistrate to interrogate you, I will return to my own house – follow me.

LES: Monsieur Daubenton, you have thrown fear and sadness into our little circle; by taking my father away from us, you will double this sadness – this fear. Remain, I pray you, my father will give his deposition here, as well as at your house.

DAUB: I would willingly, but I expect witnesses.

LES: But they may not come – give me the preference, this saloon will serve as your court: if of great importance there will be time to return to your own house.

COUR: (*aside*) If I escape, it will excite suspicion.

LES: You will consent?

JULIE: Join your entreaties to ours, Monsieur Courriol, requesting Monsieur Daubenton to remain.

COUR: (*going unwillingly towards him*) You, Monsieur Daubenton, will not hesitate – to remember – that – the dinner is waiting.

LES: (*laughing*) Good, Courriol, good; we will not pay for the guilty!

JEROME: (*aside*) What assurance! Comes it from an honest man, or a hardened ruffian?

DAUB: I will remain as you desire it, Mademoiselle.

LES: I am very glad of that! Julie, we will go to dinner, look to your grandfather, take care of him, see if he suffers from his shoulder.

JULIE: Come, grandfather!

(JEROME *and* JULIE *exeunt.* JEROME *looks dejected.*)

LES: (*to* DAUBENTON, *who is going*) A word, Daubenton. My friends, I will be with you immediately – follow them, Courriol!

COUR: (*aside*) What can he want with Daubenton? (*Exit.*)

LES: Tell me, Daubenton, will there be much trouble for my father in this sad affair?

DAUB: No, his testimony, once given, I will endeavour not to call upon him until he is required to identify the guilty party.

GUER: Lesurques, you did not tell us yesterday that your father lived at Lieursaint!

LES: He concealed it from all except me; not one in the family knew it.

GUER: It was there you were bound for on quitting us yesterday! Some kind action you wished to conceal!

DAUB: You were at Lieursaint yesterday?

LES: (*hesitating*) No! Merely taking the air – a ride to – to Vincennes.

(*Enter* JEANNE *with a letter.*)

JEANNE: Monsieur the judge, an agent and two gendarmes are below with a witness.

DAUB: (*to* LESURQUES) You see, a witness, it is necessary that I should go.

LES: This saloon is at your service. Can you not interrogate the witness here?

DAUB: True. It is a mere form. Ten minutes will suffice.

LES: (*to* GUERNEAU *and* LAMBERT) Come, we will leave Daubenton! Jeanne, bring in those that would speak to monsieur. There are pens, ink, and paper, you have there all that is necessary to convict twenty villains. Despatch them, my dear friend, quickly, the soup is getting cold. (*Exit.*)

(JEANNE *has retired, and returns with the* AGENT, *who salutes.*)

DAUB: Who have you brought?

AGENT: The witness that you intrusted me to bring from Lieursaint, the garçon of the auberge.

DAUB: He that the murderers locked up in the cellar – bring him in. (*He sits at the table.*)

(*Enter* JOLIQUET.)

DAUB: What is your name?

JOLI: Joliquet, sir, in the service of Monsieur Jerome.

DAUB: Jerome Lesurques?

JOLI: Ah! I don't know if it is Lesurques, I know that it is Jerome.

DAUB: You were there when the murder was committed?

JOLI: I was in the cellar.

DAUB: But before the murder?

JOLI: First of all a man asked me for wine, and thread to mend his spur, the villain!

DAUB: Ah, this is important! And afterwards?

JOLI: Afterwards, I saw him who –

DAUB: (*returns to table and takes notes*) Wait.

(*Enter* COURRIOL.)

COUR: (*aside*) Decidedly, the wisest plan will be to escape from here. (*To* DAUBENTON) Pardon, but – (*perceives* JOLIQUET) the garçon! (*He moves up stage.*)

JOLI: Ah! (*in terror*).

DAUB: What?

JOLI: That is one of them!

COUR: (*aside*) He recognizes me!

JOLI: It is he that locked me in the cellar!

COUR: (*aside*) If I hesitate, I am lost! (*aloud*) What is it? Who is it? (*He advances.*)

JOLI: The robber!

DAUB: Are you mad, young man, or speak you according to your conscience?

JOLI: I tell you, it is he!

COUR: This garçon has lost his wits from fear!

JOLI: I recognize his voice! Arrest him! Arrest him, gendarmes! (*He runs to* COURRIOL *and seizes him, calling*) Gendarmes!

(COURRIOL *seizes* JOLIQUET *by the throat. The* AGENT *goes to the back of the stage, and beckons on two gendarmes, who remain near the door.*)

COUR: (*shaking* JOLIQUET) Miserable wretch!

JOLI: Oh, gendarmes, gendarmes! (*The* AGENT *separates them, and reassures* JOLIQUET.)

DAUB: Sir, be patient!

COUR: Sir, such an absurd accusation –

DAUB: You can the more easily disprove it.

(*Enter* JEROME.)

JEROME: What is the matter?

JOLI: Ah, master, master! I have one of them, that is to say, we have one!
  (*Enter* LESURQUES, *followed by* GUERNEAU, LAMBERT,
  DIDIER, *and* JULIE.)

LES: What is the meaning of this noise?

JOLI: (*pointing to* LESURQUES) Ah! Here is the other (*all start*). There is the
  assassin of the courier!

LES: I?

JULIE: My father?

COUR: (*aside*) Oh, the resemblance!

DAUB: (*to* JOLIQUET) What, you also accuse monsieur? This is folly.

JOLI: It is he that broke his spur.

JULIE: His spur! Merciful heaven!

JOLI: And to whom I gave the thread to join the chain.

JULIE: The chain! Ah, my father!

JEROME: (*with dismay*) All is lost!

DAUB: (*to* JOLIQUET) But my friend has not been to Lieursaint.

JEROME: (*to* JOLIQUET) No, no!

JOLI: Ah, master! You say that – you that received his pistol shot.

JEROME: I tell you it was not him, he was not at our house.

LES: This is useless – I might have been at Lieursaint, and still not culpable. I am
  not in want of a lie to defend myself.

GUER: Were you at Lieursaint?

LES: Yes. Well, did you not see me go upon the horse I borrowed of Courriol?

DAUB: You own having been at Lieursaint yesterday with Monsieur Courriol?

LES: I did not say with Courriol, but a horse that he procured me.

GUER: ⎫
LAM: ⎭ It is true, we assert that.

COUR: But, sir, I might lend a horse to Lesurques without going to Lieursaint. I
  was not at Lieursaint!

JOLI: That's a lie!

DAUB: And you entered the house of your father as the witness declares?

LES: I did.

DAUB: You broke, and afterwards mended, your spur?

LES: Why should I deny it?

JEROME: (*aside, to his son*) Be silent, unhappy one.

DAUB: Take care, Lesurques; if you avow this you confirm this young man's
  statement and recognition.

LES: Assuredly, and I recognize him also.

DAUB: But he says you are the assassin of the courier!

LES: I!

JEROME: No, Joliquet will not say that – he did not say it.

JOLI: (*hesitating*) Why, master –

DAUB: Ah, you are not quite sure, then?

JOLI: Why, sir – you see, he's my master's son –

LES: Oh, that is not the language required; I will have no prevarication. Did you see
  me at the house of my father – yes or no?

(JOLIQUET *looks at* JEROME, *and hesitates.*)

LES: Father, let him speak the truth.

JEROME: You will be lost!

LES: Did you see me – yes or no – at my father's house; and did you give me thread to mend my spur? Why not say yes, since I say yes!

JOLI: Then, yes!

LES: You also know I left the house while you fetched some wine! During the time you were in the cellar, you sang – that you know!

JOLI: (*see* JEROME) Must I say yes?

LES: Now, father, you speak! You know what I went to your house for!

JEROME: (*astonished*) I!

LES: Yes, you must now cast aside your delicacy of feeling. Say what you found!

JEROME: What I found!

LES: In your own room – speak quickly!

JEROME: I know not what you mean.

LES: The bag containing money that I placed upon your bed.

JEROME: Upon my bed?

LES: Yes – why do you not speak, father? I was at Lieursaint, but to carry money for you. Justify me then, my father. You can do so; and let them not take me for an assassin!

JEROME: (*stammering and tottering*) No! No! Ah! (*He swoons. They place him upon the couch. There is general consternation.* JEANNE *brings a smelling bottle.*)

DAUB: Do you persist in saying you saw Monsieur Lesurques at your master's house at Lieursaint on the night of the murder?

JOLI: Yes, sir.

COUR: (*to* DAUBENTON) But then, sir, I?

JOLI: (*earnestly*) Oh! He is not one of the family! I will not hesitate about him! My head upon the block, I still say – yes, I saw him! He was there!

DAUB: Gendarmes, arrest that man! (*He rises, and touches* LESURQUES *upon the shoulder*) Lesurques, in the name of the law, I arrest you!

JULIE: (*going to* LESURQUES) Father!

LES: (*embracing her*) My daughter! (*Everyone is in consternation.*)

ACT III

SCENE 1. *A boudoir in the house of Lesurques. There are doors to either side, and a window looking out into the garden at the back. There is a secretaire with writing materials in it, a sofa, and a table with a lighted candle upon it.* JEANNE *enters.*

JEANNE: No, it is impossible! Judges, witnesses, nothing can ever convince me that he is culpable! There is some fatal mistake. Can his resemblance to Dubosc be the secret? Merciful heaven! Am I to be the means of saving a life that saved mine? The poor young girl, if I could only but save the honour of her family by my life, I would give it with joy! They have preserved a mother for her son – if it is my blessed lot to restore a father to his child! Oh, for a proof, a single proof that it is as I suspect, and you shall see if I can forget the good you have done to me, dear mistress! One single proof, and you shall see, Dubosc, that I remember the ill that you have done me!

(*Enter* JULIE, *with a letter in her hand.*)

JULIE: Jeanne!

JEANNE: (*aside*) She has been crying again, poor child. (*aloud*) Madame?

JULIE: How is my grandfather this morning?

JEANNE: The same, mademoiselle.

JULIE: Has he slept?

JEANNE: He has not slept since he has been here!

JULIE: (*going to the table, and looking amongst the papers*) No news from Monsieur Daubenton? Not one of my father's friends called?

JEANNE: No one comes here now.

JULIE: (*quickly*) No one?

JEANNE: Except Monsieur Didier, who calls every day.

JULIE: (*sadly*) Yes; but he did not come yesterday – for the first time he has abandoned me, it is but natural. If he comes –

(*Enter* DIDIER.)

JULIE: Jeanne, you will tell him – (*she sees* DIDIER) Ah!

DIDIER: (*going to* JULIE) Julie!

JEANNE: I knew he would come. (*Exit.*)

DIDIER: You receive me coldly, is it because I was not able to come yesterday? Oh, believe me –

JULIE: You need not excuse yourself – I have nothing to exact from you – I do not reproach you. (*She gives him a letter.*) In reading that, you will see, that far from accusing, I thank you. I do not accuse you, Monsieur Didier – if I were to I should be ungrateful.

DIDIER: You will leave me?

JULIE: Read! Often the hand has the courage to trace a word that the lips refuse to pronounce.

DIDIER: What word? You alarm me! Of what word would you speak? Oh, stay, Julie, I entreat.

JULIE: It is a word which places eternity between friends who are separated – it is the word adieu, Monsieur Didier.

DIDIER: Adieu! You say adieu! You have written it; you will separate yourself from me! And what for?

JULIE: Because you are an honest man; because you may have a happy future; because your name is spotless, and I – read, read, and spare me the anguish of telling you what I have written.

DIDIER: (*tearing the letter*) I will not read the word adieu, written by you, Julie. Look at me – reflect, and if you have the courage to say so to my face, then speak it.

JULIE: I tell you it is not just that you should be burthened with the weight of our shame and our misfortune. Didier, disgrace, ruin, and despair hover over this house. Fly! It is yet time – fly while I speak; tomorrow, perhaps, it will be too late.

DIDIER: Julie!

JULIE: Oh, it is not that my father is culpable – in my eyes! Of what importance is it to what say the witnesses, what say the accusers, or the decision of the jury? For eighteen years since first I took breath I have seen him, and known him to be the best, the most noble of men. I am the daughter of Lesurques – it is my duty to speak thus; you have also a father – you who have sisters – you should not share our dishonour, which will fall also upon your family. You have promised me marriage – I return you your liberty. Didier, you are free from this moment.

DIDIER: Mademoiselle, I believe that I am considered an honest man – if I take back my promise, I should cease to be so. To whom am I engaged? To your father! Of his innocence you are sure, you say? I go further – for I will prove it – even should it take all the time I have to pass on earth. I have sworn to your father to make you happy. That oath, mademoiselle, I adhere to! I will accomplish this work; and when I shall have reached the end of my task – when I have aided you, and, if possible, consoled you during the captivity of your father – when I see him free – when I know there exists not a shadow to mar your happiness – not a cloud in the future – then, mademoiselle, forget not your words: 'Didier, I marry you not because I am rich, happy – but I marry you because I love you.'

JULIE: Oh, Didier, I love you more than ever!

DIDIER: (*taking* JULIE*'s hands*) You love me, Julie – then your hand in mine. Julie, we have two inexhaustible resources that nothing can subdue – our love, which will support us through all trials – our conscience, which will plead for us before the tribunal of heaven – we must not despair. And now, dear Julie, let me ask you to summon all your fortitude, to bear the tidings I have to impart.

JULIE: A misfortune!

DIDIER: A happiness! Ah, a great happiness!

JULIE: (*with joy*) My father is acquitted.

DIDIER: Not yet, but he will be!

JULIE: Ah, take care, Didier, if you deceive me – after joy like this you will kill me.

DIDIER: Listen – whilst Lesurques vainly tried to prove that he entered Paris at seven o'clock in the evening of the 8th of May, I have been to the house of Choppard, the lender of horses, who has disappeared. His register of the sums he receives for the horses hired, contains the hour in which each horse returns; this book, this witness so many times invoked by your father had disappeared and could not be found. Ten times yesterday was I at the house of Madame Choppard, begging her to give me the book – this evening I returned again, 'Here is five thousand francs, give me the register.' 'I have it not', she replied. 'Here is ten thousand.' 'Impossible!' she said, looking at the money, 'I have burnt it.'

JULIE: Oh, heaven!

DIDIER: Her eyes were riveted upon the money, 'Remember', I replied, 'by keeping the book you become an accomplice in the murder of an innocent man.' She began to tremble. 'Well', I replied, 'It is no longer ten thousand but twenty that I offer; here – in this pocket book; give me the register, and the money is yours.'

JULIE: Well! Well!

DIDIER: She rose, and counted the notes; then breaking with her foot the horsehair cushion of the chair upon which she had been sitting, drew out the register – and it is here! (*He shows the book.*)

JULIE: Thank heaven!

DIDIER: Read, Julie: '8th May – The Blower, hired by Monsieur Lesurques – thirty sous the hour – started at four o'clock; returned at half-past seven – received five francs' – signed by the wife of Choppard. It was eight when the courier of Lyons was murdered at Lieursaint; the assassin would not be able to reach Paris before half-past nine o'clock, and this book proves your father to have returned at half-past seven. He is saved!

JULIE: (*with emotion*) Saved! Oh, blessed word!

DIDIER: There is not a moment to be lost!

JULIE: We will take this register to Monsieur Daubenton (*going*).

DIDIER: (*stopping*) Give me your father's pistols, Julie!

JULIE: (*with fright*) What to do?

DIDIER: In coming here, I have been followed!

JULIE: Followed!

DIDIER: The moment I came out of the house of Choppard, a man entered – an ill-looking fellow – I observed another in the street – I walked fast – it appeared to me in a few moments I heard someone running behind me. I then increased my speed. I will not go out with this register without arms. This book is precious; to lose it is to lose the life of your father!

JULIE: (*going to the secretaire*) You are right.

DIDIER: But, no – hold! I think we will have a coach, and go together; they will not attack a coach in Paris at half-past eight. Quick, Julie; dress yourself, while I fetch a conveyance. (*He gives the book to* JULIE.)

JULIE: Ah, Didier, how shall I ever be able to repay you for so much devotedness!

DIDIER: (*kissing her hand*) With your love. Julie, in ten minutes –

JULIE: I shall be quite ready. (*She joyfully places the register in the secretaire, and goes off.*)

(*Exit* DIDIER. JEANNE *has entered during the above.*)

JEANNE: (*alone, and placing a light upon a stand*) Now will Providence, whom I have so wrongfully accused, save the innocent, and spare me the misery of denouncing the culpable. Dubosc is the father of my child! If he is doomed, it will not be by me!

JULIE: (*off*) Jeanne! Jeanne!

(JEANNE *exit into* JULIE's *room, taking the light. As soon as the light has gone,* FOUINARD *is seen to cut the glass and open the window. He assures himself that there is no one in the room, then returns to the balcony, and beckons.*)

FOU: Now, quick!

DUBOSC: (*appearing on the balcony*) Is there no one?

FOU: No!

DUBOSC: (*entering*) Who was here?

FOU: Two women jabbering with the young man. You get the book (*going towards the window*).

DUBOSC: Where are you going?

FOU: (*on the balcony, in a low voice*) I will watch below.

DUBOSC: You are a brave man, Fouinard! Are you sure he has not taken the book?

FOU: No, I saw him put it there! (*He points to the secretaire, and opens a dark lantern.*)

DUBOSC: Here it is! (*reading*) '8th May – Lesurques – the Blower – returned at half-past seven.' (*He takes a knife from his pocket, and begins to scratch the writing.*)

FOU: Take the book – it is the easiest way!

DUBOSC: Imbecile! The book that cost them twenty thousand francs may be missed instantly on their return.

FOU: Ah, that is true! But come, come, I am getting nervous. Some one comes.

DUBOSC: Bah! Here – there is twenty thousand francs thrown away! (*He closes the book triumphantly.*)

JULIE: (*off*) Come, Jeanne!

FOU: Some one comes. (*He darts over the balcony.*)

DUBOSC: (*hiding behind a table as he cannot get to the window quickly enough*) Diable!

(*Enter* JULIE *and* JEANNE, *with a light.*)

JULIE: I think I heard the coach!

JEANNE: Yes, mademoiselle!

JULIE: Come at once! Ah, the book. (*She takes the book, kissing it joyfully.*) Oh, treasure, dear, precious book!

(*Exuent* JULIE *and* JEANNE.)

DUBOSC: (*alone*) Thirty-two thousand and twenty makes fifty-two thousand francs! By my faith, I will marry Madame Choppard when she is a widow!

(*The door opens suddenly.* JEANNE *appears with a candle in her hand.*)

JEANNE: A man here!

DUBOSC: Jeanne!

JEANNE: Dubosc. Ah!

DUBOSC: Jeanne in this house! (*He makes towards the window.*)

JEANNE: (*intercepting him*) Ah! Villain! Open not that window – or I will call for assistance!

DUBOSC: (*pointing to the door*) Then by here, make way for me to pass.

(*He strikes out her candle, and the stage is plunged in darkness.*)

JEANNE: I let you pass! When you can restore the life and honour of a family! Never! Never! (*She locks the door, and takes out the key.*)

DUBOSC: No jesting with me! You know me! I have no wish to settle our accounts here!

JEANNE: It is you, ruffian! You assassinated the courier of Lyons!

DUBOSC: The better reason that I should save myself now!

JEANNE: You do not leave this room as you entered! The measure of your crimes is full – you shall now pay for your past wickedness!

DUBOSC: Open that door!

JEANNE: (*with resolution*) You shall not escape! (DUBOSC *makes for the door, but* JEANNE *places herself in front of it.*) You do not leave, I say! Will you give yourself up to justice?

DUBOSC: That is good!

JEANNE: Will you set at liberty the innocent? Know you that there is an avenging angel?

DUBOSC: Good-bye, Jeanne! (*He goes towards the window.*)

JEANNE: (*seizing him*) You shall not escape!

DUBOSC: Let go! (*He strikes her.*) Let go!

JEANNE: (*runs to the window, and opens it*) Help! Thieves! Murder!

DUBOSC: Ah! (*He puts his hand over her mouth, but* JEANNE *hurls him from her, and screams.*) Be quiet – I will make you rich! Be still – I will make you my wife! Be still, I say!

JEANNE: (*escapes from him, and runs to the window*) Help! Help!

> (DUBOSC *seizes her, and a violent struggle takes place. He strikes her down, she rises. He draws a knife, and stabs her. She staggers and falls. He raises the window, and escapes.*)

SCENE 2. *An apartment in* DAUBENTON's *house. There are central doors, chairs, and tables, with writing materials.*

> (*Enter* DAUBENTON *and* AGENT.)

DAUB: Let the accused be conducted hither; the testimony of these new witnesses will be decisive. The man, Choppard, whom you have at last discovered, must have concealed himself to avoid affording his testimony. Lesurques has been for years my friend; I cannot believe him guilty, and will allow him every opportunity to disprove this most fearful accusation, that my duty to the public will allow. Let the accused mingle with the other parties present, and let no distinctive mark guide the witnesses in the identification of the persons accused. Should Lesurques pass this ordeal, his innocence will be at once manifest. (*The* AGENT *throws open the central doors and beckons.*)

> (*Enter four* GENDARMES *conducting* CHOPPARD. *They remain on each side of the entrance.*)

DAUB: (*to* AGENT) This man is the witness, Choppard!

CHOP: (*advancing*) Yes, sir, Pierre Choppard. (*aside*) Witness! All goes well.

DAUB: You disappeared the day after the murder – that is strange.

CHOP: Sir, it is my custom to attend the fair of Perche: the murder would not prevent me attending to my business!

DAUB: You have also business at Paris – we require you as a witness; we would confront you with the accused.

CHOP: I am ready, sir. (*aside*) Who have they taken? Courriol is the only name that I know! I care very little for him. They have not taken the grand and illustrious Dubosc, the only one of the gang in whom I am interested?

> (*Enter* LESURQUES *and* COURRIOL, *followed by* LAMBERT, GUERNEAU, *and several police* AGENTS.)

CHOP: Dubosc! Oh, they have taken him!

DAUB: (*to* CHOPPARD) Who do you recognize here?

CHOP: (*aside*) Now is the moment. (*aloud*) I? But – I recognize Monsieur Courriol. Ah, Courriol, how do you do?

COUR: Your humble servant, Monsieur Choppard.

DAUB: What have you to say, sir, relative to the 8th of May?

CHOP: Nothing in particular.

DAUB: On that day did he not hire a horse of you?

CHOP: Perhaps, yes; perhaps, no – I do not know!

COUR: I often hire horses at his house; that is not astonishing!

DAUB: Silence! (*to* CHOPPARD) There is another person here that you will recognize also?

CHOP: (*aside*) Now it's coming! Who?

DAUB: (*pointing to* LESURQUES) This gentleman, for example.

CHOP: (*going up to* LESURQUES) That gentleman? I do not know him.

DAUB: He was at your house on the 8th of May. (LESURQUES *comes forward.*)

CHOP: My house? (*He makes a sign to* LESURQUES.)

DAUB: Without doubt, sir, he has himself declared it.

CHOP: (*surprised*) Sir! (*to* LESURQUES) You have declared it? That –

LES: Declared what?

CHOP: That you came to my house.

LES: Conducted by Courriol, yes.

CHOP: The 8th of May, the day of the murder?

LES: The 8th of May.

CHOP: (*aside to* LESURQUES) Ah, you are a fool!

LES: What mean all these signals?

DAUB: Signals?

CHOP: Signals, oh, no. It's a cold I've got, sir.

LES: I do not know you; but I was at your house on that day.

CHOP: Sir, I do not say no; I did not see you, for I was not at home.

DAUB: If you were not at home, where were you then?

CHOP: (*aside*) I shall put my foot into it.

COUR: I will aid his memory if monsieur the judge will allow it. (*upon a sign from* DAUBENTON) It was about four o'clock, was it not, Lesurques?

CHOP: (*astonished*) Lesurques!

COUR: (*aside to* CHOPPARD) It is not Dubosc, it is a man who resembles him, and whom they have taken for him.

CHOP: Ah, it is not Dubosc!

COUR: It was about four o'clock, and at that hour Choppard was at home.

CHOP: Ah, yes, at that hour I was at home!

LES: But I did not see you!

CHOP: I might be there without your seeing me.

COUR: Monsieur Lesurques took a horse from your stables, Choppard?

CHOP: Yes, the horse we call the Blower.

COUR: But I – did I take a horse that day, Choppard? Was I with Lesurques?

CHOP: With Lesurques? No, I swear that –

DAUB: I did not ask you that.

COUR: Sir, it is the means to prove my innocence.

CHOP: It is true that he is innocent, like me.

COUR: Ask Lesurques again if I was with him at Lieursaint.

LES: No, he has not been there – at least with me!

CHOP: And now, sir, that you have received my deposition, I am at liberty to return?

DAUB: No, not yet.

CHOP: But, sir, this is the hour to feed the horses, and to feed myself: I'll come, sir, at any time you please to appoint, I will, upon my honour!

DAUB: I still require your presence.

CHOP: What to do, in the name of thunder?

DAUB: You will know directly. (*A noise is heard.*) Be seated, Lesurques. You, Monsieur Courriol, talk with Monsieur Lambert. Choppard, you will come to this side. I request that there may be no affectation, no constraint; and that no one will speak without my consent.

CHOP: (*aside, and sitting*) What devilish idea has he now, that he makes me stay here? Well, it is a resemblance!

> (*The witnesses are introduced: an* OLD MAN, *the postmaster, his* NIECE, *and* GARÇON.)

OLD MAN: Sir, I have been told that you desired to speak to my niece, myself, and garçon: we are here.

DAUB: You are the owner of the post-house at Montgeron, and it appears certain that the assassins of the courier of Lyons had refreshment at your house.

OLD MAN: Unhappily, sir, yes.

DAUB: You have said, I believe, that you can give some important information?

OLD MAN: Sir, I can, for I distinctly remarked all four. (CHOPPARD *and* COURRIOL *evince terror;* LESURQUES *only listens with interest.*)

DAUB: All! And if you should see them?

OLD MAN: Sir, I should know them.

CHOP: (*aside*) An old vagabond!

DAUB: Tell us anything you may have remarked.

OLD MAN: First of all, they were on horseback, all four.

GARÇON: Upon hired horses. (CHOPPARD *exhibits great terror.*)

DAUB: Ah, you believe they were hired horses?

GARÇON: That was easily known – they were so lean.

CHOP: (*aside, and in disgust*) You're a nice judge!

DAUB: And then?

OLD MAN: Speak, niece.

NIECE: And then, sir, I filled for one of them a large decanter of brandy.

CHOP: (*aside*) That's Dubosc's only weakness.

OLD MAN: (*to* GARÇON) Do not forget the brush you lent to the most gentleman-like of the four, to remove the dust from his blue waistcoat.

COUR: (*groans and buttons his coat*) Oh!

DAUB: Is that all?

OLD MAN: Ah, no. There is one circumstance which I have not related yet to anyone, which I have reserved for the court of justice.

DAUB: Well, then, relate it now.

OLD MAN: One of them repeated, constantly knocking with a whip upon the table, 'In the name of thunder, my horses will be broken winded!'

DAUB: Do you recognize him?

OLD MAN: It appears to me that I see him there. (CHOPPARD *draws back.*) When the four horsemen were gone from my house, we discovered that one of them had forgotten his whip – it is he of whom I speak. We went after them –

they had disappeared; but about half-an-hour afterwards he returned for the lost whip – it was I that gave it to him. He took it so rudely from my hands that the knob of the whip fell off.

DAUB: He picked it up, no doubt?

OLD MAN: He was in such a hurry that he did not perceive it had fallen off; when he was gone I sought for it, picked it up, and saw two letters engraved upon it – P and C.

DAUB: P and C?

OLD MAN: Sir, here it is.

DAUB: Come and look at it, Monsieur Pierre Choppard.

CHOP: (*frightened*) Sir?

DAUB: (*sternly*) Approach, sir!

        (CHOPPARD *approaches, and turns to him most reluctantly.*)

OLD MAN: (*recognizing him*) That is the man!

LES: (*starting up*) He!

NIECE: (*recognizing* LESURQUES) And that's the man that had the brandy.

GARÇON: (*pointing to* COURRIOL) And that's the gentleman who borrowed the brush. (*There is a general sensation.*)

DAUB: You see those three men, are you quite sure you recognize them?

WITNESSES: (*solemnly, raising their hands*) We swear it!

DAUB: This one is the owner of the lost whip, the one who spoke of the broken-winded horses, and to whom the handle belongs.

OLD MAN: Yes!

NIECE: } Yes!
GARÇON:

CHOP: Because there's a C engraven upon it. Am I the only man in France whose name commences with a C?

DAUB: (*signs to an* AGENT, *who gives him a whip*) Look at this – see if the handle belongs to this whip, that was found just now at the house of your wife. (*He puts the knob on the whip, and holds it up.*)

CHOP: There are ten others at the house of my wife, had your spies searched for them.

DAUB: (*taking two cheques from an* AGENT) But they have found something else.

CHOP: What?

DAUB: These two cheques of five hundred livres each upon the bank, numbers 159 and 180, which were stolen from the pocket-book of the courier of Lyons! Oh, I have watched you for a long time, Choppard!

CHOP: The devil – I am done for!

DAUB: Conduct him to prison! (*To* CHOPPARD) Have you any confession to make?

CHOP: I don't see what good that will do me.

LES: Gentlemen, in the name of heaven, own at least that I was not with you! Own that I was not at Montgeron! Own that you know me not!

CHOP: How would that serve *you*, when they won't believe *me*?

LES: (*to* CHOPPARD) But you know well that I am innocent. What have I done to you? Say, then, that I am guiltless. You know in your conscience, both of you, that I was not with you! Sir, if you have any belief in heaven – Courriol, if

there is one spark of humanity left in you – speak and say that I was not with
you.

COUR: No, you were not with me, nor I with you. We are both innocent!

CHOP: (*crying*) They will not believe it, these blood thirsty tyrants!

LES: I am lost! I am lost!

CHOP: Yes, but Dubosc is saved! It is sweet to do good (*aside*).

LES: (*to the* OLD MAN) Is it impossible that you can be my enemy? Look at me –
have I not the face of an honest man? Look at me well! I drank no brandy at
your house! Look at me, I say! There is no drop of blood in my veins, but boils
with indignation at this most foul accusation! Speak one word, mademoiselle!
(*To the* GARÇON) You, my friend – for my child's sake, for my father's sake
– speak! Say that you are mistaken! Say that you know me not! (*He falls on his
knees.*) I implore you on my knees. (*They fall back.*) You do not speak! (*rising*)
Oh, brain! Brain! I shall become mad! (*He falls powerless upon a chair.*)

DAUB: This man is a monster, or a martyr. (*To an* AGENT) Convey the prisoners
to separate dungeons. I have investigated this case – fairly; if I have been
partial, it has been in a leaning towards you, Lesurques; but all evidence
condemns you – evidence that it is as impossible to controvert as to disbelieve;
my conscience will not allow me to pause longer, unwilling, but truly, I declare
you, Joseph Lesurques, guilty!

(*Enter* JULIE *and* DIDIER *with the register.*)

JULIE: No, he is innocent!

LES: Julie! My child!

JULIE: Oh, my father, you are saved! (*To* DAUBENTON) Monsieur Daubenton,
suspend the proceedings – this proof we have so anxiously reached for – the
witness that will prove my father was far away from Lieursaint at the hour of
the murder, we have found!

LES: Great heaven!

JULIE: I feel choked – speak, Didier, speak!

DIDIER: (*to* DAUBENTON) If we prove that Lesurques was in Paris at half-past
seven on the eighth of May, will you believe him innocent?

DAUB: Yes.

JULIE: (*giving the register*) There is the register belonging to the wife of
Choppard. It contains an entry of the horse lent to Monsieur Lesurques, with
its return at half-past seven, signed by the wife of Choppard, on the eighth of
May.

DAUB: (*turning the leaves*) But – I do not see anything – no –

DIDIER: How!

JULIE: Let me show you.

DAUB: (*trying to decipher*) I see several words which resemble 'the eighth of May',
'to Lesurques' – I also see traces of figures, but all is scratched, effaced,
illegible!

DIDIER: (*taking the register from his hands*) Effaced! Illegible! Yes, yes, yes – it has
been effaced, but who has done this? (*To* JULIE) You have not quitted this
book, Julie?

JULIE: No, during the time I was dressing I placed it in the secretaire, and there I
found it.

DIDIER: Jeanne only knows, Jeanne only!

JULIE: Oh, it is impossible! Jeanne, that I have saved!

LES: Who, then? Who can have been thus my enemy – thus to steal my life and honour?

DAUB: Lesurques, this attempt to impose on justice but steels the hearts that would pity you. As a friend it is time that I should cease to know you. You are guilty! And as a murderer your fate is sealed – your judge tells you that your doom is death! (JULIE *shrieks, and faints in her father's arms.*)

LES: Now, as with my latest breath, I swear that I am innocent!

ACT IV

SCENE – *The first floor of a cabaret at the corner of the Place de Grève. In the distance is seen the Quay, and the Towers of Notre Dame. DUBOSC is sitting at a table, drinking. FOUINARD stands before him.*

DUBOSC: Some drink! I am thirsty!

FOU: (*uneasy*) You have had more than enough! Go, conceal yourself, I must go below to the shop!

DUBOSC: (*a little intoxicated*) I will not hide myself! I will not go! I will drink!

FOU: At least don't remain here. Remember the procession will pass directly underneath that window, and if you are seen –

DUBOSC: No one will come here. I hired this room for myself, to see the poor devils executed at my ease. Here I shall have a superb view!

FOU: (*drawing back*) Cruel devil!

DUBOSC: (*rising, threateningly*) Ah, is that it! Perhaps you would prefer me to appear in this procession, rather than the virtuous Lesurques?

FOU: Ah, mon dieu! I don't say that, but still one may feel some pity for this unhappy man!

DUBOSC: Pity? Curse you! You would rather it were me going to be guillotined instead of him? (*He takes* FOUINARD *by the collar and shakes him violently.*)

FOU: No, friend Dubosc, no! Now don't drink any more!

DUBOSC: (*drains a tumbler of brandy, goes to the window, and shouts.*) Come on!

FOU: Oh, murder! You must not cry out! You must not let them see you or we shall both be lost!

DUBOSC: Ah, poltroon! Contemptible sneak! (*He kicks* FOUINARD.) I will be sure that my place on the scaffold has been supplied! When a man, right or wrong, has paid his debt to society, society has no right to make another pay a second time – is that the law?

FOU: No!

DUBOSC: You lie, you cur! (*He kicks him again.*)

FOU: Ah, yes, yes – it is the law (*rubbing himself*). But do keep yourself quiet; remember we have the affair of the woman and the register.

DUBOSC: Jeanne!

FOU: Yes, you know – that little assassination!

DUBOSC: (*with a drunken air*) The only woman that I have ever loved!

FOU: (*aside*) I hear a noise – it is them! (*aloud*) Oh, heavens, if anyone comes up here! Dear Dubosc, don't go to the window.

DUBOSC: (*takes* FOUINARD *by the arm and whirls him about till he falls on the ground*) Ah, coward! Be off, cur, or I'll break your neck. This is my room. Be off, dog!

FOU: (*rising*) I go. (*aside*) If I could, I would twist his neck – but he is stronger than I am. I see he'll betray himself – it's no use – I may as well look to myself, and I will too! Good-bye, my dear Dubosc, take care of yourself. (*aside*) A dog, eh? Perhaps you'll taste the dog's teeth presently. (*Exit.*)

DUBOSC: (*closes and locks the door, then crouches down at the window looking through the balustrade*) Here they are! It is them, they approach! (*The noise of the crowd gets louder.*) Come along, come along, you devil's cart, quicker, quicker still! A few more turns of the wheel, and I am safe! (*The noise ceases.*) They stop! What's that for? Oh, they come on again. (*He advances towards the opening, then draws back again.*) Imbecile! What am I going to do? (*Renewed cries of the crowd as the cart arrives below the balcony.*)

COUR: (*from beneath the balcony*) Lesurques is innocent! (*The noise stops.*) Choppard and I are guilty! Kill us, we deserve to die, but Lesurques is innocent! (*There is a great tumult.*)

DUBOSC: (*lying on the floor*) Ah, ah, my friend – you may spare your breath – they go on. Ah, six steps more, and I am safe! Ah, hell! What woman is that? 'Tis Jeanne – yes, Jeanne – or her ghost; and Fouinard too! They are pointing to this place – they are speaking of me. Curses on you! Curses on you!

(*A frightful yell is heard outside which appears to approach the house. DUBOSC rushes backwards and forwards with wild gestures in despair. The tumult and the noise of feet ascend the stair and approach the door. He presses against the door with his back. It yields, and DUBOSC is pushed back and concealed behind it. Enter JEANNE and FOUINARD, with GENDARMES and the crowd. Other GENDARMES climb over the balustrade. DUBOSC is seized, struggling violently. Loud shouts are heard which herald the arrival of LESURQUES, who advances through the crowd with DIDIER and JULIE. Curtain.*)

IT IS NEVER TOO LATE TO MEND

It Is Never Too Late to Mend was produced at the Princess's Theatre on 4 October 1865, with the following cast:

MR WINCHESTER	Mr Tapping
GEORGE FIELDING	Mr George Melville
WILLIAM FIELDING	Mr Gascon Murray
MR MERTON	Mr H. Mellon
MEADOWS	Mr F. Villiers
TOM ROBINSON	Mr Vining
REVEREND EDEN	Mr J. G. Shore
ISAAC LEVI	Mr T. Mead
CRAWLEY	Mr Dominic Murray
HAWES	Mr C. Seyton
FRY	Mr Reynolds
EVANS	Mr Alford
JOSEPHS	Miss Louisa Moor
JACKY	Mr S. Calhaem
ABNER	Mr Bentley
GEOFFRIES	Mr R. Cathcart
HITCHIN	Mr Chapman
BOB HUDSON	Mr Andrews
BLACKWELL	Mr James
JEM	Mr Dowlins
JACK	Mr Hummerston
CARTER	Mr Swerdon
GROOM	Mr Tressider
SUSAN MERTON	Miss Catherine Rodgers

Poster for a Manchester production of
It Is Never Too Late to Mend

ACT I

SCENE – *The Grove farm house, and its stable. In the background, a stubble-field.*
Enter MR WINCHESTER *and* GEORGE FIELDING. *They have been riding;*
WINCHESTER *wears boots and spurs,* FIELDING *carries a whip.*
WINCH: The Grove is a bad farm, Fielding.
FIELD: Don't say so, sir.
WINCH: Go with me to Australia, and you shall have five hundred sheep and a run
for them; and cost you nothing.
FIELD: It's a handsome offer, sir, and like yourself. But emigrate? Leave England
and the plough to keep sheep in the wilderness? Why, la, sir, you might as well
try to transplant an old oak-tree, as a Berkshire farmer. Besides – you know,
sir – there is my cousin Susanna (*he looks down*).
WINCH: I know there is. And there is my cousin Flora. Why, what do any of us go
to Australia for? To lay our bones there? No. To make a lot of money; and
then come back and marry our Susans and Floras.
FIELD: That is common sense, sir.
WINCH: I am serious, farmer; but we can talk about it as we go along. Please to
show me the blacksmith's shop: I'm going to Australia; so I must learn to shoe
a horse.
FIELD: Well, I never. The son of an earl, and the first nob in Berkshire, a learning
to shoe horses.
WINCH: Why, an earl's son has got an arm, and ten fingers: so why not learn to use
them?
FIELD: That is commonsense again. This way, sir. (*Exeunt.*)
        (*Enter* CRAWLEY, *peeping.*)
CRAW: Another year gone by, and (*with amazement*) I'm not struck off the rolls! I
can't acccount for it. (*Snaps his fingers.*) That for the rolls! I have got Mr
Meadows. That is to say, he has got me. A great man. A wonderful man. The
way he enlisted me shows that. He saw I was a clever man – a clever *little* man;
but *unfortunate*; fond of a drop. He bought up my debts, took out execution,
held the axe of the law over my head with his right hand, and with his left
offered me his friendship – on one condition; that I should be his slave, his
white nigger. Well, I am. This great man and I, we do a deal of dirty work
together. But I get all the credit. I am an attorney of wood, a puppet attorney;
he pulls my strings out of sight and I do the movements. Where shall we all go
to? My orders today were to meet him here, and keep out of sight till I see him
alone. I have been close to him once, and heard him tell old Mr Merton –
Humph! Here he comes alone at last.
        (*Enter* JOHN MEADOWS)
CRAW: (*obsequiously*) Good morning, Mr Meadows.
MEAD: Seen George Fielding?
CRAW: Yes, Mr Meadows, just caught sight of his back, Mr Meadows.
MEAD: Follow him. And serve him with this. His rent is half a year behind. (*Gives
him a writ.*)
CRAW: (*examining it*) Why, your name is not here, sir.
MEAD: My name, fool? Am I a man to leave my footprints everywhere I walk?

CRAW: Oh, no, Mr Meadows, you are a wonderful man, an invisible man. You
   have but one little, little fault; you trust nobody, not even your faithful
   Crawley.
MEAD: (*sharply*) What do you want to know? And why?
CRAW: Well, sir, with a view to co-operation, sir, and not impertinent curiosity, I
   should like to know why you ran down the Grove farm to old Mr Merton just
   now, and why you told him Will Fielding was at the bank this morning, and the
   bank wouldn't cash their draft, and why –
MEAD: (*sternly*) So you have been listening to me.
CRAW: (*frightened*) Being ordered to play peep-bo; and – and – with a view to
   co-operate; not impertinent curiosity.
MEAD: (*reflecting*) You ask – me – to tell you what I scarce dare whisper to myself.
   Well: I will. For it burns my heart; and you will not betray me.
CRAW: Count on my fidelity, Mr Meadows!
MEAD: I count on this: if you opened your lips, I'd – (*he stamps on the ground as if
   crushing something.*)
CRAW: (*trembling*) That is about it, I believe.
MEAD: The secret is this. Come this way. I love George Fielding's sweetheart,
   Susan Merton.
CRAW: You love a woman? What are we all coming to? A great man, an iron man
   like you, love so small a thing – compared with yourself – as a woman?
MEAD: Crawley, I love her with all my heart, and soul, and brain. I love her with
   more force than such as you can hate.
CRAW: Oh, Mr Meadows, little men can hate pretty hard. And I suppose you hate
   George Fielding.
MEAD: Not I; he is in my way, that is all. And whatever gets in my way –
CRAW: Gets kicked out of your way, Mr Meadows.
MEAD: (*sternly*) You see the game. Serve the writ. Go!
CRAW: I fly, sir. Oh, how sweet to be trusted by a great man, (*aside*) and get him
   into my power in turn. (*Exit.*)
         (MEADOWS, *his hands behind him, begins to walk off thoughtfully
         when he is hailed by* HITCHIN, *the village constable, and a*
         LONDON POLICEMAN *in plain clothes.* HITCHIN *is heated.*)
HITCH: Master Meadows, sir, I have news for you. Your pocket was picked last
   Martinmas Fair?
MEAD: Yes.
HITCH: Should you know any of the money?
MEAD: I could swear to three notes of the Farnborough Bank.
HITCH: (*showing a note*) Is this one of them?
MEAD: It is. Who passed it?
HITCH: George Fielding's lodger, Robinson, if that is his name: but I suspect he is a
   London thief, taking an airing. Gentleman from Bow Street, come to see if he
   knows him.
MEAD: Is he at home?

Gentleman from Bow Street: Bow Street was a main police station in the West End of London.
A policeman is indicated.

HITCH: No – he is out fishing. We'll hang about the farm till he comes back, and
then we'll take him.

POLICE: You had better be at hand, sir, to identify the notes.

MEAD: I will not leave the premises. Stop – be cautious! If he is an old hand, he
will know the officer.

POLICE: Oh? I am dark, sir. He won't know me till I have got the darbies on him.
(*Exeunt* POLICEMAN *and* HITCHIN.)

MEAD: Here's luck! This stone will kill two birds: get me back my notes, and sting
George Fielding. He has often been warned against this Robinson; but he
never would listen. His friend a thief? He will be ready to fly the village for
shame. Hallo! Here comes another rival I am putting out of my way; the old
Jew.
(*Enter* ISAAC LEVI.)

LEVI: (*bowing low*) Good morning, sir.

MEAD: (*abruptly*) Good morning! If it is about that house, you may keep your
breath to cool your broth. The house is mine now.

LEVI: It is, sir. But I have lived there twenty years. I pay a fair rent; but if you think
anyone would give more, you shall lose nothing by me. I will pay a little more;
and you know your rent is sure.

MEAD: I do.

LEVI: Thank you, sir. Well, then –

MEAD: Well, then, next Lady Day you turn out bag and baggage!

LEVI: Nay, sir, hear me, for you are younger than I. When the hair on this white
head was brown, I travelled in the east: I sojourned in Madras and Benares, in
Baghdad, Ispahan, Mecca, and Bassora, and found no rest. When my hair
began to turn grey, I traded in Petersburg, and Rome, and Paris, in Vienna
and Lisbon, and other western cities, and, like my nation, found no rest. I
came to this little town, where least of all I thought to pitch my tent for life.
But here, sir, the god of my fathers gave me my wife, and here he took her to
himself again.

MEAD: (*roughly*) What the deuce is all this to me, man?

LEVI: Much, sir, if you are what men say – for men speak well of you. Be patient,
and hear me. In the house you have bought, two children were born to me,
and died from me; and there my Leah died also; and there at times in the
silent hours, I seem to hear their voices and their feet. In another house I shall
never hear them – I shall be quite alone. Have pity on me, sir, an aged and a
lonely man! Tear me not from the shadows of my dead! (*pause*) Let me prevail
with you.

MEAD: No.

LEVI: No? Then you must be an enemy of old Isaac Levi.

MEAD: Yes.

LEVI: Ha! What have I done to gain your enmity?

MEAD: You lend money.

LEVI: A little, sir, now and then; a very little.

---

the darbies: handcuffs.
next Lady Day: Lady Day was one of the traditional quarter days for the payment of rents.

MEAD: That is to say, you have no money in hand when the security is bad; but, when the security is good, no person has ever found the bottom of Isaac Levi's purse. Well, what you do on the sly, I do on the sly, old sixty per cent.

LEVI: The world is wide enough for us both, good sir.

MEAD: It is, and it lies before you. Go where you like; for the little town of Farnborough is *not* wide enough for me and any man that works my business for his own pocket.

LEVI: This is not enmity, sir; it is but a matter of profit and loss. Let me stay there, and I swear to you by the tables of the law you shall not lose one shilling per annum by me. Trust me!

MEAD: I'll trust you as far as I can fling a bull by the tail. You gave me your history – here's mine. I have always put my foot on whatever thing and whatever man has stood in my path. I *was* poor; I *am* rich – and that is my policy.

LEVI: It is a frail policy. Some man will be sure to put his foot on you sooner or later.

MEAD: What? Do ye threaten me?

LEVI: No, sir; but I tell you what these old eyes have seen in every nation, and read in books that never lie. Goliath defied armies, yet he fell by a shepherd boy's sling. Samson tore a lion with his bare hands; but a woman laid him low. No man can deny his kind. The strong man is sure to find one as strong, and more skilful; the cunning man one as adroit, and stronger than himself. Be advised, then; do not trample on one of my people. Nations and men that oppress us never thrive. Let me rather have to bless you. An old man's blessing is gold. See these grey hairs! My sorrows have been as many as they are; his share of the curse that is on his tribe has fallen on Isaac Levi; I have been driven to and fro, like a leaf, many years; and now I long for rest. Let me rest in my little tent, till I rest for ever. Oh! Let me die where those I loved have died, and there let me be buried!

MEAD: If you like to hang yourself before next Lady Day, I give you leave; but after Lady Day, no more Jewish dogs shall die in my house, or be buried for manure in my garden.

LEVI: (*giving way to his pent-up wrath*) Irreverent cur! D'ye rail on the afflicted of heaven? The founder of your creed would abhor ye, and I curse ye. Be accursed (*he throws his hands up*). Whatever is the secret wish of your black heart, heaven wither it! Ah, ha! You wince already! All men have secret wishes. May all the good luck you have be wormwood, for want of that – that – that! May you be near it – close to it – upon it – burn for it – and lose it! May it sport, and smile, and laugh, and play with you (*re-enter* GEORGE FIELDING, *attracted by the speaker*) – till Gehenna burns your soul upon earth.

MEAD: (*whose wrath has been visibly rising*) I'll smash your viper's tongue! (*He aims a blow at* LEVI *with his stick.*)

FIELD: (*coolly parrying the blow*) Not if I know it! You are joking, Master Meadows. Why the man is twice your age, and nothing in his hand but his fist. (*To* LEVI) Who are you, old man? And what do you want?

MEAD: He insults me because I won't have him for a tenant. Who is he? A villainous old Jew.

LEVI: Yes, young man, I am Issac Levi, a Jew. (*To* MEADOWS) And what are you? D'ye call yourself a heathen? Ye lie, ye cur! The heathen were not without their starlight from heaven: they respected sorrow and grey hairs.

MEAD: You shall smart for this. I'll show you what my religion is.

FIELD: Now don't you be so aggravating, daddy. And you, Master Meadows, should know how to make light of an old man's tongue. It is like a woman's – it is all he has got to hit with.

LEVI: See – see! He can't look you in the face. Any man that has read men from east to west, can see 'lion' in your eye, young man, and 'cowardly wolf' in his.

MEAD: (*trembling with rage*) Lady Day, Master Isaac; Lady Day!

FIELD: Lady Day? Confound Lady Day, and every day of the sort! There, don't be so spiteful, old man. Why, if he isn't all of a tremble! (*He calls.*) Sarah! (SARAH *opens the door.*) Take the old man in, and give him the best that is going, and his mug and his pipe; and don't go lumping down the chine under his nose, now. Forget all your trouble by my fireside, my poor old man.

LEVI: I must not eat with you, but I thank you, young man. Yes; I will go in and compose myself; for passion is unseemly at my years. (*He stops suddenly at the door.*) Peace be under this roof, and comfort and love follow me into this dwelling! (*He turns suddenly and gives* FIELDING *his hand.*) Isaac Levi is your friend. (*Exit into house,* FIELDING *looking after him.*)

MEAD: (*aside*) One more down to your account, George Fielding. (*Exit.*)

FIELD: Old man's words seem to knock against my breast. Master Meadows – gone, eh? That man has everybody's good word; parson's and all; but somehow I never thought he was the right stuff, and now I'm sure . . . Oh, here's Bill at last with the money, thank heaven! (*Enter* WILLIAM FIELDING.) Better late than never.

WILL: I couldn't get away before. Here's the money for the sheep – thirteen pound ten. No offer for the cow. Jem's driving her home.

FIELD: Well, but the money: the eighty pounds?

WILL: I haven't got it. Here's your draft: the bank wouldn't take it.

FIELD: They wouldn't take it? Ay, our credit's down: the whole town knows our rent is overdue. What's to be done? I suppose you know money must be got some way.

WILL: Ask a loan of a neighbour.

FIELD: Oh, Bill! To ask a loan of a neighbour, and be denied! It is bitterer than death! Who can I ask?

WILL: Uncle Merton, or Meadows, the corn factor. It would not be much to either of them.

FIELD: Show my empty pockets to Susanna's father? Oh, Will! . . . And I've just offended Meadows a bit. Besides, he's a hard man; a man that never knew trouble or ill luck. They are like flints, all that sort.

WILL: I'll ask him, if you will try Uncle: the first that meets his man to begin.

FIELD: That is fair: I agree.

(*Exit* WILLIAM. *Enter* MR MERTON.)

MERT: George, you are threshing out new wheat!

FIELD: (*looking down*) Yes.

MERT: That is a bad look-out: a farmer has no business to go to his barn door for rent.

FIELD: Where is he to go, then? To the church door, and ask for a miracle?

MERT: No, to his ship-fold, to be sure.

FIELD: You can do that: you have grass, and water, and everything to hand.

MERT: And so must you do it, or you won't die a farmer. Now, George, I must speak to you seriously: you are a fine lad, and I like you very well; but I love my own daughter better. I have seen a pretty while how things are going here; and, if she marries you, she will have to keep you instead of you her. You are too much of a man, I hope, to eat a woman's bread; and, if you are not, I am man enough to keep the girl from it.

FIELD: Those are hard words to bear, so near my own door.

MERT: Well, plain speaking is best when the mind is made up. Good morning, George. (*Exit.*)

FIELD: Good morning, *uncle*! My mother took him out of the dirt, or he'd not have a ship-fold to brag of – the ungrateful old hunks.

(*Re-enter* WILLIAM, *peeping.*)

WILL: Well, will he lend it you?

FIELD: I never asked him. Bill, he begun upon me at once – he sees we're going down hill – and he as good as bade me not to speak to Susan any more.

WILL: It was your business to own the truth, and ask him to help us over the stile. A bargain's a bargain. I asked Meadows, and he said no: you fell talking with uncle about *Susan*, and never put the question to him at all. Who is false, eh?

FIELD: If you call me false I'll knock your ugly head off, sulky Bill.

WILL: You're false, and a fool into the bargain, bragging George.

FIELD: What! You will have it, then?

WILL: If you can give it me.

FIELD: Well, if it is to be, I'll give you something to put you on your mettle. The best man shall farm the Grove, and the second best shall be a servant on it – for I'm sick of this.

WILL: And so am *I*! And have been this two years.

(*They shake hands, and then begin to spar. Suddenly* FIELDING *drops his hands, looking very sheepish.*)

FIELD: Susan! (WILLIAM *puts his hands in his pockets, looks uneasy, and takes a step or two.*)

(SUSANNA MERTON *enters rapidly, and stands between* WILLIAM *and* FIELDING.)

SUSAN: What is this?

FIELD: Oh, nothing. William was showing me a trick he learned at the fair; that is all Susan.

SUSAN: That is a falsehood, George. You were fighting, you two; I saw your eyes flash. (*They exchange a rueful look.*) Oh, fie, fie! Brothers fighting in a Christian land, within a stone's throw of a church where brotherly love is preached as a debt we owe to strangers, let alone our own kin. What a ruffian you must be, to shed your brother's blood.

FIELD: La, Susan, I wasn't going to shed the beggar's blood – I was only going to give him a hiding for his impudence.

WILL: (*calmly*) Or take one for your own. (FIELDING *shakes his fist at* WILLIAM.)

SUSAN: Take his hand this instant.

FIELD: (*deprecatingly*) Well, why not? Don't you go in a passion, Susan, about nothing. (*They take hands.*)

SUSAN: Now, you stay so, whilst I speak a word to you. You ought both to go on your knees, and thank providence, that sent me here to prevent so great a crime. Your character must change greatly, George Fielding, before I trust myself to live in a house of yours.

FIELD: Ah! It is always poor George that does all the wrong.

SUSAN: Oh, I could scold William too, if you think I am as much interested in his conduct as yours.

FIELD: No, no! Don't scold anybody but me, Susan! I couldn't bear that. I'll tell you, Susan, and then, perhaps, you'll forgive me – and Bill, I ask your pardon.

WILL: No more about it, George, if you please.

FIELD: Susan, you don't know all I have to bear. My heart is sore. Uncle twitted me this morning with my ill luck, and as good as bade me speak to you no more; and that is why, when William came at me on the top of such a blow, it was more than I *could* bear; and, Susan, Uncle said you would stand to whatever he said.

SUSAN: George, I am sorry my father was so unkind.

FIELD: Thank ye, Susan, kindly; that is the first drop of dew that has fallen on me today.

SUSAN: But obedience to parents is a great duty, and I *hope* I shall never disobey my father.

FIELD: (*testily*) Oh! I don't want any girl to be kind to me that doesn't love me. I am so unlucky, it wouldn't be worth her while, you know.

SUSAN: (*sharply*) Well, I don't think it would be worth any girl's while, till your character and temper undergo a change.

FIELD: Enough said! I have no friend upon earth. I am in everybody's way here (*turning up stage*).
(*Enter* ROBINSON.)

ROB: Everybody is, in this country. It is so small: two steps, and into the sea. For the fiftieth time, will you come to California, and make your fortune?

SUSAN: You have been there, and did not make yours.

ROB: I beg pardon, miss, I made it – or how could I have spent it?

WILL: Ay! They say what comes by the wind goes by the water.

ROB: Alluding to the dust?

SUSAN: Gold dust especially.

ROB: That is not bad for Berkshire; but the ladies are sharp in every latitude. Miss Merton, a crop of gold does not come by the wind any more than a crop of wheat; gold takes harder digging than your potatoes. You should have seen our shirts in California after a day's digging; if we had wore them in the river they wouldn't have been wetter, and the little boys in California wanted two shillings a shirt for washing them: so we sent them to China in ships; she did 'em for fourpence. We sent them Monday morning, just as we do here – only, in stead of Saturday, we get 'em back Saturday six weeks.

SUSAN: Two shillings a shirt? Why they make them, and wash them, and sell them for that here.

ROB: Very much to the credit of the old country – over the left. Well, you see, miss, work is rewarded in California: here it is snubbed. This very morning, I heard one of your clodhoppers say, 'The squire is a good gentleman: he often gives me a day's work' – *Gives* me a day's work! I should think it was the clodhoppers *gave* the gentleman the day's work, and the gentleman give him a shilling, and he made five by it. (WILLIAM *scratches his head.*) Ay, rake that idea into your upper soil, Master Will. And that is why I want my friend George to take his muscle, wind, pluck, backbone, and self out of this miserable country, and come where the best man has a chance to win.

SUSAN: It is very interfering of you.

ROB: Oh? I'll bring him back again. Come, George, England is the spot, if you happen to be married to a duke's daughter: and got fifty thousand a year – and two horses – and a coach – and a curricule – and a brougham – and ten brace of pointers – and a telescope, so big, that the stars have to move for *it*, instead of *it* for the stars – and no end of pretty housemaids – and a butler, with a poultice round his neck, and whiskers like a mophead – and green peas all the year round – and a pew in the church, warmed with boiling eau de cologne – and a pianoforte in every blessed room in the house – and a silver tub full of rose-water to sit in and read the 'Morning Post'. But this island is the Dead Sea to a poor man. Open one eye, George. This hole you are in is all poor, hungry, arable land, without a blade of grass – you can't work it; cut it. Beg, borrow, or take five hundred pounds. Carry out a cargo of pea-jackets and fourpenny bits, to swap for gold dust; a few tools, a stout heart, and a light pair of – oh, no! 'Their name is never heard' – and we'll soon fill both pockets with the shiners in California.

(*Enter* SARAH *from the house, ringing a handbell.*)

ROB: (*stopping his ears*) Come, dinner! dinner! Oh, that horrid bell will never stop. (*Exit* SARAH.)

SUSAN: I want to speak to George first.

(*Exeunt* WILLIAM *and* ROBINSON.)

SUSAN: That is a very bad acquaintance for you, I'm sure. Father says he has no business or trade, and he is not a gentleman: so he can't be good for much.

FIELD: Uncle is not my friend. Robinson is my friend: that is his fault. He is the only creature that has spoken kind words to me today. Oh! I saw how bitter you looked at him for taking my part.

SUSAN: (*whimpering*) You are a fool, George. You don't know how to read a woman, nor her words, nor her looks either (*going, with her handkerchief to her eyes*).

FIELD: Forgive me, Susan! My heart feels like lead. And words have been said to me that will never go out of my heart. Your father has turned my blood to gall.

---

over the left: on the credit side of a financial balance sheet.
pea jackets and fourpenny bits: a sailor's short woollen overcoat of coarse cloth, and a small silver coin, both of which would be useful to trade.
'Their name is never heard': perhaps an advertising slogan.

I begin to hate the place where I was born. I loved it well till today. And I feel as if everything was turning cold and slippery, and gliding from my hand in spite of me!

SUSAN: (*uneasily*) Nonsense, George! You want to make me cry. Now you take my hand, and come to dinner. (*Exeunt, hand in hand.*)

(*Enter* MEADOWS *and* CRAWLEY.)

MEAD: Now before I turn you off, and beggar you, and send you to prison, for dawdling with my business, have you any excuse to make?

CRAW: (*trembling*) Yes, Mr Meadows. The weakness of human nature. I have watched George Fielding like an eagle; and I have followed him – like a dog; but I couldn't serve the distress.

MEAD: Why not?

CRAW: He had his horsewhip in his hand. He would not put it down.

MEAD: What is that to me?

CRAW: Oh, nothing, Mr Meadows. You are a great man; you don't serve your own writs. But I am a little one, and do. And it was a big horsewhip; and it is a legal maxim, 'Never serve a little writ on a big horsewhip.'

MEAD: Coward! (*He reflects.*) Run down to the river-side and you will see the constable with a stranger. Tell them from me, their man is come home.

CRAW: Yes, Mr Meadows.

MEAD: Don't you wait for them, but run back here, and serve the writ on George Fielding before them all. I'll be here and protect you, horsewhip or no horsewhip.

CRAW: You *are* a great man, Mr Meadows. (*Exit hastily.*)

(*Enter a* CARTER, *dragging in* JOSEPHS.)

CART: Oh, here ye be, master. We ha' found how the taters went out o' the cart. This young shaver took 'em. So I ha' took he; and here he be.

JOSEPHS: Oh, please forgive me this once; oh, pray let me go.

MEAD: I'll let you go to jail, you young thief. You have been at my potatoes this fortnight. There has been a hole made in them every night.

(*Enter* ROBINSON.)

ROB: What do I hear? A thief. What, are there thieves down here among the daisies?

MEAD: Weeds grow on every land, Mr Robinson.

JOSEPHS: No, no! I'm not a thief. (*To* ROBINSON) Oh, good gentleman, speak for me. Mother has nothing to eat. I only took a handful for her, no more than a meal.

ROB: Naughty little boy! What, steal a handful of potatoes? That is degrading the business.

MEAD: There, lock him in the stable till the constable comes this way; he won't be long.

JOSEPHS: Oh, no, no, no! Oh, pray don't send me to prison. I will be a good boy. I'll starve sooner than take a tatoe for mother again. I will be a good boy! (*He struggles with the* CARTER.)

ROB: (*coming close to him*) Hold your tongue, you young rogue. (*aside*) I'll let you out, boy. (*He makes himself very busy locking* JOSEPHS *in the stable.*)

MEAD: (*ironically*) Much obliged for your assistance, Mr Robinson.

ROB: (*politely*) You are welcome, Mr Meadows. Should be happy to do as much for
yourself. You hardened brute.
      (*Enter* SUSAN, *followed by* FIELDING *and* WILLIAM.)
SUSAN: Why, what is the matter? We heard someone crying.
ROB: Only a poor little fellow that has been taking a few potatoes out of a rich
man's cart, without leave.
      (*Enter* CRAWLEY.)
SUSAN: (*looking him keenly in the face*) We call that stealing here, sir.
CRAW: He has dropped his whip. I have got something for you, Mr Fielding.
      (CRAWLEY *serves his writ.* FIELDING *takes it, reads it, and*
      staggers.)
SUSAN: George!
FIELD: A distress on the farm! On my father's farm; where we have lived honest so
many years. (*He hides his head in his hands.*)
SUSAN: George! George! Don't despair! Can nothing be done? Where is my father
gone? He is rich; he will help you. (*She runs up stage calling.*) Father, father!
Ah, there he is. Father! (*Enter* MERTON.) Oh, father! Poor George!
MERT: Lawyer Crawley here! I guess how it is. You had better come home with
me, girl.
SUSAN: What, when he is in trouble? No, father, I am too uppish with him in
prosperity to be unkind in hard times. I shall stay.
CRAW: (*aside to* MEADOWS) Do you hear that, Mr Meadows?
MEAD: Curse it.
MERT: Well, George, I told you how it would end.
FIELD: (*fiercely*) What, do you come here to insult over me? I must be a long way
lower than I am, before I shall be as low as you were when my mother took
you out of the workhouse and made a man of you!
SUSAN: Oh, George, stop, for pity's sake, before you say words that will separate
us for ever! Father, how can you push poor George so hard? Hush! Hush!
      (*Enter a* SERVANT *with a letter for* FIELDING.)
SERV: You are to send an answer, if you please.
FIELD: From the Honourable Mr Winchester.
MERT: What, does he write to you?
FIELD: So it seems. (*reading*) 'George Fielding, my fine fellow, do think of it again.
I have got two berths in the ship that sails from Southampton tomorrow; you
will have every comfort on the voyage. I'll do what I said for you, and after
one year, you will farm on your own account.' He promised me five hundred
sheep and a run for them. (*reading*) 'I must have an honest man, and where
can I find as honest a man as George Fielding?' Thank you, Mr Winchester –
thank you, sir. (*He looks round on them all.*) 'You saved my life; I can do
nothing for you here, and you are doing no good – everybody says so.'
Everybody says so! 'My heart is pretty stout, but home is home; and I wait
with some anxiety to know whether my eyes are to look on nothing but water
for the next four months, or are to be cheered by the sight of something from
home; the face of a thoroughbred English yeoman; and a friend and – and –'
(*he falters*).
SUSAN: (*taking the letter from him she reads*) 'An upright, downright honest man.'

And so you are, George! 'If the answer is favourable, a word is enough. Meet me this evening at the "Crown" at Reading, and I will drive you tomorrow morning in Lord Tewkesbury's trap, which is gone forward for that purpose.'

FIELD: (*to* SERVANT) The answer is 'Yes!' (*Exit* SERVANT.)

SUSAN: Yes? What do you mean by yes? He is asking you to leave us all and go to – oh, George!

FIELD: This gentleman respects me, if worse folk don't; but it isn't the great bloodhounds and greyhounds that bark at misfortune's heels, it is only the village curs, when all is done. There lies my path – I'll pack up my clothes and go. (*Exit* FIELDING.)

SUSAN: Oh, father, what have you done?

MERT: No more than my duty, girl, and I hope you will do no less than yours.

WILL: George will forget her out there, and she him. Heaven forgive me for being glad of my brother's going.

ROB: Go to Australia? He's mad! There's no good to be done there. I wouldn't go there (*re-enter* HITCHIN *and* OFFICER, *cautiously*) if my passage was paid, a new suit of clothes found me, and a house provided for my reception, and the governor's gig to take me from the ship. Australia!

> (*The* CONSTABLE *and the* OFFICER *take him.* SUSAN, *who was about to follow* FIELDING, *looks back in dismay.*)

ROB: (*with a look of disgust*) Ugh!

POLICE: To Australia you'll go, Tom Lyon, alias Scott, alias Robinson, and you'll have the new suit of clothes, and voyage paid, and a large house ashore made ready for your reception (*he puts handcuffs on* ROBINSON).

ROB: (*with dignity*) What am I to understand by this violence, from gentlemen who are perfect strangers to me?

CONST: (*taking bank notes out of his pocket*) Mr Meadows, what were the numbers of the notes you were robbed of?

MEAD: 381, 2, and 3.

CONST: 382 passed by this gentleman at the 'White Lion', and the others found upon him. Better leave them with the officer for the present.

ROB: (*snuffling*) Appearances are against me, Miss Merton, but my innocence will emerge all the brighter for this temporary cloud.

SUSAN: Oh! (*Turns away from him and exit.*)

ROB: (*drily*) Well, Jacobs, you seem pleased, and I am content. I would rather have gone to California, but any place is better than England. Let chaps that never saw the world, and the heavenly countries there are in it, snivel at leaving this isle of rocks and fogs, and taxes and nobs; the rich man's paradise; the poor man's ... I never swear, it's vulgar.

> (*Re-enter* FIELDING *and* SUSAN.)

FIELD: A thief? Have I taken the hand of a thief?

ROB: It is a business, like any other.

FIELD: If you have no shame, I have. Oh, how I long to be gone from this nest of insults.

ROB: Did ever I take tithe from you, George? You have got a silver caudle-cup, a heavenly old coffee pot, no end of spoons, double the weight the rogues of silver-smiths make 'em now. They are in a box under your bed – count 'em

– they are all right; and, Miss Merton, your bracelet, the gold one with the cameo, I could have had a hundred times. Miss Merton, ask him to shake hands with me at parting. I am so fond of him; and, perhaps, I shall never see him again.

FIELD: Shake hands with you? If your hands were loose I should ram my fist down your throat. But there, you are not worth a thought, at such a time. You are a man in trouble, and so am I. I forgive you, and I pray heaven I may never see your face again (*he turns his back scornfully on* ROBINSON, *and exit*).

ROB: Well, Mr Jacobs, am I to be put in the pillory here? You should spare the feelings of an old friend – I may say a brother – for you were in my line once, you know. I say, do you remember cracking the silver-smith's shop in Lambeth, along with Jem Salisbury, and –

POLICE: There, enough chaff! On you go!

MEAD: (*opening stable door*) Here is another: you can take the two rogues together.

ROB: We leave worse rogues behind us. Don't snivel, boy. You will only get three months.

> (*Music plays. A* LAD *comes out of the house with a carpet-bag, followed by* SARAH. *She puts a bottle into the bag, then raises her apron to her eyes, and exit. The* LAD *crosses the stage, and exit. They all turn and watch him.*)

SUSAN: Father, I thought it was a dream; but he is going; he is really going. Oh, have mercy on us both! Speak him fair – his spirit is so high, father!

> (*Re-enter* FIELDING.)

MERT: Susan, the lad thinks me his enemy, but I am not. My daughter shall not marry a bankrupt farmer; but you bring home a thousand pounds, George – just one thousand pounds, to show me you are not a fool – and then you shall have my daughter, and she shall have my blessing.

FIELD: Your hand on that, Uncle, before heaven and earth! (*Takes his hand.*) You give me new life.

SUSAN: But your words are sending him away from me, father.

FIELD: Susan, I am to go. My path is clear. But don't forget, it is for your sake I go, my darling Susan.

> (*Re-enter* ISAAC LEVI *from the house.*)

LEVI: No. You shall not wander forth from the home of your fathers. I have sat in your house, and watched my friend and my enemy; and these old eyes have seen deeper than yours. You are honest; all men say so; I will lend you monies for your rent (*sharply*) upon fair interest; and the maiden who loves you will bless me.

CRAW: All our web undone in a moment, Mr Meadows.

FIELD: (*after a long pause*) No, sir! I *am* honest, though unfortunate; and proud, though you have seen me put to shame in my own homestead. To borrow without a chance of paying is next door to stealing. And I should never pay you. My eyes are open in spite of my heart. I can't farm 'The Grove' with wheat at forty shillings. I have tried all I know, and I *can't* do it. Bill, there, is dying to try; and he *shall* try – and heaven speed his plough better than it has poor George's.

LEVI: Young man, think what you do! You leave enemies behind you. A word in your ear (*they whisper, and glance towards* MEADOWS).

MERT: Good-bye, George, and good luck be with you!

MEAD: (*uneasily*) I'll go with you, Mr Merton.

FIELD: (*thoughtfully*) No, sir; stay if you please: you are as good a witness as I could choose of what I am going to say to my brother William.

MEAD: (*aside*) I doubt what is coming. The keen old Jew has blown on me. I wish I could sink into the earth!

FIELD: William!

WILL: (*uneasily*) George! (*aside*) It is about the farm. Oh, yes, it must be about the farm!

FIELD: I've often had it on my mind to speak to you, but I was ashamed – now that's the truth. But now I am going away from her, I must unload my heart, and I will. (*pause*) William!

WILL: George!

FIELD: (*very slowly and deliberately*) You have taken a fancy to my lass, William. (WILLIAM *looks up suddenly, then covers his face with his hands.*)

SUSAN: George – what nonsense! I am sure poor William . . .

        (FIELDING *points to* WILLIAM, *and* SUSAN, *in silence, looks down ashamed.*)

FIELD: Oh, it isn't to reproach you, my poor lad. Who could be near her, and not warm to her? But she *is* my lass, Bill, and no other man's. It is three years since she said the word, and though it was my hard luck there should be some coolness between us this bitter day, she will think kindly of me when the ocean rolls between us, if no villain undermines me.

WILL: Villain! George, that is a hard word to come out of your mouth.

FIELD: So 'tis, Will. But ye see, I must speak in time. It shan't be a *mistake*, or a *misunderstanding* – it shall be villainy, if it is done. Speak, Susan, before these witnesses, Mr Meadows especially.

SUSAN: Oh, George, you shall not go in doubt of me! We are betrothed this three years, and I glory in it; and now I give you my word again, in the sight of heaven, and these men, William, and good Mr Meadows: so long as you are true, I live for you – take my ring, and my promise, my own George – there was no coolness between us, dear; you only fancied so; you don't know what fools women are – how they delight to tease the man they love, and so torment themselves. I always loved you dearly, but never as I do this day. *So* honest! *So* proud! So *unfortunate*! I love you, I honour you. I adore you! (*She clasps him in her arms, and kisses him; he kisses her.*)

CRAW: Do you see that, Mr Meadows?

MEAD: Ay, and all my joy is wormwood.

        (FIELDING *wipes* SUSAN's *eyes, and she his, with the same handkerchief.*)

FIELD: Do you hear, William?

WILL: I hear, George.

FIELD: (*to* SUSAN) Then, Susan, here's your brother. (*to* WILLIAM) William, here's my life. Let no man rob me of it, if you believe one mother really bore us two.

WILL: Never! S'help me God! She's my sister – no more, no less; and may the red blight fall upon my heart and arm, if I, or any man, rob you of her. A man? Sooner than a hundred men should take her from you while I am here, I'd die at their feet a hundred times!

FIELD: I believe you! I trust you! I thank you! (*He goes to shake hands, but throws his arm round* WILLIAM's *neck.*)

CRAW: (*whispers*) Do you see that, Mr Meadows?

MEAD: (*whispers*) I see it, and I am in hell. But yet she shall be mine.

FIELD: And now, Will, you have given me strength to go, and I'll go; farewell, friends and well wishers all. Farewell, enemies, if I have got any, and may they never feel what I feel this day! Bless all the village, from the oldest man in it down to Luke Dodd's little girl that was born yesterdaynight. I never knew how I loved it till now. (*From here to the fall of the act drop, the air 'Home Sweet Home' is played softly in full orchestra.*) Good-bye, little homestead where I was born. Good-bye, little village church where I went to church, man and boy. Good-bye, churchyard where my mother lies. There will be no church bells, Susan, where I am going, no Sunday bells to mind me of my soul and home. (*Bells ring a merry peal.*) Why, what is that for? Are they mocking me? No. I mind it is Tom Clerk and Esther Borghirst married today. They have only kept company a year, and Susan and me we have kept company three years; and Tom and Esther are married today. But what are George and Susan doing today? (*He sobs.*)

SUSAN: Oh, George, my pride is all gone! Don't go! Don't think to go! Have pity on us both, and don't go!

FIELD: Shame on me! I that ought to comfort her! Bless you, Susan, darling (*he kisses her*). William, help me! I'm cold as ice. (*He beckons to* WILLIAM, *who comes and takes* SUSAN's *hand.*) Heaven help us both!

    (*He tears himself away, and runs sobbing out.* SUSAN *sinks fainting on* WILLIAM's *arm.* LEVI *turns and lifts his hands in blessing upon* FIELDING.)

MEAD: (*advancing towards* SUSAN) Mine! Mine!

LEVI: (*turning suddenly, and striking his staff on the ground between* MEADOWS *and* SUSAN) No!

    (MEADOWS *recoils one step, and they eye each other defiantly.*)

ACT II

SCENE 1. *A small apartment,* MEADOWS's *study, late that of* ISAAC LEVI.

MEADOWS *is discovered seated, and writing.*

MEAD: I am one against two. Will Fielding watches me, and if ever I get alone with Susan, up he comes and sticks to us like a leech. Old Levi has bought the neighbour house to this, and he watches me. I'll outwit them both. I am creeping to my mark by a by-road their shallow cunning will never think of; patiently, patiently, slowly, slowly: like a mole in the ground. Meantime, I'll remove the smaller obstacles, Will Fielding among them. (*He takes up a whistle from the table, and whistles cautiously.*)

    (*Enter* CRAWLEY *who stands beside him.*)

MEAD: (*without looking up or ceasing to write*) Is Will Fielding in the
town?

CRAW: Sure to be, sir; why, it's market-day.

MEAD: You got him to sign judgement for that money we lent him?

CRAW: Fell into the trap like a lamb.

MEAD: You had better take him at once. He is in my way.

CRAW: (*joyfully*) I will. I'll teach him to get in a great man's way.

MEAD: (*looking suddenly up, and eyeing him keenly*) You have got a spite against
this man.

CRAW: No, sir; nothing to speak of.

MEAD: Crawley, who are you trying to deceive?

CRAW: The devil. Well, sir, he did put a little affront on me. Called me a
pettifogger.

MEAD: Oh, is that all?

CRAW: No, he warned me off his premises: and threatened to horsewhip me next
time he caught me there.

MEAD: Oho. Is that where the shoe pinches?

CRAW: No, but he altered his mind – and did horsewhip me then and there –
without witnesses, curse him!

> (MEADOWS *seizes* CRAWLEY *by the collar.* CRAWLEY *goes
> instantly from fury to mean terror.*)

MEAD: And do you mix your paltry quarrels up with my business? How dare you
go in a rage?

CRAW: I am not: I'm in a fright.

MEAD: (*relaxing his hold*) Come out of it then!

CRAW: I'm c-c-coming as fast as I can.

MEAD: You are my instrument. You shall have no more anger, nor fear, nor any
other passion than my razor has.

CRAW: Well, I won't. You are a great man, Mr Meadows; for you I put my
passions in my pocket.

MEAD: (*reflecting*) I shall postpone his arrest.

CRAW: Oh, don't say that, Mr Meadows; have some mercy. I'll *take* him as genteel
as if he had never leathered me. (*clasping his hands*) What would life be worth
to a little man if he could never serve a big one out? (*aside*) I hope to serve
you out *some day*, Mr Meadows.

MEAD: What are ye muttering? And you have been drinking too.

CRAW: Drinking, sir? Not a drop has passed these lips this two days, *u-pon my –
soul*! (*aside*) Where shall we all go to?

MEAD: Liar! Why the smell of it comes through your very skin.

CRAW: Oh, Mr Meadows; you have got a nose like a hawk, Mr Meadows.

MEAD: The next time a public-house tempts you, say to yourself, Peter Crawley,
that is not a public-house to you: that is a workhouse, a gaol, a hospital, a
dunghill. For if you go in there, John Meadows that is your friend, will be your
enemy, and trample you to perdition.

CRAW: Don't mention trampling, Mr Meadows; it makes my blood run cold. (*with
enthusiasm*) Sooner shall the poor little moon snap her fingers at the sun,
which keeps her from going out altogether, than I disobey you, Mr Meadows:

only if you would but let me – now and then – have a glimmer of a notion *what* I am doing, and why I am doing it, I could co-operate better.

MEAD: I doubt it. A tool is a tool. However; I'll give you a trial. What do you want explained?

CRAW: Well, sir, If you would condescend so far as to give me a glimpse, why I have been decoying old Mr Merton into rotten speculations, and why I have made him from a man of wheat-ricks to a man of straw. But above all, why I keep going on lending him your money; as if he was still a man of wheat, instead of a man of straw.

MEAD: Are you really so shallow as not to see why you are ruining old Merton?
(*Enter* SERVANT GIRL.)

SERV: Mr Jeffries, the postmaster, sir. He says you sent for him.

MEAD: I did. Show him up. (*Exit* SERVANT.) Now stand aside there, and watch the game close.
(CRAWLEY *goes and listens from behind a door. Enter* JEFFRIES, *speaking.*)

JEFF: Well, sir, don't keep me long; for I have got a letter for Miss Merton, and she is next door.

MEAD: You will not deliver that letter then.

JEFF: Won't I, though? What, when I know a pretty girl has been waiting months for it? Why, Mr Meadows, for what do you take me? Would you have a government officer keep a letter back?

MEAD: It would not be the first. Do you know this note? (*Shows him a bank note.*)

JEFF: Not I.

MEAD: Why it passed through your hands.

JEFF: A good many do that. I wish some of them would stop on the road.

MEAD: This one did: it stuck to your fingers.

JEFF: (*violently*) Take care what you say, sir I'll bring my action of slander against you in half a minute if you dare to breathe a word against my official character.

MEAD: Hold your tongue, you fool, and don't trumpet yourself into gaol. One or two in this town lost money coming through the post. They complained to me. I took a thought, and I said, 'Jeffries is a man that often talks about his conscience: he will be the thief.' I baited six traps, and you took five. This note came from Ireland. Don't you remember it now?

JEFF: I am ruined! I am ruined!

MEAD: The letter from Australia. (*He holds out his hand, and* JEFFRIES *reluctantly hands it over.*) You changed the note at the grocer's (*opening the letter slowly*).

JEFF: Why, you wouldn't ever open Miss Merton's letter?

MEAD: (*smoothing the letter to read it*) The other baits were single sovereigns, all marked; you spared three, and nailed two. Ah!

JEFF: Oh, Mr Meadows! Have pity on an unfortunate man, and his family.

MEAD: Talk to Crawley, talk to Crawley. (*Exit hastily, reading the letter.*)

JEFF: (*walking wildly to and fro*) What will become of me? Madman! To think I could escape detection! Ruined! Undone! He has me in his power; I cannot escape him. (CRAWLEY *appears, and stands watching him.*)

CRAW: Of course not; he is too great a man.

JEFF: Oh, Mr Crawley! No body knows my *misfortune* but you and Mr Meadows. Do pray stand my friend, sir. Get me off this once and I'll take an oath on my bended knees never to make such a mistake again.

CRAW: Well, Jeffries, it is not easy to turn such a man as Meadows. But if anybody can, I can. You see I'm at the bottom of all his secrets. (*aside*) Where shall we all go to?

JEFF: Bless you, sir! Bless you!

CRAW: What will you do for me if I should succeed?

JEFF: Anything, sir – anything – your own terms.

CRAW: Well, then, every letter that comes from Australia you must bring to Mr Meadows with your own hand.

JEFF: (*sadly*) I will, sir.

CRAW: And (*aside*) humph! I'll help myself as well as Meadows – (*aloud*) You must find me ten pounds.

JEFF: Ten pounds! I must pinch to get that.

CRAW: Pinch away! And let me have it directly.

JEFF: I will, sir. Before the day's out.

CRAW: And you mustn't tell Meadows you feed me to plead your cause, or he will be angry with me, and smash you.

JEFF: No, sir, I won't. Is that all?

CRAW: That is all.

JEFF: Then I'm very grateful. I'll go and get the money.

CRAW: The sooner the better. (*Exit JEFFRIES.*) That's a shuttlecock (*pointing after him*). And Meadows and I are the battledores, and knock him to and fro. Bang! Bang! Bang! (*contemptuously*) Fancy being a shuttlecock.
      (*Enter MEADOWS hastily, with his hat and whip.*)

MEAD: Crawley, you wanted to see to the bottom of my plans.

CRAW: Ah, Mr Meadows, it is too far for any man to see with the naked eye.

MEAD: Not when it suits my book. Have I told you the object of my heart, and of all my schemes?

CRAW: Oh, yes, Mr Meadows, I'm down upon *that*; but what puzzles me is, how you mean to succeed, with Mr Levi, and Will Fielding, and the girl herself against you.

MEAD: By using two hands instead of one. My right hand shall work here in Berkshire. Thus. I have got the post-office under my thumb. (CRAWLEY *nods*.) I stop every letter to Susan from Australia. Then in four months I raise a report George Fielding is dead.

CRAW: (*roaring*) Capital. (*in a low voice*) Where shall we all go to?

MEAD: In two months more comes a letter from Australia, telling somebody – not me – that George Fielding isn't dead but *married* (*going*).

CRAW: Beautiful! But who is to write it?

MEAD: (*at the door*) My left hand. (*Exit MEADOWS.*)

CRAW: His left hand? (*suddenly pretending to understand, and bawling after him*) Sublime! What a fool I was to think that old Jew was as great a man as Mr Meadows. (MEADOWS *returns with a bottle and two glasses.*)

MEAD: Next I make some tool of mine threaten old Merton with gaol. Then I step in and offer to pay his debts and start him afresh, if he will be my father-in-law. I own to Susan I always loved her, but hid it for conscience while George was true. She will be mine.

CRAW: She will. She is. (*Fills his glass.*) There, ring the church bells for the beautiful Miss Merton, and the great Mr Meadows!

MEAD: Stop a bit. Suppose George Fielding should come home with the thousand pounds?

CRAW: (*depressed*) Why, he'll kick all our schemes into toothpicks, that is all. (*violently*) He mustn't come home. He shan't come home; and – (*dejectedly*) who is to hinder him from coming home?

MEAD: My left hand.

CRAW: Your left hand? (*He looks at* MEADOWS*'s left hand.*) Oh, this is lovely. It is like looking down into the deep, deep sea (*he drinks*).

MEAD: (*Tapping* CRAWLEY *on the shoulder*) *You* are my left hand.

CRAW: (*puzzled*) Honoured and proud! (*He inspects his own left hand.*)

MEAD: This paper contains full instructions. My very brains lie here. Put it in your pocket.

CRAW: Your brains in my pocket, sir! (*He pockets the paper.*) Ah, if I could only keep 'em there!

MEAD: And this is a cheque-book. You will draw on me for a hundred pounds a month.

CRAW: (*excited*) No. Shall I? Mr Meadows, you are a king. (*He puts the cheque-book in his breast pocket and slaps it.*)

MEAD: You are going a journey.

CRAW: (*in high spirits*) All the better. Changes are lightsome.

MEAD: A long journey.

CRAW: The longer the better. (*aside*) I shall be the farther from you, and the nearer the public house.

MEAD: My left hand must not fear a little sea and wind.

CRAW: (*exalted*) The sea be hanged, and the wind be blowed! With your talent in my eye, and your cheque-book in my bosom, and your courage in my heart (*he slaps his bosom*), and your brains in my pocket (*he slaps his pocket*), I could – I feel – I feel – I could kick the world over the moon. (*He kicks.*) Come, when shall I start? When shall I start?

MEAD: This afternoon.

CRAW: (*Drinks.*) All right. Where to?

MEAD: To Australia. (CRAWLEY *drops the glass and breaks it.*)

CRAW: To Aus – stra – I – I – beg your pardon. Where (*rising*)?

MEAD: Australia.

CRAW: Oh, certainly! To Australia. (*aside*) Ugh!

MEAD: What, daunted already?

CRAW: (*violently*) Not a bit, sir; not a bit. Look! See? I'm off. (*He walks rapidly and confusedly to the wrong door, and opens it.*)

MEAD: (*calmly*) That is not Australia; that's my bedroom.

CRAW: Cur–cur–curious mistake! Here g–g–goes for Australia.

MEAD: Australia. And (*quietly and grimly*), as you seem confused, I will attend you to the rail.

CRAW: What an honour. (*aside*) No escape.

MEAD: And take you to London, and put you on board the ship, which sails tonight.

CRAW: (*faintly*) How kind! Sails – for – Australia?

(CRAWLEY *makes for the remaining glass, but* MEADOWS *interposes sternly and points him off with his riding-whip.*)

MEAD: For Australia.

CRAW: It is where w–we are all g–going to.

(*Exeunt* CRAWLEY, *with uneven steps, and* MEADOWS *walking slowly and calmly behind him.*)

SCENE 2. *A line of cell doors in the corridor of the borough gaol. Enter* SUSAN *and* EVANS, *reading a card.*

EVANS: Oh, then, it is the chaplain you want to see, miss?

SUSAN: Yes, sir, if you please. He lodged with us when he was curate for a little while in our village; and I have made bold to bring him some home-made bread, and some fresh eggs, and some flowers, if he will accept of them.

EVANS: I'll take you to his study, miss. Step aside a moment till these prisoners pass.

SUSAN: Oh, sir, please stand by me. I'm afraid of them.

(*Mournful music plays. Enter a* TURNKEY, *followed by several prisoners wearing their caps, who pass slowly and in silence across the scene, and then exeunt.*)

SUSAN: Poor things!

EVANS: Now, miss, if you please. (*Exeunt.*)

(*Enter, meeting,* MR HAWES *and* FRY. FRY *touches his cap, and hands* HAWES *a paper.*)

FRY: Reports, sir

HAW: Humph! No. 7; refractory in chapel.

FRY: Will persist in saying the responses. I tell him we are on the silent system here; but he says he has always been used to say 'amen' in church, and it will pop out.

HAW: Then pop him – into the black-hole.

FRY: (*writing in his memorandum book*) Yes, sir. Seven, for saying 'amen', after hex–pos–tu–lation; black-'ole.

HAW: Eleven and twelve refractory at the crank.

FRY: Not done their full number. Eleven says he is sick; twelve says he won't.

HAW: Sick and sulky: I'll grind them. What is this? Nineteen has been defacing his slate? (FRY *nods.*) What, destroying the Queen's property? Break her slate?

FRY: I didn't say break it, sir. I said deface it; drew a figure on it.

HAW: With his knife?

FRY: Knife, sir, no. With his slate pencil.

HAW: Humph! Well, after all, that is defacing it: for if I was to draw another face on your face, that would be defacing you.

FRY: That is how I argee, sir. Besides, it was a hugly figure, a very hugly figure, and one as smelt refractory. (*lowering his voice, and looking askant at the other turnkey*) Figure of a prisoner a hanging himself, con*trary* to law.

HAW: What did the young viper mean by that?

FRY: That is just what I asked him, sir: and says he, 'Why, sir, it is what you are driving us all to, ain't ye?', and looks up in my face as innocent; shut me up, the young varmint did; for (*lowering his voice*) certainly they do hang themselves in this gaol uncommon.

HAW: What, Fry, do *you* falter? Do you doubt the *system*? The great *separate* and *silent system*, which is working such wonders on the convict mind?

FRY: Laws forbid, sir. The *system* is a grand *system*, a beautiful *system*, dissolves the varmints into tears, and grinds 'em into bible texts and bone dust; but somehow they do hang themselves *systematic*, to get out of the *system*. I book all such hirregularities; and (*inspecting his book*) here's fourteen of 'em has tried it on since you came to the gaol; and (*lowering his voice*) four *done it*.

HAW: The ruffians only hang themselves to spite *me*. (*calling off*) Hy! Evans, you send eleven and twelve here to me.

FRY: Now he is out o' hearing, sir, keep your eye on that Bill Evans; he is turning soft. Ever since he had the fever, and the chaplain went twice a day and palavered by his bedside, he fawns on his Reverence like a dog; and you know his Reverence is not a friend to *the system*.

HAW: Oh, hang him. The visiting justices will be here tomorrow. At my request they are going to turn his Reverence out of the gaol. And I'll kick Evans out at the parson's heels.

FRY: And good riddance of bad rubbish, both of 'em.

> (*Enter* ROBINSON *with a moody, depressed air. He salutes* HAWES *and remains silent.* HAWES *eyes him.*)

HAW: So, number twelve, you have been refractory at the crank again; only done 3,350 revolutions out of your 3,500.

ROB: (*trembling*) I did my best, sir, believe me.

HAW: No excuses. Hold your tongue.

ROB: And be belied; what shall I gain by that?

HAW: You'll gain that you won't be put in the black-hole. Separate and silent – that is the system. Twelve, you have been refractory at the crank; and –

ROB: But, sir, you don't know; I am only just recovering from a fever; it has left me very weak, and my crank is a heavy one, or I should have done my whole task to the minute; upon my honour.

HAW: A prisoner's honour! (*coldly*) Fry, bread and water for three days, and short allowance of that.

ROB: Man, man! How is a poor fellow to get back his strength to do such hard work if you starve him at top of his fever?

HAW: And take away his gas ten nights for answering me!

ROB: (*whispering*) May the eternal curse –

HAW: And take away his bed for muttering. (ROBINSON *gasps, but says nothing, and goes out dejected.*) Curse 'em, I'll break 'em. (*Enter* JOSEPH, *with* EVANS.) So, eleven, refractory again!

JOSEPHS: Me, sir?

HAW: Ay, ay, sham innocent! You told Fry here you wouldn't turn the crank.

---

take away his gas: the gas-light which illuminates his cell.

JOSEPHS: Oh, Mr Fry, how can you say that? You know I never said I *wouldn't*; I said I *couldn't*; that crank is a man's crank; it is too heavy for a lad like me.

HAW: Did eleven say *wouldn't* or *couldn't*, Fry?

FRY: I am not very sure.

HAW: Very well, couldn't or wouldn't, it comes to the same thing; for I say you can and shall. Give eleven the punishment jacket.

JOSEPHS: Oh, no, no, no, anything but that! It chokes me, it cuts me, it robs my breath, it crushes my heart, it makes me faint away. It kills me by inches: I cannot go on like this – first the jacket till I faint away; then buckets of water thrown over me, and to lie all night in my wet clothes; then starved, and then the jacket again, because you have starved me down too weak to work. Oh, pray, pray have mercy on me and hang me! You mean to kill me; why not have a little, little, little pity, and kill me quicker! (*Sobs and clings to* HAWES'*s knees.* FRY *hangs his head.*)

HAW: You refractory young vagabond: how dare you break the system, kicking up this row? You will get it double for that! Take him away, I tell you. (FRY *and the* TURNKEY *tear him away.*)
        (*Enter* MR EDEN.)

JOSEPHS: (*struggling*) Oh, no, no! Murder! Murder! Murder! (*Exeunt.*)

EDEN: (*gently, but with emotion*) What has the poor boy done, sir?

HAW: What is that to you?

EDEN: Everything. I am here to see the laws of heaven and of man respected. And it is my painful duty to tell you that they are constantly violated by your order.

HAW: Have you done preaching? Then hear me! Whenever you come between a prisoner and me, it shall always be the worse for the prisoner. I'll show you who is master here, you or I.

EDEN: Neither, Mr Hawes. The law is your master and mine; and since my repeated, and, permit me to add, courteous though earnest remonstrances are met with contempt, I shall not trouble the visiting justices; for they, alas, see only with your eyes, and hear with your ears.

HAW: Oh, you have found that out, have you?

EDEN: But I shall appeal to the Home Secretary.

HAW: Ay, do. Write to old Circumbendibus. And he will tie your letter up in lots of red tape and send it round back down to the visiting justices; and they will refer it to me.

EDEN: In that case I shall appeal to the Crown.

HAW: And suppose the Crown takes you for a madman?

EDEN: Then I shall appeal to the people. I give you my honour this great question, whether or not the law can penetrate a prison, shall be sifted to the bottom.

HAW: Do your best – do your worst – and be –

EDEN: (*interrupting him calmly and politely*) I'll do my best, Mr Hawes. (*He salutes* HAWES *politely, and exit.*)

HAW: Won't I serve the prisoners out for this. I'll make their lives hell.
        (*Exit.*)

SCENE 3. *A double scene, representing a line of cell doors, with a corridor in the centre. Gas-lights over the cells are not lighted. The interiors of* ROBINSON'*s and*

JOSEPHS's *cells are visible to right and left.* JOSEPHS *is discovered strapped to the wall.* ROBINSON *is seated gloomily in the cell.*

ROB: If what they say is true, that the devil walks the earth, and grins at his children's works, let him look in here, and take a hint for improving his prisons below. They keep a poor fellow from the sound of his neighbour's voice, ay, even from his own. They hide the light of day. The seasons change outside that gloomy wall, but no change pierces here; our summer is winter, and our day is night. (*He sighs.*) Overworked, and then starved for not being able to do more than a man's work, then on the top of starvation set a heavier task. Driven to despair, and then punished for despairing. When I first came here, I hadn't a bad heart, though my conduct was bad. I was a felon, but I was a man. And I had a secret respect for the law; who hasn't? Unless he is a fool as well as a rogue. But here I find the law as great a felon as any of my pals. Here the law breaks the law; steals a prisoner's food contrary to the law, and claps a prisoner in a black-hole contrary to the law, and crucifies him against a wall contrary to the law, and forces him to self-murder contrary to law. So now (*he starts to his feet*) I despise the law; because it is a liar and a thief. I loathe the law; because it is a murderer. I hate the human race; and but for good Mr Eden, I should hate Him who made them the heartless miscreants I find them here. (*He sits down shuddering.*) Ah, I am going mad: that is how we end under Hawes and his system. Mad? – Mad!

EVANS: (*coming down*) What is all this, number twelve? Why, you are *communicating*!

ROB: I was not communicating. I was muttering. Mayn't I commune with my own heart?

EVANS: (*Scratches his head.*) I don't know. I'll ask the governor. But you mustn't commune with your own art hout loud. You mustn't do nothing hout loud. It's against *the system*.

ROB: (*softly*) Curse *the system*. There, that is not loud, but deep.

EVANS: Come, drop it, my lad: and, number twelve, why is your door ajar? 'Prisoners to shut their own doors', see rule nine.

ROB: Oh, every man to his own turnkey. And what shall I gain by that?

EVANS: You'll gain as you won't be put on bread and water in the black-hole, *refractory*.

ROB: Curse you all (*he slams the door*).

EVANS: (*shaking his head*) You will break out before long. I know the signs. (*He inspects* JOSEPHS.) Ah, my poor little bloke, yours is a hard time. (*Exit slowly.*)

ROB: If I was not to get a peep at the corridor now and then, I should go melancholy mad. Their new-fashioned doors shut with a spring like a mouse-trap. But a cracksman's science can beat theirs. I've nicked the tongue of the spring bolt, and when I shut the door, in goes my bit of string with it. (JOSEPHS *groans.*) And now I pull the string – back comes the bolt and open comes the scientific mouse-trap. (JOSEPHS *groans.*) Ah! What is that? (*He recoils.*) (*in a whisper*) It is only some poor soul they are tormenting. Why, it is in this corridor. Are they watching? (*He steals cautiously out, and peeps.*) Oh, the villains! If I dared, I'd loose him. His head droops; he is choking. I must risk it. (*He runs to* JOSEPHS, *and begins to undo his straps.*)

JOSEPHS: (*after a look of surprise*) Why, it's Robinson. No, no, let me alone! You will catch it if you unloose me.

ROB: But you'll die, boy, you'll die.

JOSEPHS: No such luck: no such luck. I am only fainting. Many's the time I've done that in this terrible jacket; but I can't die. Oh, dear, I can't die.

ROB: Die? Why of course not. Keep up your heart. I'll loose the straps anyway. I daren't take you down. But they won't find out I've loosened you.

JOSEPHS: Oh, what a relief! Bless you!

ROB: Poor soul! Josephs, don't you give way to despair. Listen. I've broken a great bit of stone in the floor of my cell; and it is ready at a moment's notice.

JOSEPHS: (*with curiosity*) What to do?

ROB: Why, to smash that beast's skull.

JOSEPHS: Oh, Robinson, why that would be murder!

ROB: And isn't he murdering us inch by inch? It is his life or mine.

JOSEPHS: Oh!

> (*Enter* HAWES.)

HAW: Why, what is this? Prisoners *communicating*!

ROB: (*hastily*) No, sir, but he was choking, and no body was by. So I thought you would be angry if I stood looking, and did nothing.

HAW: (*stamping*) Turnkey! (*Enter* FRY *and* EVANS.) Seize number twelve. (*They seize him.*)

ROB: Well, you need not be so rough, am I resisting?

HAW: And take him to the black-hole.

ROB: Oh, no, no, not to the black-hole! Any torture but that. Leave me my reason, if you take my life.

HAW: To the black-hole!

> (ROBINSON *gives a cry of despair, then trips* FRY *and* EVANS, *and takes a posture of defence.* HAWES *blows on a silver whistle.* EVANS *and* FRY *run at* ROBINSON, *one after the other. He knocks* FRY *down with his fist, and butts his head into* EVANS's *stomach, who staggers back. Enter two more* TURNKEYS, *at the sight of whom,* ROBINSON *strikes* HAWES *in the face, and dashes into his cell, slamming the door in the face of* EVANS *and* FRY, *who are close at his heels.* ROBINSON *then takes up a great stone from the floor of his cell, and stands with it uplifted.*)

HAW: Oh, oh, oh! (*He whistles.*) Oh, oh! (*He whistles.*) Open his cell.

FRY: Hadn't we better wait till he cools?

HAW: Cowards! Give me the key and you stand by.

> (HAWES *goes softly and peeps through the hole made in the cell door for that purpose.* ROBINSON *takes a stride forward, stone in hand.* HAWES *recoils.*)

HAW: Strap up the boy!

JOSEPHS: Oh, no! Pray don't give me any more. I didn't do it.

HAW: Hold your tongue! If you break *the system* with your noise, I'll strap you up in the black-hole, and ten times tighter. (JOSEPHS *moans.*) Now, mind, turnkeys, the door of that cell is not to be opened by anybody but me. (*He marks* ROBINSON's *door with a piece of chalk.*) And no food enters in there till he goes on his knees and begs for the black-hole, and then he shall have it,

and six ounces of bread and water to live on in it. D'ye hear that, ye vagabond? (ROBINSON *who has been listening, groans.* JOSEPHS *moans.* HAWES *looks from one to the other.*) Now, who is master here?
> (*Enter* EDEN, *quietly.*)

EDEN: The law! (*They all turn round.*)

HAW: The devil!

EDEN: How is it, Mr Hawes, you have inflicted this illegal punishment? Poor child! I can feel the straps cutting into his young flesh.

JOSEPHS: Oh, Mr Eden, oh, oh, oh! (*He bursts out crying.*)

HAW: Mind your own business, parson.

EDEN: I will. The law is my business; and the Gospel is my business; and – in both their sacred names – I loose this victim of unchristian, lawless, tyranny. (*He takes down* JOSEPHS, *whom he has loosed while speaking.*)

HAW: Turnkeys, do your duty. Part those two.

EDEN: (*calmly*) Stand behind me, Josephs. (*The* TURNKEYS *hesitate.*)

HAW: I command you to seize that prisoner, and let those who protect him take the consequences.
> (*The* TURNKEYS *reluctantly step forward.* EVANS *suddenly interposes.*)

EVANS: (*sulkily*) That won't do, sir. They mustn't lay a finger on his Reverence.

HAW: What, mutiny in my own officers! Stand aside, Evans, or you are ruined for life.

FRY: (*aside to* HAWES) Have you lost your head?

HAW: (*stamping*) In the name of the Crown, seize William Evans, and Francis Eden!

EDEN: (*sternly*) In the name of the law, forbear all violence, or you shall answer it to the law.

ROB: (*opening his door, stone in hand*) Didn't I hear some scoundrel threatening his Reverence? (HAWES *slips out alarmed.*)

EDEN: (*gravely*) You will be so good as to retire into your cell, and not get yourself into worse trouble than you are in at present.

ROB: (*meekly*) Yes, your Reverence. (*He retires.*)

EDEN: Turnkeys, oblige me by returning to your duties in the prison. (*Exeunt* TURNKEYS *after saluting* EDEN. *Then, to* JOSEPHS) My dear, go to your cell and pray heaven to forgive your own sins, and the cruelty of your persecutors. (JOSEPHS *kisses* EDEN's *coat, and exit into cell, but staggers at the cell door.*)

EVANS: A card for your Reverence. I had almost forgot it with all this row.
> (*The lights are gradually lowered.*)

EDEN: (*reading*) 'The Honourable Charles Elliott'.

EVANS: (*mysteriously*) Gentleman from the Home Office; I have not told anybody.

EDEN: Good Evans, worthy Evans: all this misery and cruelty will end today. (*Exit hastily, followed by* EVANS.)

JOSEPHS: (*who has been kneeling with his face on his bed*) I don't know how it is, but all my right side seems cold. I think it is dead. Perhaps if I lie on it I may get it warm (*he coils himself up on his bed*).

ROB: What a fool I was to obey his Reverence! But somehow there is no disobeying him. That man would lead old Nick to heaven with a packthread.

(*Enter EVANS with a light. He lights the lamps in the corridor, and the small gas-light in JOSEPHS's cell. Then he whistles at ROBINSON's cell, opens a plate in the door, and throws in a lucifer match. Exit.*)

ROB: (*groping for the lucifer, and finding it*) Bless you! Bless you, bless you, whoever you are! (*he strikes the lucifer, and lights the small gas-light in his cell*). Welcome little spark of light: you keep hope alive in my darkened bosom.

(*Enter HAWES who goes to JOSEPHS's cell, and opens it.*)

HAW: Why, how is this? Gas! Didn't I order you should have no gas for fourteen days?

JOSEPHS: No, sir. What for? Oh, please don't rob me of my gas. It is the only bit of comfort I have in this dreadful place.

HAW: Oh, it is, is it? Then to teach you not to defy me, out goes your comfort. (*He turns off the gas, and exit.*)

JOSEPHS: I won't live this life much longer. There's one way out of this, and any way is better than no way. Dark! Dark! Dark!

(*Enter EDEN, who opens ROBINSON's cell.*)

EDEN: Robinson, your troubles here are at an end. In a few minutes you leave for Portsmouth, where your ship lies, bound for Australia.

ROB: What, what? The open air, the sun, the sea, the blue sky! Ha, ha, ha, ha, oh, oh, oh!

EDEN: Be calm. You have often told me you repent, and will labour with your hands, and will steal no more.

ROB: Oh, never, your Reverence, never. I'll never take another farthing, nor farthing's worth while I live – for your sake.

EDEN: Alas, many such a vow has been made to me in this very cell; made in sincerity, but broken in weakness.

ROB: No, no, sir. If I could but have an honest pal! But what honest man would take up with me now? That is where we poor fellows are beat. Honesty gives us the cold shoulder, and theft opens its arms to us; then comes drink and does the rest.

EDEN: I know it. You shall have an honest companion. There is a friend of mine, a young lady, in my room, writing a letter to a very honest man, one George Fielding.

ROB: George Fielding! Oh, that is like your Reverence! But no, George will never speak to me.

EDEN: What, not when you take him a letter from his sweetheart? Come, you shall see her.

(*EDEN opens the door, and beckons ROBINSON out, but ROBINSON hesitates.*)

ROB: But what will Hawes say? He will black-hole me for life.

EDEN: Mr Hawes will lose this very day the power he has abused. (*Exeunt.*)

(*Enter FRY, peeping.*)

FRY: Now you have put your foot in it, Master Parson. I'll just execute my orders in this cell, and then I'll bring the governor down on you. (*He goes into* JOSEPHS's *cell.*) Now then, youngster, I want your bed (*he lays hold of it*).

JOSEPHS: Oh, no! Oh, pray don't rob me of my bed.

FRY: Rob you, you young dog! Why it isn't your bed. It is the Queen's.

JOSEPHS: Then how dare *you* steal it?

FRY: (*Staggered, scratches his head.*) Well, it is the governor's orders. You are to have no bed, nor gas, for fourteen days.

JOSEPHS: Ha, ha, ha!

FRY: What, that makes you laugh, does it?

JOSEPHS: Yes, I laugh at your thinking you can rob me of light and sleep for fourteen days – a poor worn-out boy like me. You tell the governor I'll find a bed in spite of him long before fourteen days.

FRY: Come, you mustn't sauce the officers. The governor will serve you out quite enough without that. He says he has got another rod in pickle for you – tomorrow.

JOSEPHS: Oh, tomorrow, eh? There is my hand, Mr Fry. (FRY *looks at his hand.*) Come, take it. Surely, surely, if I can take your hand after all you have done, you can take mine. (*with sudden dignity*) Take it, sir, or you will never rue it but once, and that will be all your life.

FRY: (*puzzled*) Why, Josephs, you needn't spit fire. I don't say no. Only it seems odd to take your bed, and then take your hand. There it is. (*giving his hand; aside*) He is turning cranky. Now what good will that do you? (FRY *takes his bed out.* JOSEPHS *sinks to his knees.* FRY *has gone a little way, when suddenly he stops.*) It goes against me, and him taking my hand. I was born of a woman, though this place have hardened me to stone. I'll take the bed no farther than the next cell; and I'll leave his door ajar: he must be a precious fool if he doesn't take the hint. (*He approaches softly and unlocks* JOSEPHS's *door.*)

JOSEPHS: (*in a whisper*) They are watching me. (FRY *retires.*) Now is the time. Tomorrow there is to be some new torture for me. Well, tomorrow I'll be beyond their reach. I'm going the road so many have took to get out of this gaol. (*He gets up on a stool with much difficulty.*) There is the moon; how beautiful she shines! Who wouldn't go up to where she is, rather than bide in misery here by night and day? But will they let me come up there, a poor wicked boy like me? Perhaps they will serve Hawes out for this instead of me. Anyway, they can't be as cruel up there as they are here. I must look sharp, or I shan't have the strength. One side of me seems dead. (*He takes his handkerchief from his neck, and, while speaking, ties it to the bars, stopping every now and then.*) Some folks live to be eighty, I am only fifteen. (*sadly*) That is a long odds. (*doggedly*) But I can't help it. Hawes won't let me live. Mr Eden will be sorry. *But I can't help it.* Bless him! Mother will fret (*he weeps*). But I hope someone will tell her what I went through, and then she'll say better I should die so than live to be tortured every day. Heaven forgive me; *for I can't help it.* Oh, dear! What is this? The power is all out of me – my other side is turning cold now. Ah, they have got me! They have got me still. (*He falls against the door, which flies open and leaves him lying half in and half out of his cell.*)

(*Enter hastily* HAWES, FRY, *and a* TURNKEY.)

HAW: (*looking sharply round*) Why there are *two* cells open: you only told me of one.

FRY: (*aside*) Confound the little fool!

(HAWES *runs into* ROBINSON's *cell, and comes out again immediately.*)

HAW: Gone, sure enough. I'll give it him. (*He runs to* JOSEPHS's *cell.*) I'll give it them both. (*Enter* EDEN *and* ROBINSON.) Hallo! (*uneasily*) What is the little vagabond up to now? (EDEN, *concern marked in his face, moves quickly to* JOSEPHS *whom he raises in his arms.*) Ah, he heard us coming, so now he is shamming, eh!

EDEN: (*solemnly*) No, sir, he is not shamming; he is dying.

FRY: Dying?

EDEN: (*to* HAWES) And you are his murderer.

ROB: Dying? Then may the eternal judge torture you as you tortured him. (*He falls suddenly to his knees.*) May your name be shame, may your life be pain, and your death loathsome; may your skin rot from your flesh, your flesh from your bones, and your bones from your body, and your black soul split for ever on the rock of –

EDEN: (*sternly*) Silence, miserable man! Who are you that invoke curses on your fellow sinner, and disturb a soul that is passing away from earth and its evil passion? (*gently*) Peace, all of you: be still; we are in the presence of death.

JOSEPHS: (*feebly*) That is his Reverence's voice, my only friend.

EDEN: No, not your only friend, nor your best friend. Oh, Josephs, die like a Christian boy, forgiving your enemies.

JOSEPHS: I will; I do.

EDEN: Then put your poor hands together and pray for them as I taught you.

JOSEPHS: (*putting his hands feebly together*) Heaven forgive me, as I forgive Mr Hawes and the rest. Good-bye, your Reverence; bless you! Good-bye, dear Robinson. Oh, dear, he is crying! Never mind me, Robinson. I am happy now: no more pain; no more trouble. Only I feel so tired.

HAW: (*aside*) The young viper has done it to spite me. (*aloud*) But I won't be insulted by *you* – I'll soon have you in the black-hole (*he whistles*) for breaking out of your cell. (*Enter* EVANS *and* TURNKEY.) Seize that prisoner!

EDEN: No. Conduct Mr Hawes out of the prison instead. (*He gives* ROBINSON *the office paper to give to* HAWES.) He is dismissed Her Majesty's service.

(HAWES *takes the paper, reads it, and staggers back.*)

HAWES: (*after a long pause*) Discharged! Is this the end of all my faithful services? Curse you! Curse all the world! (*Exit, followed by* EVANS, *pointing to the door.*)

VOICE: (*off*) Prisoners for Portsmouth. The van is at the gate.

EDEN: Leave Robinson alone a moment with me – and with him. (*They retire softly to the back of the stage, except for* ROBINSON. *Then, in a broken voice*) My poor erring brother, you are going far from me; you are going to Australia – kneel there. (EDEN *signs to* ROBINSON *to kneel on* JOSEPHS's *other side.*)
(*Music plays softly to the end of the act.*)

EDEN: Take your dying comrade's hand (ROBINSON *trembles, but obeys*), and by that pledge promise me to live, as he is dying now – penitent.

ROB: (*sobbing*) I promise.

EDEN: But, above all, never despair. Despair, it is the soul's worst enemy. My last word to you here – perhaps my last word to you in this world – is *it is never too late to mend.*

> (*At these words* ROBINSON'*s face expresses high resolve, and rapturous hope.*)

ACT III

SCENE 1. *The interior of* FIELDING'*s hut. There is a rude truckle bed, a chair, and a table. Enter* GEORGE FIELDING, *staggering, and sinking into a chair.*

FIELD: It is no use: the sheep are all tainted. I've done the work of three, anointing and washing them night and day. I'm spent, and Susan lost. (*Enter* JACKY *with a pair of coat-sleeves turned into bags, and carried round his neck like a yoke.*) Jacky, you and Abner must do my work today – why, what have you done with your sleeves?

JACK: Made bags ob 'em. You and Jacky, carry pertatoes home. Pertatoes a good deal troublesome to carry outside black-fellow; so Jacky make bags. (*He lumps the bags down on the table.*) Now, suppose you want pertatoes to eat, Jacky undo bags in a little while direckly. (*He falls on them with sudden fury, and hacks one of the bags with his tomahawk.*)

FIELD: That will do. (*with a feeble smile*) I don't eat 'em mashed. Where's the coat that owned these sleeves?

JACK: Oh, thrown *him* away: he was a good deal hot.

FIELD: (*angrily*) Thrown it away? Why it was bran' new.

JACK: Yes, Massa George, he was *ban* new, but he was *dam* hot. So Jacky threw him in the river. Dat cool him. Den the fishes dey can wear him if dey like.

FIELD: Now, Jacky, it was only hot because it is noon. It will be cold at night, and then you will come shivering again to me as you did last night.

JACK: (*after scratching his head*) When Jacky a good deal hot here (*feeling himself*) he can't feel a berry little cold a berry long way off there (*he points with his heel backward*). Jacky not a white-fellow.

FIELD: Little I heed the colour of a friend: give me the skin with gratitude beneath it before the skin that is fair and false. You haven't forgotten Twofold bay, Jacky, have you now?

JACK: (*puzzled*) Two fool bay? Yes: sometimes I hunt near Two fool bay.

FIELD: Nay, but the time I mean, you weren't hunting; you were being hunted. (JACKY *scratches his head.*) Why, if he hasn't forgotten the very shark that was swimming after him, and nearly made a meal of him.

JACK: Shark? Shark? No; I see him a good way behind. Jacky in water, so (*he swims on the floor, looking fearfully behind him*). Shark, he come after – so – and open um mouth for Jacky – so. (*He turns on his back.*) They you come roaring with stones (*he jumps up, and acts* FIELDING'*s part*). And fling, and fling, and say dam a good deal cos you a white-fellow; den one stone hit shark on um nose a good deal debbilich hard, so, and down he go (*he falls suddenly flat*), so. Den Jacky dive with knife in um hand, and tickle shark a good deal so – and so – and so. Den he float up dead, so. Den we light a fire, and Jacky roast shark, and eat him: that a good deal more delicious than shark eat Jacky. Yah, yah, yah, yah, yah! (*with sudden pomposity*) Jacky turn white man – Jacky see a good deal dam long way off behind um back this time.

FIELD: I am glad of it; for now you will do me a kindness in return. Jacky, all my poor sheep must be slaughtered directly, and boiled down before they pine their grease away. (*He groans.*) Now I'm of a breed that is good at work, but bad at bloodshed. I'm man enough to take a Leicester ewe in these two hands, and fling her in the water for her good; but I'm not man enough to cut her throat for my own. But you can bear the sight of blood, you know.

JACK: Iss, Massa George (*cheerfully*); a little blood now and den, dat a good deal good for Jacky.

FIELD: Well then, while you and Abner spill their blood, and my means, like water, I'll lie here. For, oh, Jacky, I'm bad – I'm bad this day. I've abused my strength, flinging ten score sheep into the water, without help. You say it is a hot day: well I declare I'm as cold as ice: and, Jacky, my head swims, and I've got such a pain in my back, it cuts my breath.

JACK: Den you send away dat pain direckly, or you make Jacky a good deal angry. When black man have that pain in um back, he always die.

FIELD: (*solemnly*) Like enough, like enough! (*Enter* ABNER.) Come, take your knife, Abner; there is no way left but that.

ABNER: I am a poor man myself, and must look out for the best.

FIELD: (*struggling with his indignation*) Ay, but there is a time for everything. You let somebody's tainted sheep in among mine by bad management. And now you can't ever think to leave me in the trouble your want of skill has brought me to. If ye do, don't hope to thrive, go where you will.

ABNER: Words, words! There is no agreement between you and me. However, as you're down in the world, I'll stay just a week, to oblige you.

FIELD: You'll oblige me, will you? Then oblige me by taking your ugly face out of my sight. Stop, there are your wages up to twelve o'clock. (*He flings them at* ABNER – ABNER *stoops for them, and* FIELDING *starts to his feet.*) Now begone, or I may be tempted to dirty my hands with your mean carcass. (*Exit* ABNER *hastily.* FIELDING *follows, and cries after him.*) And wherever you go, may sorrow and sickness – No, I leave that to heaven. (*As he turns round,* JACKY *puts the double-barrelled gun into his hands.*) What is that for?

JACK: (*calmly*) Shoot um!

FIELD: What, take his life?

JACK: Iss, Massa George. He got too much bungality and impudence; shoot him dead. After dat you feel so comfortable (*he smiles affectionately*).

FIELD: Oh, fie! Heaven forbid I should do the man any harm. But when I think how kind you and I were to him in his sickness, and now to leave us in so sore a strait. Oh! (*He sits on the bed and sighs.*)

JACK: (*sitting close beside him, gravely*) Now you listen a me: this one time I speak a good many words. Massa Abner know nothing, and because you no shoot him you very stupid. One, he know nothing wid dese (*pointing to his eyes*), or else he see the bad sheep come among your sheep. One more, he know nothing wid dis (*touching his tongue*), for when Jacky speak him good words, he speak Jacky bad words. One more, he know nothing wid dese (*indicates his hands and arms*), for after you do him good things, he do you bad things. All this make Jacky a good deal angry. Since Jacky know you, Jacky turn good, very good (*proudly*), dam good; a good deal gooder dan other black-fellows. But when that stupid fellow know nothing, and now you cry, dat make good Jacky angry, and good Jacky go hunting a little, not much, direckly. (*He snatches up a spear, and is about to go off immediately.*)

FIELD: What, today? Oh, don't desert me today. Don't set me against flesh and blood altogether.

JACK: Jacky *must* hunt a little deal (*whining*). Jacky feel so very uncomfordable.

FIELD: I say no more. He knows no better. Poor Jacky, take my hand. I shall never see you again.

JACK: That is a good deal very ridicalous – you will see me when I've done hunting a very little, not a great deal, close behind this very minute direckly. (*Exit* JACKY.)

FIELD: He thinks he will come back. But when he gets on the track of a Kangaroo or a wild turkey, his poor shallow brain will forget his sick friend. Oh, my head, how it swims. My father was a strong man, like me; but he abused his strength, and he was took just like this, one Wednesday night, and was gone in four-and-twenty hours. And I've abused my strength, and now I'm laid low. (*gasping*) Dover Cliffs – Farnborough Steeple – I am not to see you again. (*very feebly*) My poor Susan . . . (*he becomes unconscious. 'Home Sweet Home' is played very softly.*)

(*Enter* JACKY *radiant.*)

JACK: Dere, Massa George, me comfordable now. Hunting soon done. Massa Abner he not go a great deal fast. (*angrily*) Dat stupid fellow always know nothing: dis time he not know hunter behind him. Jacky come crawling a good deal soft, and go so (*he strikes with his tomahawk*), and Massa Abner (*falls flat*) go so, and Jacky feels so comfordable. (*He looks towards* FIELDING.) What for you say nothing? Dat a good deal bad manaahs. (*He goes to inspect him.*) White-fellow gone asleep before the sun. Yah, yah, yah! Massa George! (*He shakes him.*) Massa George! (*alarmed*) Oh, dear! Massa George! Massa George! Jacky's getting a good deal ex–pos–tulated at your sleeping so dam sound before de sun, Massa George! Massa George! Massa George! How white he feels! How cold he look? (*He runs to heap blankets on* FIELDING, *horror-struck.*) Massa George! Massa George! (*He shakes him.*) Massa George! (*with sudden calmness and solemnity*) He has left Jacky. He has gone to the happy hunting fields where de good white-fellows go. (*whispering*) What do I do for him now to show I lub him? I put his make-thunder by his side. (*He tip-toes to fetch it.*) Den he shoot a good deal and neber be hungry in that country. And what else he want? (*Whispers.*) Here his book what he speak good words out ob to Jacky. Dat book often make him comfordable: so I put that close to him hand. Poor George! Dere, now I go away bery swift. (*peevishly*) I so very uncomfordable here. Something hurt me inside in my middle. I go hunt in de big woods a great way off. (*He goes rapidly to the door, and then returns.*) Why I go hunting that stupid Massa Abner? Why I leave

good white-fellow, and not hear him last word before he go? Oh, I so
uncomfortable; no more can breathe, and want to do like the gins do; but
don't know how. My troat – he bite me a good deal. Oh, Massa George! Why
you go away so swift? Why you leave poor Jacky all alone like dat? Oh, oh,
oh, oh, oh! (*He bursts into violent sobbing, and buries his head in the clothes.*)
     (*Music plays. Enter* TOM ROBINSON, *who peeps into the hut.*)

ROB: Anybody at home? (*He enters the hut, peering about, and at last discovers*
JACKY.) Hallo, Blacky! Does George Fielding live here?

JACK: (*without moving*) Yes, Massa white-fellow, oh, oh!

ROB: Where is he?

JACK: (*sorrowfully*) Gone away, so swift as a bird.

ROB: Gone! Where to?

JACK: Gone dead. Oh, oh, oh!

ROB: Heaven forbid! Why there he lies. (*He uncovers* FIELDING'*s face.*) What is
this? Have I come all this way to bury him? No; I can't think he is dead. Did
you close his eyes?

JACK: No. Dey shut themselves all at one time, while I go hunting a very little deal.
(*He sobs.*)

ROB: All the better. Stay, I've got a bit of a glass. (*He takes out a round mirror
about the size of his hand, and holds it to* FIELDING'*s lips.* JACKY *watches
with great curiosity.*) Hurrah; he is in the world yet. Come, jump out of that,
you darkie, and light a fire; he is frozen.

JACK: Yes, Massa Nobody, I make fire in one moment, a good deal swift, direckly.
     (JACKY *runs and gets a light by friction, after the manner of savages,
and lights a fire.* ROBINSON *takes out his flask, and sprinkles*
FIELDING'*s face with it repeatedly.* FIELDING *sighs, and comes
gradually to consciousness.*)

FIELD: Who are you, kind sir?

ROB: (*putting his hand over his eyes*) The doctor. Drink. (FIELDING *drinks.*)

FIELD: It runs through me like fire. Why, it is neat brandy, doctor.

ROB: Bad food, but first-rate physic, George.

FIELD: Why, Robinson! Well I never thought to see *you* under a roof of mine.

ROB: That is just the welcome I expected. Well, when I've delivered my message, I
won't trouble your house long.

FIELD: (*humbly*) I meant no offence, sir. 'Twould be much mistimed. Jacky, warm
some soup for Mr Robinson and me, if *you* please.

ROB: (*apart, and grinding his teeth*) Mr Robinson! I dare say you'll think me a great
fool, but I've walked one hundred and sixty miles just to bring you a letter, Mr
Fielding.

FIELD: (*feebly*) Then I call that very kind of you. Who from? Not from her – not
from my dear Susan?

ROB: Well, it is like to be from some pretty girl or other. I'm not the post. (*He
fumbles in his pocket for the letter.*) I don't carry waste paper from Jack to Jill
all round creation. (*He gives the letter to* FIELDING.)

FIELD: (*suddenly reviving*) It is – it is! (*He opens the letter eagerly and reads and
kisses it alternately.* ROBINSON *smiles.*)

JACK: How you's eyes spark. White-fellow not dead yet.

FIELD: You're a good fellow to bring me such a treasure in the wilderness. (*He kisses the letter again. Then, firmly*) I'll never forget it as long as I live. (*He reads.*) Why, there's something about you in it! Susan says you never had a father – not to say a father.

ROB: She says true, George.

FIELD: And – poor fellow – she says they came between your sweetheart and you. (ROBINSON *sighs.*) No wonder you went astray after that. What would become of me if I lost my Susan?

ROB: Bless her little heart for making excuses for a poor fellow; but she was always a charitable, kind-hearted young lady.

FIELD: Wasn't she, Tom.

ROB: And what sweet eyes! Brimful of heaven. And when she used to smile on you, Master George, oh, the ivories she brought to light!

FIELD: Now you just take my hand: and don't be long about it. There, I'll let you read it yourself, that I will, for your goodness in bringing it to me.

ROB: (*reading*) 'And, George, Mr Eden says he is well-disposed, but weak; do keep him by you – to oblige me, George.'

FIELD: Will you stay with me, Tom? I'm not a lucky man; but while I've a shilling, there's a sixpence for the man that brought me this dew in the desert.

ROB: I will, George; and I'll be even with you and Susan for this, or say I'm not a man (*he walks excitedly, and full of thought*).

JACK: Now Jacky want to speak words; not many, but a good deal wise.

ROB: Hear, hear! Go it, darky!

JACK: A little behind, dis white-fellow whiter nor ever; cos um dead, bery dead, extremely dead as mutton. Den dis Susan come here in a physic paper; den dis dead man not eat dat paper, he only bite the words a little, and speak 'em out; and now he a good deal red, and talk like a gin, chatter, chatter, chatter, and not die neber no more. Amen.

FIELD: Die? I never was better in my life.

JACK: Den Jacky says, says Jacky, dis Susan what is made of black and white paper, he is a bery good doctor, yah!

ROB: And no mistake.

JACK: A bery unmassiful, good doctor, an uncommon, abominable, ridicalous, dam good doctor. Yah, yah, yah!

ROB: And let us drink that doctor's health (*he gives* JACKY *the flask*).

JACK: Dat am one more good physic. Paper doctor good for white-fellow. Dis doctor best for Jacky. (*He puts the flask on his other side, and drinks from it from time to time.*) Now Jacky want to talk to that other lilly doctor what tell you Massa George not quite dead yet.

ROB: The mirror! Hand it him, George. Always encourage laudable curiosity.
(ROBINSON *takes out a box of lucifer matches and his pipe.* FIELDING *gives* JACKY *the mirror.* JACKY *looks into it, utters a loud yell, flings it down, hacks it to pieces with his tomahawk, and dances round it in great excitement.*)

FIELD: What is that for? Ye little mischievous monkey.

ROB: (*good-humouredly, but not best pleased*) Come, I say, furniture is cheap where you come from.

JACK: Oh, Massa George, Massa Tom; Jacky seen the dibble (*he glares horribly*).
ROB: Where?
JACK: In dere. Him nasty, ugly, ingenious beast, so black as never was.
ROB: Compliments pass when gentlefolks meet.
FIELD: He, he! Why, Jacky, it was yourself you saw.
JACK: (*with a haughty wave of the hand*) Massa George, you not quite alive yet; you
  a little dead as mutton still: why, dat a good deal stupid: when I here, how can
  I be dere? Tellee twas a nasty, ugly, black debble. But I doctor him, yah, yah,
  yah! Dis is de physic which cures 'em of live too long (*he flourishes his
  tomahawk*). Cure Massa Abner of dat, bery near, not quite, almost.
    (FIELDING *and* ROBINSON *look at one another and burst out
    laughing, in the midst of which* ROBINSON *lets off a lucifer match on
    the floor, close to Jacky's nose, who is on his knees, gravely inspecting
    the fragments of the glass.* JACKY *rolls head over heels with a howl,
    then springs to his feet and dances round* ROBINSON, *flourishing his
    tomahawk.*)
ROB: (*snatching up the box*) Come, none o' that now. My lucifers ain't devils; and if
  you tomahawk me – (*calmly*) I'll punch your head. (ROBINSON *lights his
  pipe.* JACKY *retires to a corner and sits amazed, and glaring at the lucifer box.*
  FIELDING *still reads and kisses the letter.*) Now then, to business. (*He
  smokes.*) How far have you got towards your thousand pounds?
FIELD: Oh, Tom, I shall never make it. Here my sheep are all dying, and I'm
  forced to boil them all down into a tallow and sell them for the price of a wild
  duck. Why did you remind me? I have left my Susan, and I've lost her.
ROB: I am glad of it.
FIELD: What d'ye mean?
ROB: Because now I shall be the one to find you the thousand pounds. You shall
  bless the hour you listened to your own good heart, and that sweet girl's letter,
  and gave a penitent thief the warm hand instead of the cold shoulder. Listen,
  George: you know I was a miner in California; well, of course I know the signs
  of gold; and here they are in this part, thick and three-fold.
FIELD: Gold? What, hereabouts? Nonsense, Tom. What signs?
ROB: The shape of the hills, for one thing. You could not tell them from the golden
  range of California; the stuff they are made of for another: granite, mica, and
  quartz. And scarce a stone-throw from your door I picked up a pale old Joey.
  Here it is (*he shows him*).
JACK: (*aside*) Punch your head? Punch your head? I never heard *him* before. Punch
  your head!
FIELD: (*after inspecting it*) Why, it is only a shell: I can show you them by the score.
ROB: By the score? Don't, George, don't! You put me all in a flutter. Wherever
  these shells lie beside mica and quartz, there is gold to be found by those that
  know how to look for it.
FIELD: I don't believe there is an ounce of gold in all Australia. But drowning men
  catch at straws. If you are game to look for it, I am.
ROB: Then take your spade and give me that iron pan, and we'll go prospecting this
  very minute.
FIELD: So be it. (*He shoulders his spade.*) Come along, Jacky. (*to* ROBINSON)

I never leave him alone in the hut; he is no more to be trusted than a child.

JACK: (*following, deep in thought*) Punch your head! (*Exeunt, JACKY last.*)

(*Music plays. JACKY slips back and eyes the lucifer box: he makes ready his tomahawk, he goes on all fours and creeps cunningly till he gets within reach of it; then he raises his tomahawk, and threatens it, but finding it does not resist, he takes hold of it gently with his left hand. He then sits down, and with considerable nervousness, strikes the ground with the wrong end. He throws it away indignantly.*)

JACK: Dat one look at me and see I not a white-fellow. Dat why he not make fire for me. (*He takes another.*) Suppose you not make fire for me, *I punch your head.* (*He ignites it, and is startled.*) Loramassy! (*He ignites another.*) Loramassy! Jacky clebber fella, make fire like white man.

(*He proceeds to ignite them one after another as fast as he can, laughing and crowing all the time, and flinging the burning matches recklessly about. Enter FIELDING and ROBINSON, who watch him.*)

FIELD: (*pointing to him*) Didn't I tell you? He will burn the house to tinder, if we don't mind. (*They each take one of JACKY's arms, and quietly march him off.*)

JACK: (*to ROBINSON, as they go out*) I like you a good deal, Massa Tom! You clebbaar fellaar. I punch your head.

ROB: (*drily*) You'd better.

(*Exeunt arm in arm, JACKY in the centre. The white men stoop a little; JACKY as erect as a dart.*)

SCENE 2. *A front scene. Enter CRAWLEY, shabby and tattered, with a flask slung round his neck, and a large umbrella.*

CRAW: Little men be warned by me, and keep clear of great ones. Don't you think to creep into their schemes ankle deep, and then out again: for, presently, souse you go over head and ears. Here am I, Mr Meadows's left hand – only his left hand – yet already I'm accessory to a pair of felonies. When I left England I little thought to go in for *the indictable.* But this country does look so beautiful, all mountains and valleys and purling streams, and no Newgates nor Horsemonger Lanes to sully the prospect, that one feels unprofessional, and frolics with the law. Ah, what is that? What is that? That is the worst of it: I am always seeing something, or hearing something, when there is nothing. This is the cause (*he taps the flask*). And this is the cure (*he drinks*). Where shall we all go to?

(*BOB HUDSON, who has entered on tip-toe, touches him quickly on the shoulder, then passes quickly by.*)

CRAW: Ah! Oh! Ugh. (*recovering himself*) Where are you going so fast?

BOB: What is that to you?

CRAW: Now, that is polite, Mr Hudson. You seem in a communicative mood; tell me where I can find Black Will and the rest of the gang – I beg pardon – the confederates.

No Newgates nor Horsemonger Lanes: prisons.

BOB: Take my advice, and keep out of their way just now.

CRAW: Can't afford it. In a word, there is £50 waiting for them; and nothing to do for it but burn a hut and rob the inmate.

BOB: Well they won't leave their work for a dirty little fifty pounder, and I've no time to waste gabbling. (*He runs off.*)

CRAW: Leave work? Work? Why, they would die sooner than work, every man Jack of them. Here's some strange mystery. A dirty little fifty pounder? Where do you expect to go to, Master Bob? I'm all curiosity. I must fathom this. I'll find them, if they are above ground. (*Exit on tip-toe.*)

SCENE 3. *A ravine, seen in perspective, crossed at the back by a bridge, underneath which there is a meandering brook, and above it the outline of distant hills. There is a heap of quartz boulders intermixed with moss, and a large flowering bush. At the back there is a section of a large and lofty gum-tree. There is a bank of earth and stone, and the gurgling of water is faintly heard. BLACK WILL, JEM, and JACK, stripped to their shirts and trousers, and plastered all over with clay, are discovered at the back of the scene, washing for gold. One shovels the quartz gravel into a heap, another transfers it with a trowel into a calabash and shakes it, and pours out the water which a third pours in from a bucket. The scene opens in dead silence. The men, when they do speak, show, by their earnest whispers, as well as by their anxious and eager deportment, that their souls are in their work. Music plays at the opening of the scene.*

B. WILL: Water!

JEM: Here. (*They wash for gold.*) I see a speck. How does it feel?

B. WILL: Pretty heavy. More water; we shall soon know.

JEM: Ah! It is all right. (*He draws a knife from his girdle, puts the gold dust on it, and holds it up to his mate.*) What d'ye think of that? Half an ounce at one washing.

JACK: (*at some distance*) Ah!

B. WILL: What is it?

               (*Enter CRAWLEY softly.*)

JACK: A nugget, a nugget, as big as a bean! (*He throws it down. The other two inspect it eagerly.*)

CRAW: (*laughing*) Oh, that's the mystery, is it?

               (*They rush on him furiously with uplifted knives; he sinks, yelling, on his knees.*)

CRAW: Mercy, mercy! It is Smith. It's your friend. What have I done?

B. WILL: Dug your own grave, ye prying fool.

CRAW: No, no, I won't betray your secret; I don't know what I have found out – never, never, never, mercy!

JEM: He *must* die, or else take the oath.

CRAW: I'll take a thousand oaths sooner than be killed once.

               (JEM *and* WILL *whisper together.* JACK *holds* CRAWLEY, *who is shaking with terror, and whining like a dog.*)

B. WILL: If you had been a stranger, nothing should have saved you: but as we have drunk together – give him a knife, Jem. (*A knife is given to him.*) Get up, ye cur! Cross steel with us. (*They cross their knives – CRAWLEY's hand trembles.*) Swear never to tell that there is gold in this country, on pain of death.

CRAW: (*bawling*) I swear. (*Whimpers aside.*) Oh, dear!

B. WILL: Swear to cut the throat of brother, friend, or pal who shall betray this secret.

CRAW: I swear. (*aside*) Where shall we all go to?

B. WILL: Now you are one of us: you will have to clean our boots, and cook our vittels: there's the cross-sticks, go and set the pot on. (CRAWLEY *goes feebly in the indicated direction, and disappears.*) After all, pals, we wanted a servant. Come, waste no more time. (*They recommence their work.*)

CRAW: (*peering into the wings*) Why, it is: it is Fielding and his new visitor.

B. WILL: Who are you prying into now?

CRAW: Two strangers coming this way.

JEM: Where? Where? (*They all come to look off.*)

B. WILL: Remember our oath!

JEM: Nonsense: dozens pass this way and are none the wiser.

B. WILL: Ay, with their noses in the air, but one of these is a notice-taking fellow; his eyes are forever on the ground, in the creeks and gullies. He have been in the same oven as us.

JEM: Not likely; but if it is so, there are no two ways (*he touches the knife in his girdle*). A secret is no secret when all the world do know it.

B. WILL: They are coming this way, curse them! Hide in the cave and watch them. (*Exeunt.*)

CRAW: Something horrible will happen. I feel it. It – it – it's not my fault. (*He crawls under a bush.*)

> (*Enter over the pass* ROBINSON, *with an iron pan, and* FIELDING *with a spade.*)

ROB: Hallo! Where have they vanished to? I don't like gentlemen that vanish into the bowels of the earth like that.

FIELD: What, bushrangers again! You suspect everybody. You'll end by going about armed to the teeth, as some of our farmers do.

ROB: Not so green. I carry my sting out o' sight like a bumble-bee. This looks well; but I see a place that is like the mouth of a purse. Look yonder at that old dried up watercourse; well, that was a river and washed gold down a hundred years before Adam was born. I'll look at it a little closer. (*He goes slowly past* CRAWLEY, *who shrinks in.*)

FIELD: Go without me, Tom, or I shall spoil your chance. I'm so unlucky; if I want rain, comes drought: if I want sun, look for a deluge: if there is money to be made by a thing, I am out of it: to be lost, I am in it. If I loved a vixen she'd drop into my arms like a medlar. I love an angel, so I shall never have her, never, never! From a game o' marbles to the game of life and love I never had a grain of luck like other men: Hallo, here's a calabash.

ROB: (*turning round*) Eh?

FIELD: And here is a spade. Who belongs to this, I wonder.

> (ROBINSON *comes to him, and after a moment's eager inspection gives a great shout.*)

ROB: Ah! Miners been prospecting here. D'ye believe me now? George, they must have found *something*, or they wouldn't have stayed so long at one place. (*He uses the calabash.*) Here's a sediment in this calabash. Water! Quick, let us test it. Ah! A speck, a seed; but it is the stuff – it is the true stuff. Here is more. Why, the quartz is full of it. These bunglers don't know where to look for the heavy gold. They are only washers. We are in the very home of the gold here. The quartz is like a honeycomb with it. Gold! Gold! I've found it. I, Tom Robinson, a thief that was, offer it to its rightful owner, and that is all the world. Here, gold! Gold! Gold!

FIELD: Oh, Susan, gold, gold! (*Excitedly they shake hands over it.*)

        (BLACK WILL, JEM, *and* JACK *run on with drawn knives.*)

ROB: (*whipping out a revolver*) Ah! (*The men recoil a little.* FIELDING *lifts the spade in an attitude of defence.*) Ay, where there's gold there's blood.

B. WILL: (*grinding his teeth*) You noisy, babbling idiots, it's your lives or ours.

ROB: (*sadly, but never taking his eye off the men*) Why need it come to that? (*He cocks another barrel.*) There's enough for us all, and thousands more. Keep cool, George, no running in among their knives. Keep 'em out.

B. WILL: How long will you do that? (*to* JACK) Go round.

        (*As* JACK *is going round, and the other two are making sham advances to divert the attention of* FIELDING *and* ROBINSON, JACKY *leaps onto the stage with one bound and a ferocious yell, and fells* JACK *with a blow of a club. He poises a spear which he is about to throw at* BLACK WILL. *At the same time* FIELDING *and* ROBINSON *advance on* WILL *and* JEM.)

B. WILL: Quarter, quarter!

ROB: On your knees, then, ye scoundrels. (*They fall on their knees.*) Throw down your knives. Throw 'em down, I say, or I'll blow the roof off your skulls. (*He presents the revolver: they throw down their knives.*) Spread your wipe, George. (FIELDING *spreads his handkerchief.*) Now, my lads, you wanted to take our lives, which didn't belong to you, so we'll take something from you which doesn't belong to us; out with the swag, or – (*He presents his pistol. They take several small nuggets out of their pockets and throw them sulkily down.*) Now, mark my words: I take this creek, and I warn you off it.

B. WILL: Why, there's enough for us all. Won't you let us live as well as yourselves?

ROB: Yes, but not at our door, ye blood-thirsty varmint. Do you see that ridge half a mile west? It is full of gold. Work there. If we catch you this side of it we'll shoot you down like wolves; and if we catch one of you alone we'll hang him to the first tree like a wild cat. Come, mizzle. (*He presents the revolver.*)

B. WILL: Our turn next.

        (*They go off, crestfallen. Meantime* JACK *has come to, and looks about him with a dazzled air.*)

ROB: (*with his hands on his knees*) Oh! What, you are too honest to cheat the gallows, you are! I thought you had settled his hash, darky.

JACKY: I punch his head – yah, yah!

ROB: Oh, did you? Then next time I'll trouble you to punch it a little harder. (*The man gets up, and runs off staggering after his comrades.*)

Come, mizzle: 'To mizzle' means 'to go', 'to decamp'.

JACKY: Now, please, you tell Jacky what you white-fellows fight for dis time?

ROB: For this, my lad, for the king of metals (*showing him a nugget*).

JACKY: (*inspecting it*) For dat little yellow stone? Den white-fellow more bigger great fool dan black-fellow – dat's all. I find you good deal bigger yellow stone dan dat without fighting for him at all. One day I see him not far off. Dar, you sit down and do nothing at all. I go look 'bout for yellow stone. (*carelessly*) Massa Tom, suppose I find him so big as your head, what you give me for him?

ROB: (*incredulously*) As big as my head? I'll give you my box of lucifers. He! He!

JACKY: (*excited*) Den I find him a good deal soon, all at one time direckly.

> (*While speaking he runs to the tree and mounts it rapidly by cutting nicks with his tomahawk and putting his toe in each nick alternately, and grasping the tree. Meantime* FIELDING *and* ROBINSON *seat themselves on the heap of boulders.*)

ROB: He is poking fun at us, of course.

FIELD: I am not so sure of that, Tom. These poor savages have got an eye like a hawk for everything in nature; and Jacky is on his mettle now; he is dying for those lucifers.

JACKY: (*high up in the tree*) Yah, yah, I find him. (*He descends.*)

ROB: What, a nugget up a gum-tree, like an opossum; none o' your chaff, darky. (JACKY *comes towards them.*)

JACKY: There he is, look!

> (FIELDING *and* ROBINSON *turn round and round where they sit.* JACKY *puts his tomahawk in between them – they look down with incredulous amazement.*)

JACKY: Dis moss grow over him nose a lilly bit since I saw him last, hide all but one yellow eye.

> (FIELDING *and* ROBINSON *fall on their knees and, tearing the moss away, reveal part of a nugget imbedded.*)

ROB: All right; here is a pound weight of gold if there is an ounce. Come, my lad, out you come! Out you – (*he examines it closer, and trembles*) – why this is only the point of the nugget, it lies perpendicularly, not flat, George. I can't move it. (*roaring*) The spade! The spade!

FIELD: (*shouting*) Stand clear! (*He drives the spade down and presses slowly on the handle.*) Is it jammed any way?

ROB: No, no, it is its own weight.

FIELD: Well, then, it is over a hundredweight.

ROB: (*agitated*) Don't be a fool, now; there's no such thing in nature.

FIELD: Tell 'ee there's a hundredweight of something over my spade. Now she comes; catch hold 't.

ROB: Oh, oh, oh! (*He rolls it out.*) We are made men; we are gentlemen for life.

FIELD: Oh, Tom, is it worth a thousand pounds?

ROB: (*contemptuously*) A thousand fiddles! Say six thousand pounds, and more. (*He kneels down and turns it over.*) It is the wonder of the world.

FIELD: (*kneeling on the other side*) You beauty, I see my Susan's eyes in you. (*He kisses the nugget.*)

ROB: Hush! Quick, throw your wipe over it; hide it or it will cost us our lives. The sight of it will turn honest men to rogues. (*They throw the handkerchief over it.*)

FIELD: Shake hands over it, old fellow. (*They shake hands over it and dance round it.*) Stop a bit! Oh, dear! It is Jacky's, he found it.

JACKY: What for you dance? What for you pull one another? First you bite yellow stone, den you red, den you white, den you kick up such a bobbery, all because we pull up yellow stone. All dis a good deal dam ridicalous. (*with majestic indifference*) Jacky give him all to you.

ROB: (*Embraces him.*) You are a noble fellow. (*agitated*) George, here is a true philosopher. Here's Ebony despises Gold. My dear boy, accept as a faint tribute of my respect, this box of lucifers. (*JACKY rubs his hands with delight. They both dance: one round the gold, the other round the box.*)

FIELD: And, dear Jacky, accept my hut and furniture, and all my sheep, and all my cattle, and my blessing, with all my heart. Come, let me pack up my bundle, and away to England and Susan! Hurrah, hurrah! (*Exeunt.*)

(CRAWLEY *creeps out.*)

CRAW: A hundredweight of gold! It made the perspiration run down my very back. And going home to Susan directly. What will Meadows say to that? What will he do to me? I'll tell the gang. I beg their pardon, my masters (*shivering*) – my very worthy, and approved good masters. And if I do, there will be murder: the wholesale article. Ugh! I won't do it, Mr Meadows. I'm losing all taste for felony: the best dish gets insipid in time. You have got a right hand, Mr Meadows, take and murder folk with that! Ah, but the one he'll murder will be me, if they get home safe with their weight in gold. I'll tell the gang; it is no business of mine what they do. I wash my hands of the coming felony. (*Exit, then he returns.*) These knives are awkward things lying about. Some honest men might cut themselves (*he picks them up*). These are only fit for such fellows as Black Will – Where shall we all go to? (*Exit.*)

(*Staccato music plays. Enter* JACKY, *crawling. He jumps yelling into the bush, and hacks furiously with his tomahawk. Then he brings out* CRAWLEY's *umbrella.*)

JACKY: Where de oder? Dis not the same white-fellow I see hiding dere, when I up dat gum-tree. Oh, dear, I bery uncomfordable. I come back all alone a good deal soft to punch his head, cos Massa George not like too much punch; and now him gone, head and all, and now I not punch nobody nothing. (*whining*) I bery uncomfordable. (*He sits down disconsolate, and plays with the umbrella. Then, brightening up*) Dis like a bird's wings; first him open, den him shut, den him open – now like a pigeon; now like a crow; now like an eagle, now him – Loramassy! (*The umbrella having opened entirely with a snick,* JACKY *drops it, starts to his feet, and dances round it, flourishing his tomahawk and threatening it.*) Yah, yah, now I know him. Dis is de lilly tree what grow all at one time out of a white-fellow, when it a good deal wet. Rain make dis tree grow bery swift. Call him a rumberelle. Always I see him a good deal fat like so: nebbare I see him thin. (*He reflects with his finger to his forehead.*) He makes himself thin to hide in that dere lilly bush dere. (*He utters shrill savage whistles.*)

(*Enter male and female savages.* JACKY *stands with his back to the audience, his umbrella up, and his tomahawk held behind his back. He waves them majestically to be seated, and they sink suddenly down on their hams in a semicircle.*)

JACKY: Listen a me, you black-fellows, and also likewise you gins into the bargain. White-fellows call me Jacky; black-fellows call me Kalingaloonga. (*The* SAVAGES *incline their heads gravely.*) In de next place, the consequence is my white name is called Jacky, my black name Kalingaloonga are a great chief – he are a bery great chief – a regular unscrupulous good chief. (*He goes to the* SAVAGE *at the extreme right of the semicircle.*) Now, sar, me ask you lilly question: who de most great comparative big chief you ebbare see?

SAV: Kalingaloonga!

JACKY: Dat you was answer true. Bery good. Who de most iniquitous, good, abominable chief *you* know, sar?

SAV: Kalingaloonga!

JACKY: Dat was true answer. (*To one of the* GINS) Who de most unreasonable, good, expeditious, dam long, venerable, bandy-legged chief *you* know? Speak loud, lilly lub. I not hear. (*At the least hesitation the tomahawk wags behind his back in a threatening way.*)

GIN: Kalingaloonga.

JACKY: Who de most preposterous, good, sanguinary, delicious, obscene chief *you* know?

SAV: Kalingaloonga.

JACKY: Dat a good deal curious, how you all know the right question to what I answer you, quite correct. (*aside*) Suppose one not know, den I punch dat one's head. (*He seats himself under his umbrella.*) Lilly black-fellow, you watch up gum-tree, see nobody come to bother dis here un-justifiable chief when he want to chatter. (*A little* SAVAGE *runs and mounts the tree.*) Now listen a me. White-fellows give me a good many tings. But I give you all one half a piece cos I a most avaricious good chief. One, he give me him house – dat bery good useless ting – cos – suppose him dark; time to sleep: den you put dat house between you and de wind, and dat house keep off wind most as good as a rock, or a lilly high bank. Suppose you cold, den dere a good deal wood in de house, which is called tables and chairs: you bring out dis here table and chairs, you burn him, and he make you a good deal warm. Suppose you hungry, you go up softly to one of the sheep which was de white-fellow's by and by, but presently it is Kalingaloonga's, and you punch his head, and he make haste and die: after dat you eat him first and den roast him wid white-fellow's fire sticks. (*He produces the lucifer box.*) Yah! Now you shut your eyes wide open, and see Kalingaloonga make fire like a white-fellow.

> (*They glare with expectation. He strikes a lucifer. They shriek and roll over – all but a* GIN *who pinches one* SAVAGE, *and sinks gracefully on the shoulder of another. The box is passed gravely round the semi-circle and back, like a snuff-box, several times, each enjoying the felicity of igniting one of the matches, till the little* SAVAGE *in the tree gives an alarm.*)

JACKY: What dat?

L. SAV: (*pointing off*) White-fellows coming this way – one, two, three, four, five. Got knives: seen um shine.

JACKY: What dat for? Lie down you, a good deal quick. (*They all fall flat.* JACKY *cuts a hole in the umbrella, and raising himself, cautiously peers through it. Then, angrily*) How they dare come here after Massa Tom tell 'em stay there? What for they come here with knives – ah! (*with a wild and savage snarl*) War!

SAVS: War!

JACKY: Give Kalingaloonga his war-paint. (*A* GIN *gives him colours from her purse.*) Soft – soft – soft! (*They glide off the stage.*)

    (*The air, 'Home Sweet Home' is heard, soft at first, but louder by degrees, in orchestra.*)

FIELD: (*off*) It is pretty heavy to carry, Tom.

ROB: The heavier the better for us.

    (*Enter* FIELDING *and* ROBINSON, *carrying a carpet-bag on a short pole.* FIELDING *has a staff.*)

FIELD: Well, change shoulders, then, to cross the bridge. (*They let down the load, and when they have resumed it and taken one step forward.* FIELDING *stops and looks about him.*) I say, Tom, didn't we leave those vagabonds' knives somewhere hereabouts?

ROB: Ay, we thought of nothing but the gold – nobody ever does. What is come of them knives, I wonder?

B. WILL: (*off*) They are here.

    (BLACK WILL, JEM, JACK, BOB HUDSON, *and* ABNER *enter, running with drawn knives. At the sound of* WILL's *voice,* FIELDING *and* ROBINSON *drop the carpet-bag with a cry of dismay. It falls heavily. The men attack at the run without an instant's pause.* ROBINSON *fires, and* ABNER *falls wounded.* FIELDING *fells his first assailant with his staff, and thrusts it in another's face, causing him to stagger back. Then he seizes the hands of* BLACK WILL *which are raised to stab him. They struggle.* ROBINSON's *pistol misses fire the second time, but he strikes one assailant down with the butt; another recovers from* FIELDING's *blow and closes with* ROBINSON: *they struggle a long time.* ABNER, *wounded in the thigh, crawls to* FIELDING, *and, seizing his legs, pulls him down.* ABNER *raises a knife to stab* FIELDING, *whose hands are occupied still with* BLACK WILL. *Suddenly the* SAVAGES *come leaping in from all sides. They are fully armed, and horribly painted.* KALINGALOONGA *springs, yelling, on* ABNER, *and knocks him flat. Another disables* ROBINSON's *adversary.* FIELDING *wrenches the knife from* BLACK WILL, *throws it away, and thrusts* WILL *off with his foot. They start up, and* WILL *strikes at* FIELDING *with his fist.* FIELDING *parries the blow, and strikes* WILL *with his fist;* WILL *staggers back towards* ROBINSON, *who hits him on the neck and drives him forward towards* FIELDING. FIELDING *then deliberately knocks him down. Meantime the others, except* ABNER, *have got up, but after a short engagement are overpowered by the* SAVAGES. ABNER *lies motionless. A* SAVAGE *darts off with a whoop.*)

FIELD: (*breathless*) Don't kill them, Jacky; but keep them close prisoners – till – our gold – and our lives – are beyond their reach.

JACKY: (*with dignity*) Kalingaloonga want to punch their heads a good deal more, but he will do what you say, because after dis he tinks Massa George will speak no more good words to him friend Kalingaloonga.

> (JACKY *hangs his head sorrowfully, and motions to the other* SAVAGES *who drag and drive the men, except* ABNER, *into the centre, and encircle them with extended weapons.* FIELDING *and* ROBINSON *take up the bag and go out. A great outcry is heard, and* CRAWLEY *enters, screaming and writhing, with a spear sticking in his back like a tail, followed by the* SAVAGE *who has thrown it; he falls on his knees.* JACKY *kicks him into the circle. This done,* FIELDING *and* ROBINSON *appear on the bridge going homeward; they stand triumphant and wave their caps.*)

FIELD: Hurrah for home and Susan, hurrah!

ROB: Hurrah!

> (*The orchestra plays a very spirited 'The Girl I Left Behind Me', and the caps are waved during the music. The tune is played again after the act drop falls, to prolong the leading sentiment.*)

ACT IV

SCENE 1. MR MEADOWS's *study, a girl enters with candles and letters. She places them on his desk, orders them, dusts his chair etcetera, and exit.* MEADOWS *enters, throws himself into his chair, and buries his head in his hands a moment.*

MEAD: Ay, Susan is cold as marble. She believes me; she marries me; but she shrinks from me. It is my wedding eve; and I am sick of my life. (*He opens his letters.*) What is this? Will Fielding was in the town today, and vows he will stand at the church porch tomorrow and part the bride and bridegroom with his horsewhip. Says if she *will* take a dog instead of a man, it shall be a beaten dog. Will ye so? Will ye so? After the wedding I'll cram your brag down your throat with my fist. But, meantime – (*He touches his hand-bell, and writes a hasty note. Enter the* SERVANT.) Send Jem with this to lawyer Smeaton on the instant. (*Exit* SERVANT. MEADOWS *rises.*) He'll part Susan and me tomorrow? Tonight I put him in the county gaol. I have spared you this eighteen months, Master Will, but you will have it; take it, then. Ah, that has done me good. Susan's pale face and cold words unman me; but threats and difficulties they turn me to steel.

> (*Enter* SERVANT.)

SERV: Mr Jeffries, sir. The postmaster.

MEAD: Send him up. (*Exit* SERVANT.) My mind misgives me. What does he want?

> (*Enter* JEFFRIES *wildly, and holding out his hand at* MEADOWS *in a threatening way.*)

JEFF: I can carry this game on no longer; and I won't. To see the poor girl come to me, month after month, with her pale face and begging eyes, 'Oh, Mr Jeffries, do have a letter for me!' Better to sleep in gaol with a clean breast, than to lie all night without a wink as I do, tasting eternal torment before my time, and your villainy; yes, yours; for you are the tempter. I'm but the tool, the miserable tool.

MEAD: (*calmly*) I, Jeffries? What d'ye mean? It is you that have abused the public
confidence, not I. So, if you are such a fool and a sneak as to cut your own
throat, and your family's, by peaching on yourself, I'll cry louder than you,
and show you have emptied letters as well as stopped them. Go home to your
wife, and keep quiet, or I'll smash both you and her.

JEFF: Oh, I know you are without mercy; and I dare not speak out while I live; but
I'll beat you yet, you cruel monster. I will send my wife this moment to Miss
Merton, to confess all, and tell her George is true, and you are the false one;
and I'll blow out my brains tonight in the office.

MEAD: (*aside*) I'm lost. (*He puts his hand in his breast pocket.*) Jeffries, I don't
think you are *game* to take your own life.

JEFF: Tomorrow will show.

MEAD: I must know before that. (*He seizes* JEFFRIES *in an iron grasp and puts a
pistol barrel to his head.*)

JEFF: Oh, no! Mercy, mercy! No! No!

MEAD: (*coolly*) All right: you won't kill yourself – you are fool enough to do it, but
you are too great a cur. Give over shaking like an aspen, and talk sense. You
are in debt; you have accepted bills; I've bought 'em. Here they are (*shows
them cautiously*). Come to me *after the wedding* tomorrow, and we'll light our
pipes with them.

JEFF: Oh, Mr Meadows, that would be a load off my mind. (*He sighs.*)

MEAD: You are short of cash, too. Come to me *after the wedding*, and I'll hand you
a fifty pound note.

JEFF: You are very liberal, sir. Would it were in a better cause.

MEAD: Now go to bed; and don't be a sneak, and an idiot, till *after the wedding*; or
I'll sell the bed from under your wife's back, and send you to the stone-jug. Be
off! (MEADOWS *points him off, then draws himself up to his full height and
shouts.*) Are there any more of you that hope to conquer John Meadows?
Then come on! Come at me a thousand strong, with the devil at your back –
and then I'll beat you. (CRAWLEY, *now shaved, and neater in his dress,
opens a secret door.* MEADOWS *hears him, turns quietly, and sees him.*)
Crawley!

CRAW: (*softly*) Yes, Mr Meadows.

MEAD: Hush! I had better close the staircase door. (*He disappears for an instant,
and then returns to confront* CRAWLEY. *In a half whisper*) Well? Well? Well?

CRAW: Well, sir, I give you joy. They say two heads are better than one. But I say
two hands are better than one; your two have done the trick between them.

MEAD: But why did you come back without orders? Tell me all.

CRAW: All, Mr Meadows? Why it's volumes. I've served you as no great man was
ever served before. I bribed his shepherd, and his sheep all died. I tempted
Black Will and Co. to rob him, and that nearly led to – murder – ugh! For you
I flung the professional to the winds, and went in for *the indictable* like
mother's milk; and (*opening his eyes*) swam in felony. But there, they go safe
to Sydney by a miracle, and on board for England: and then I crawled into the
ship after them, stiff and sore – for I was wounded in your service. Wounded?

the stone-jug: a prison.

I was skewered like a fillet o' veal. Six inches of a bone-headed spear in me, and cut out with a cheese knife, and bled a bucketful – and there I lay all the voyage, scheming in vain, and groaning, and saying, 'How shall I ever face that great man?' I came down here to warn you. But the first thing I saw was you and Miss Merton at a distance, walking arm in arm. I knew it was all right then; I went to the barber's crying, oh, be joyful! Well, sir, and when did the event come off?

MEAD: What event?

CRAW: The happy event, the marriage, you and the lady. She is worth all the trouble she has cost us.

MEAD: You fool, we are not married.

CRAW: Don't say so! Now don't say so.

MEAD: No matter, we shall be tomorrow morning.

CRAW: We are ruined! We are undone! Why, man alive, they are in the town.

MEAD: Who?

CRAW: Why, George Fielding and his mate.

MEAD: Are you drunk?

CRAW: No. I wish I was. They are not ten doors from where we sit. They are at the Red Lion. It was a sharp race. I beat them by an hour. But by then I had gone to the barber's and civilized myself to visit you – *there they were.*

MEAD: (*leaning his head on his hand*) What is to be done?

CRAW: Do, sir? Why – nolle prosequi!

MEAD: (*confused*) Do what?

CRAW: Nolle prosequi – abandon the suit. The lady won't marry *us* if defendant is sitting at the wedding breakfast; and he will be. These farmers rise with the sun. Luckily no blood has been spilt, except mine; so there is no harm done. Go and say you are de–light–ed to find George Fielding has been belied by some *villain*. Lay particular stress on the *villain*, to divert suspicion; and go give the girl up with a flourish; keep dark, and nobody will ever know the little game we have been at.

MEAD: What, soil myself with all these crimes for nothing; lie, and feign, and intercept letters; and rob, and all but assassinate – and fail? Wade in sin up to my middle, and then wade back again without the prize? Never. Do you see this pistol? If she and I are ever parted it shall be this way – I'll send her to heaven with one barrel, and myself to hell with the other. There, you need not look so scared; ten to one if it ever comes to that. I shall try all I know first. You look tired, my good Crawley: you shall have a bottle of my old port: and I am a little staggered myself, but it is only for a moment. My heart is often sick and cold; but my will is unconquerable. (*Exit, and is heard to descend, his heavy tread becoming fainter and fainter. The lights dim.*)

CRAW: Mr Meadows is getting wildish. It frightens me to see a cool hand like him burst out like that. He is not to be trusted with a loaded pistol. Ah, and I am in his secrets; deep in them! Great men often sweep away little rubbishy men, that know too much. I never saw him with a pistol before. (*He takes off the caps.*) I'll take off the caps for fear it should go off by accident, and kill me on purpose.

(*Enter* MEADOWS *with a bottle and two glasses. He motions*

CRAWLEY *to be seated, lights a candle, and pours out some wine, keeping the bottle on his side. NOTE: no comic business is admissible just here.*)

MEAD: (*thoughtfully*) The loss of his sheep must have ruined George Fielding. So at all events he comes back without the thousand pounds.

CRAW: What, haven't you heard of the great nugget of gold? Why, London was ringing with it when I came through.

MEAD: Yes, I read it in the paper. But what has that to do with George Fielding?

CRAW: Why, he is the finder. He and his mate. Mr Meadows, I lay hid in a thornbush and saw those two pull that nugget out of a heap of stone that five hundred shepherds had sat on, five thousand times, eating bread and cheese, and seen nothing; the idiots! I've sat on it myself often, and none the wiser.

MEAD: What will they get for that one nugget? Not the – the – thousand pounds?

CRAW: (*groaning*) They sold it in Sydney for seven thousand pounds. (*coaxing*) Come, come, what can't be cured, must be endured. Nolle prosequi.

MEAD: You must have been four months in one ship with them – and could you think of nothing?

CRAW: You underrate my zeal, sir. When force failed, I tried skill. I retained a returned convict that I found in the ship; he agreed to hocuss them and then rob them. Look here! (*He puts a small white substance on the table.*) Put that in a man's glass of grog, and in ten minutes you might take the clothes off his back. Well, sir, we soon found where the money was.

MEAD: Where?

CRAW: His friend carries it in a square pocket-book inside his shirt. Well, the gentleman I retained watched and watched all the voyage for a chance. It was no go. Teetotal, or next thing to it. Mr Meadows, the last card is played. Give the girl up. She is like all the women; costs a great deal more than she is worth.

(MEADOWS *fills his own glass and* CRAWLEY's, *and while the latter is drinking, quietly puts the white substance in his waistcoat pocket. He then rises and empties his own glass at a draught.*)

MEAD: (*sternly*) Stay here, Crawley, till I come back. (*at the door, gloomily*) On my return I shall perhaps take your advice and resign her I love: if I do, I shall leave the country tomorrow and take you with me. (*Exit* MEADOWS.)

CRAW: Thank you, Mr Meadows. Well, and so he ought. (*He drinks.*) I hope he won't be long gone. I can't bear to be alone. How dark it is. (*He lights the other candle.*) I hate night-time. For then it is I see such cu–rious sights. I know they are only brandybubbles. But they are awful ones (*he drinks*). Sometimes it is a judge, with furrowed brow and flowing wig, and grey shaggy eyebrows, and, oh, such a strike-me-off-the-rolls-and-give-me-ten-years-penal-servitude eye, like a cold, grey diamond. Sometimes it is a policeman, all of a colour, and all of a piece, with a pair of handcuffs bright as silver; there he stands stock-still, like Fate clear-starched, calm, inevitable, immoveable, half in, half out of the wall, as much as to say, 'Go on, go on, Peter; run out to the end o' your little chain, Peter; *Bobby can wait*: to these iron bracelets you must come at last.' (*He drinks eagerly.*) But the worst is when the air seems to fill with a thin blue smoke: it clears, and then out comes, plainer and plainer,

blacker and blacker, a horrible figure (*he lowers his voice to a whisper*), with
hoofs – and horns – and eyes like rubies afire, and teeth of white-hot iron, and
a grin, oh, such a grin, it freezes your soul! (*He covers his face with his hands.*)
It is only the drink. But what am I the better for its being only the drink? I see
these horrible things as plain as I see this bottle, or that wall there. (*He fills a
glass and is about to drink, but stops, and points with trembling hand at the wall
in an awe-struck manner.*) Something is coming *now*; that is how it mostly
begins; the wall opens gradually, and the phantom sits or stands in it, and eyes
me, and eyes me, and eyes me, till I am dead with terror. (*He shrinks flat
against the wall as a panel is opening very slowly indeed.*) Curse Meadows for
leaving me! No – running away makes them stronger. Your only chance is to
face them, go at them! (*He puts his arm before his face and goes staggering at
the panel.*) Go at 'em, and butt 'em like a ram! (*He runs his nose nearly against
ISAAC LEVI's face which is protruded through the open panel.*) Ah, ah! (*He
runs and tumbles over. LEVI closes the aperture noiselessly, CRAWLEY looks
fearfully around.*) Vanished, thank heaven! Go at 'em is your only chance!
(*Looking over his shoulder, he goes to his chair, and sits down.*) That was a
new one. (*He drinks.*) My little stock of 'em is increasing. It was an apparition
of that terrible old Jew. I'd as soon see Old Nick any day. (MEADOWS *bursts
in through the secret door, pale and wild.*) No, no! Mercy, mercy! (*He runs
away.*)

MEAD: (*sinking into a chair*) Perdition seize the hour I first saw her!
CRAW: (*gasping, and aside*) It is only my captain. I thought it was our
Commander-in-chief.
MEAD: (*with an unnatural calm*) Crawley, when the enemy of man buys a soul, how
much does he give? A good round lump I hear. (*He flings down a roll of
banknotes. Then, furiously*) Count those, and tell me what mine has gone for.
CRAW: Why, they are all hundred pound notes, new and bright as silver. Oh,
beautiful, beautiful! However did you get them? (*He counts them carefully.*)
MEAD: (*shaking his head*) Too easily. I used that drug you gave me. I drugged their
liquor in the bar. George Fielding was in bed. The other was alone and fast
asleep – a sleep like death. I took them out and stuffed the pocket-book and
put it back into his breast. Crawley, he I robbed – of thousands – was
Robinson, the man I sent to prison for picking my pocket of fifteen pounds.
(*He groans.*)
CRAW: (*who has been counting while MEADOWS was speaking*) Report spoke true
for once: it is seven thousand pounds.
MEAD: Seven thousand! This will be a dear job to me.
CRAW: Say a dear job to them, but a glorious haul to you.
MEAD: Why, you fool, do you think I am going to keep the man's money?
CRAW: Keep it? Why, of course: or why take it at all at such a risk?
MEAD: You are as blind as a mole. Don't you see I have made George Fielding
penniless again, and that old Merton will not let him have Susan. He was to
come back with a thousand pounds: 'stead o' that, he comes back without a
penny. And, as he can never marry her, I shall, soon or late; and that same
afternoon seven thousand pounds will be put into George Fielding's hand; he
won't know by whom, but you and I *shall*. I am a villain, but I am not a thief.

(CRAWLEY *gives a dissatisfied grunt.*) Enough chat. There's the fire: burn them this moment; then they will tell no tales.

CRAW: (*agitated*) No, no, sir; don't think of it! Talk of crime? What are all the *little* crimes we have done together compared with this? You would not burn a wheat-rick, sir, not your greatest enemy's, I am sure you would not, you are too good a man. But this is as bad: the good money, the great money, the beautiful money that heaven has given, in its bounty, for the good of man.

MEAD: Come, no more of this folly! Burn them this moment! (*He seizes* CRAWLEY.)

CRAW: (*falling on his knees*) Mercy, mercy, think of me, of your poor faithful servant, who has risked a halter, and been pierced with a javelin, and has stuck at nothing for you. Oh, how ungrateful great men are!

MEAD: Can you look me in the face and tell me that?

CRAW: Never till now, but now I can. (*He rises, and with desperate courage, screaming*) To whom do you owe them? To me. You would never have had them but for my drug. Yet you would burn them before my eyes: a fortune to poor me.

MEAD: To you? Give them you?

CRAW: Yes, What does it matter to you, so he never sees them again? Give them me, and in twelve hours I will be in France with them. You won't miss me. My work is done; and it will be prudent of you, for since I left you I have taken to drinking. (*threatening*) I might let out something we should both be sorry for. Send me away to foreign countries, where I can keep travelling towards the sun, and so make it always summer. I hate the long nights; for when it is dark I see such curious things. O pray let me go and take them away with me, and you shall never see them nor me again! (*He kneels.*)

MEAD: Humph! On conditions.

CRAW: Yes, sir; yes.

MEAD: (*taking out his watch*) That you go to London by the mail train which starts in one hour, and over to France this evening.

CRAW: (*starting up*) I will, sir. Hurrah! Hurrah!

MEAD: Wrap them in paper, hide them next your skin, and begone. Oh, I am worn out; I must snatch an hour's sleep, then off to Grassmere and make Susan mine. Farewell, my poor Crawley, for ever! (*Exit with a candle.*)

(CRAWLEY *comes down stage, runs his fingers over the notes, folds them, and puts them in his bosom. During which, the panel opens, and a hand comes out and points at him.*)

CRAW: (*during the business*) Is it a dream? No; I have really got seven thousand pounds. They are mine, honestly mine! For I have saved them from destruction. Good-bye, England. They call you a cold country; you are too hot for me. (*He takes a candle, and exit by the secret door on tip-toe.*)

SCENE 2. *A front scene, opposite a railway station, lighted by two feeble lamps, and with a central door. Enter* CRAWLEY *in a great-coat, with a small bag. He walks to and fro.*

CRAW: Half an hour to wait. Office shut: no fire; no light. Confound these railways! I'll write to the 'Times' from Paris. (*He stamps to warm his feet.*) Call those lamps, the winking, blinking owls? (*A POLICEMAN appears at the side.*) Who are you? (CRAWLEY *recoils a step, and glares.*) Oh – I see – only a small trifle – of – an apparition. Got a bull's eye this time. Left – your – handcuffs – down below – eh? Bub a bub a Bobby? (*with a ghastly attempt at humour*) Your most obedient: good-bye till the sun rises. (*Another POLICEMAN appears noiselessly at the other side and confronts him as he turns that way.*) Another 'Bobby can wait'. (*violently*) N–n–now what is the use of this – my good – souls? It is only done to harass the defendant. The sun is just rising, and then you know you *must* walk your chalks, ye cursed blue devils; whether you like or not (*despairingly*) They will make me cut my throat some dark night.

> (ISAAC LEVI *enters softly through the door, and stands in the centre of the stage.*)

CRAW: (*stealing a look to right and left, and seeing the POLICEMEN motionless*) Oh, very well; then I shall just turn my back on both of you till daylight, that is all. (*almost screaming*) Curse the sun! Why don't he rise? (ISAAC LEVI *motions with both hands and the two POLICEMEN advance a step or two.*) Coming nearer? Oh, Gammon! Shadows don't wear nailed boots. (*He shuts his ears with his fingers.*)

> (*The POLICEMEN each take one of CRAWLEY's wrists, and CRAWLEY trembles violently, his knees shaking. The POLICEMEN each raise a bull's-eye lantern with their disengaged hands, and throw the full light on to CRAWLEY.*)

CRAW: (*aside*) It is only flesh and blood! (*haughtily*) Well, what is it? Don't ye know me? (ISAAC LEVI's *hand glides over CRAWLEY's left shoulder, tapping him here and there. CRAWLEY eyes it with terror.*) What, a Bobby with three hands! Fiends! Demons! (*He slews his head round and sees LEVI.*) Ah, ah, ah, ah! (*The POLICEMEN produce hand-cuffs.*) Oh, oh, oh! (*They hand-cuff him. LEVI waves to them to take him off. They each put an arm under him and almost support him off. In a faint voice*) Let me say a word to Mr Levi. Mr Levi, you are a much greater man than that amorous fool Meadows. I enter your service; my great uncle was a Jew. You see my zeal; it only wants guiding with your sagacity. Do retain me, Mr Levi. I ask no fee, only the honour of the connection. Mercy!

> (LEVI *stands with his back to the audience, and waves him contemptuously off. Exeunt CRAWLEY and the POLICEMEN. LEVI follows thoughtfully with his arms folded.*)

SCENE 3. *In front of MERTON's farm. The lights are gradually raised as day dawns. Birds are chirping, and music plays. Enter MR MERTON, calling.*
MERT: Here, Josh! Josh!

> (*Enter JOSH, the carter's lad.*)

Got a bull's-eye: a kind of lantern used by the police.
Bub a bub a Bobby: a 'Bobby' is a slang term for a policeman. Beezelbub, the devil, is probably indicated by 'Bub a bub'.
walk your chalks: 'chalks' is slang for 'legs'. The phrase means 'run away'.

JOSH: Here I be.
MERT: Got the ringers?
JOSH: Ay.
MERT: Mind and see they have plenty o' beer.
JOSH: That I wool. And 'elp 'em drink it.
     (*Enter* RUSTICS, *male and female, cheering, and looking off.*)
MERT: Who is it?
JOSH: Bridegroom's party just drove up.
     (*Enter* SUSAN MERTON, *dressed for a wedding.*)
SUSAN: Oh, father, please don't leave the table: they congratulate me, and they
    make jests. Jests, and I am expected to smile! Pray don't leave me. I need to
    see your dear face all the time, to remind me that I am making *you* happy, at
    all events.
MERT: That you are, girl. (*Church bells ring in the distance, and* SUSAN *bursts
    out crying.*) Don't let the bridegroom see you cry, whatever. He'll be
    affronted.
SUSAN: (*sobbing*) No, no. I won't cry before the folk.
MERT: There, I'll come to you in a moment. (*Exit* SUSAN.)
     (*The* RUSTICS *cheer.*)
MERT: Who is that?
JOSH: Parson has gone into the church. (*The bells ring.*)
     (*Exit* MERTON, *but his voice is presently heard saying:*)
MERT: Come now, make the line. Let us go in form.
     (*Enter the wedding party.* MERTON *arranges the procession, headed
     by* SUSAN *and* MEADOWS. *They move in line. A faint cheer is
     heard outside, followed by a murmur of voices. Enter* FIELDING *and*
     ROBINSON, *meeting the procession at the wing.*)
FIELD: Susan, dear Susan!
SUSAN: Ah! (*She withdraws her arm from* MEADOWS, *and, starting back, stands
    paralysed.*)
FIELD: Why, what's in all this? And what are you doing on that man's arm?
SUSAN: What am I doing? What have *you* done? You deserted me and married
    another. Father, neighbours, ask this man why he comes here *now*, to disturb
    my peace, and make me insult the honest man who honours me with his
    respect. Oh, my face, where shall I hide it? (*She covers her face with her
    hands. The whole party gets out of order, and stare, and pry, and interchange
    whispers.*)
ROB: Stop a bit! Stop a bit! George false to you, miss? Why, all his cry night and
    day has been Susan! Susan! And when he found the great nugget, he kisses it;
    and, says he, that is not because you are gold, but because you take me to
    Susan.
FIELD: Hold your tongue, Tom; who puts me on my defence? Has any man here
    been telling her I ever had a thought of any girl but her? (*He looks round
    defiantly.*) If there is, let him stand out now and say it to my face if he dares.
    (*There is a pause.*) There's a lie without a backer, it seems. (*very gravely*) And
    now, Susan, once more, what are you doing on that man's arm?
SUSAN: Kill me! Kill me!

MEAD: Miss Merton and I are to be married this morning; that is why she is on my arm.

FIELD: She thought me false. But now she sees I am true. Blindfold choice is *no* choice at all, Mr Meadows. (*He advances to* SUSAN.) Susan, I say nothing about the promises that have passed between us, and the ring that you gave me. (*turning sharply*) Haven't I one friend in all this parish to stop those bells a minute?

　　　　　(JOSH *runs off*.)

SUSAN: You have kept my ring?

FIELD: Here 'tis. No man ever loved a woman truer than I love you, Susan; but, for all that, I would not give a snap of the finger to have you if your will is towards another – would *you*, sir? So, please yourself, my girl, and don't cry like that. I could cry myself when I think all that has passed between you and me; but this must end, and end it shall; I won't live in doubt a moment, no, nor half a moment. You are free as air, Susan (*he flings down the ring*). And, being free, choose between John Meadows and George Fielding.

SUSAN: Oh, George, what choice can there be? The moment I saw your face, and truth still shining in it, I forgot there was a John Meadows in the world. (*She tears off her gloves, and, becoming hysterical, is supported by the* BRIDESMAIDS. FIELDING *picks up the ring again. The bells stop*.)

JOSH: (*running in*) Hurrah!

MEAD: Curse them!

MERT: But I am to be consulted too. George, I have been an imprudent fool. It is no use hiding what can't be concealed. I owe two thousand pounds. We heard you had changed your mind: and Meadows offers to clear his wife's father.

MEAD: Why, of course, sir. My wife's father is my father; I know no odds.

FIELD: Your word, Uncle. I crossed the seas on the faith of it. Says you, bring back a thousand pounds, to show me you are not a fool, and you shall have my daughter, and she shall have my blessing.

MERT: Did I say so?

FIELD: Ask Mr Meadows. He was there.

MEAD: (*hanging his head*.) I can't deny it. Those were the words.

MERT: Well, but you haven't brought it.

ROB: Oh, hasn't he? But I say he has brought, not one thousand, but seven thousand pounds. (*exclamations*) They are not all his; but they should be sooner than true lovers be parted. (*He takes out a very plump pocket-book. The bridal party surrounds him. Slapping it*) There is a buster. (*There is laughter*.) Here they are – seventy new hundred-pound notes. (*The* RUSTICS *cheer*.) All as crimp as a parson's neck-cloth. Why, I never put these in! (*He takes out square pieces of newspaper, and lets them fall*.) Oh!

FIELD: Why, Tom!

ROB: Robbed!

FIELD: Robbed?

ROB: Robbed! Am I dreaming. It has never left me a moment, night or day. Robbed, robbed! Kill me, George; I have ruined you! (*Murmurs*.)

FIELD: I can't speak.

MERT: But I can. Don't tell me of a London thief being robbed. You are a couple of impostors. Ye haven't got a thousand *pence*, and never had. So if you are a man at all, nevvy, leave things as they are. I say – if so be you don't hate Susan, as well as me – then don't stand in the poor girl's light. Do, for pity's sake, leave me and my daughter in peace.

FIELD: You are right, old man. My head is confused. But I seem to see it will be kindest to Susan for me to go back to Australia. Come, Tom, *honest* Tom. That for their gibes and their mean suspicion – let us, you and I, go back together.

SUSAN: (*quietly*) And if you do, I shall go with you. Friends, I am a simple girl. I have been blinded by one I now see to be a monster of deceit; but I was never false-hearted, nor inconstant. I am yours, George, for better for worse, if you think me still worthy to be your wife; and, oh, for my part, I am glad you have not a farthing. What signifies wealth to us? We have willing hearts to work for one another, and we have our youth, and our health, and our love – and this is the only happy moment I have known since we parted, two weary years ago. (*They embrace. The* RUSTICS *cheer loudly.*)

MEAD: My patience is gone. Since you scorn my love, let us see how you can bear my hate. (*Furious, he goes to leave, but is stopped by a* POLICEMAN.)

POLICE: Stay a moment, Mr Meadows!

MEAD: What for?

POLICE: Why, I don't exactly know; but I believe you are wanted. (*Meantime,* HITCHIN *has entered, and pauses close to* ROBINSON *in passing.*)

HITCH: (*to* ROBINSON) All right. Keep dark, and let *us* work. (ROBINSON *looks amazed, but hopeful.*) There is a warrant taken out against you, Mr Meadows, by one Robinson.

MEAD: Is this a jest, Hitchin?

HITCH: You know best, sir. Is it you that were robbed of seven thousand pounds at the Red Lion?

ROB: I and my mate.

FIELD: How did *he* know?

ROB: Hush, George. Let the Bobbies work.

FIELD: No, I won't hush! If he knows we have been robbed, he may know who is the thief.

(*Enter* ISAAC LEVI.)

LEVI: The thief is – Mr Meadows! (*There are exclamations of 'Meadows!'*) He drugged your liquor, and stole your money in the coffee-room of the Red Lion.

ROB: It is true. It must be true. I awoke in that coffee-room at past midnight, with my head splitting, and my feet as cold as ice.

MEAD: Well, malice goes a long way. Mr Levi is my known enemy. Now, I ask you, is this credible? I have got sixty thousand pounds. Why should I steal? (*There are assenting murmurs from the* RUSTICS.)

LEVI: To beggar your rival. Why did you stop Susannah's letters at the post-office? We don't know what any man will do till he is tempted, Mr Meadows. (*More assenting murmurs.*)

---

nevvy: nephew.

MEAD: That is an old saying, and true to slanderers, Mr Levi. Where did you pick up *that* tale of my intercepting letters?

LEVI: You drove the old Jew from his house, and from the shadows of his dead, and this you did, not from need, but hate. So he made that house a trap; he took the next house, and bored a hole in the party wall, and caught you in your villainy. I saw you give Crawley the notes.

MEAD: How generous! I might as well have kept them to myself. (*aside*) Crawley is hundreds of miles off by this. Well, you find Crawley with seven thousand pounds, and then I'll believe I have been walking in my sleep, and picking people's pockets for other people's benefit. (*The* RUSTICS *laugh, incredulously.*)

LEVI: So be it, Mr Meadows. The test you propose is fair. (*He pauses, and then, loudly*) Bring in the prisoner! (CRAWLEY *is brought in, handcuffed.*) Is he as he was when you took him? (*The* OFFICER *nods.*) If the missing notes be not found in that man's bosom, on the left side thereof, then I am a slanderer, and Mr Meadows is not a thief.

ROB: Stop, sir – to make sure – the notes ran from number 1560 to number 1629. (HITCHIN *takes the notes out of* CRAWLEY's *bosom, and holds them up, then examines them.*)

HITCH: (*to* ROBINSON) They answer to your description. (*He gives them to* ROBINSON, *who crams them with ludicrous haste into* FIELDING's *hands, saying:*)

ROB: Confound them. (*There are general exclamations.*)

MEAD: (*aside*) If I could but catch his eye.

LEVI: Crawley, where did you get them?

CRAW: I had them from a man of property, a wealthy man. How could I suspect any harm? Mr Meadows gave them to me to take to his banker in London.

MEAD: Liar! Ungrateful miscreant!

LEVI: A word with Mr Meadows before he goes to gaol. You had no mercy on the afflicted of heaven.

MEAD: Yes, you have caught me, but you shall never cage me. (*He levels his pistol at his head. The women scream. Both barrels miss fire. With a despairing cry*) Foiled, foiled! (*He hangs his head.*)

CRAW: *I* took the caps off, Mr Meadows. (*They begin to handcuff* MEADOWS. *There are low murmurs.*)

MEAD: Ay, take me to gaol, but you can't make me live there. Respected all these years, and now to be a felon. Take me where I may hide my head and die. (*He moves off in despair.*)

CRAW: (*running after him*) A fine end of all your manoeuvring, you poor bungler. Here am I, an innocent man, ruined through knowing a thief – a thief – a thief! (MEADOWS *turns at the wing, and lifts up his handcuffed hands with a mute expression of anguish and reproach.* FIELDING *strides up to* CRAWLEY *and takes him by the shoulder.*)

FIELD: Ye little snake. (*He sends* CRAWLEY *spinning.*) Let the man alone. (*Exit* MEADOWS, *guarded.*)

CRAW: (*after a malignant look, obsequiously*) Yes, Mr Fielding. You are a good natured man; don't appear against us at the assizes, Mr Fielding. What is the use? We are harmless. You've got the lady and the money; and you deserve them nobly, Mr Fielding. (HITCHIN *bundles him off, struggling and shouting*) I'll draw your marriage contract, for nothing, Mr Fielding. (*Exeunt* CRAWLEY *and* POLICE.)

(*The bells ring again, louder than at first.*)

SUSAN: Ah, it is for your return they are ringing now, George. Oh, Mr Levi, bless you, bless you!

LEVI: Susannah, man sees but a little way before him; my revenge, so long desired, gives me no joy, now it is come. But warms my aged breast to see the roses come back to your pale cheek, and to hear the sweet bells ring – (*He takes her hand and* FIELDING'*s, and joins them*) – for these two constant hearts made happy.

FIELD: (*with emotion*) Happy? Sir, there's my hand, read it if ye can, for the words ain't made that can speak my heart to you. (*He turns to the* RUSTICS.) Neighbours, Mr Meadows was an able man, and I a poor simple fellow; yet you see he ends in trouble, and I am in heaven, or next door to it. So let us take to heart the old adage, 'Honesty is the best policy.'

ROB: And when you look at me, yokels, you may see the truth of another old saying, 'It is never too late to mend.'

Curtain

THE PLAYS OF CHARLES READE

The Ladies' Battle	(from Scribe and Legouvé): Olympic, Farren and Mrs Stirling, 7 May 1851.
Angelo	(from Victor Hugo): Olympic, Farren and Mrs Stirling, 11 August 1851.
Masks and Faces	(with Tom Taylor): Haymarket, Webster and Mrs Stirling, 20 November 1852.
A Village Tale	Strand, Mrs Seymour, 12 April 1852.
The Lost Husband	(from Annicet Bourgeois): Strand, Mrs Seymour, 26 April 1852.
Gold	Drury Lane, 10 January 1853.
Two Loves and a Life	(with Tom Taylor): Adelphi, Webster, 20 March 1854.
The Courier of Lyons	(from Moreau, Siraudin, and Delacour): Princess's, Charles Kean, 26 June 1854.
The King's Rival	(with Tom Taylor): St James's, Mrs Seymour and Isabel Glyn, 2 October 1854.
Honour Before Titles; or Nobs and Snobs	St James's, J. L. Toole, 3 October 1854.
Peregrine Pickle	St James's, November 1854.
Art	(from Fournier): St James's, 17 April 1855.
The First Printer	(with Tom Taylor): Princess's, Charles Kean, 3 March 1856.
It Is Never Too Late to Mend	Princess's, George Vining, 4 October 1865.
Dora	(from Tennyson): Adelphi, Kate Terry, 1 June 1867.
The Double Marriage	(from Maquet): Queen's, Fanny Addison and Ellen Terry, 24 October 1867.
Foul Play	(with Dion Boucicault): Holborn, 28 May 1868.
Free Labour	Adelphi, Henry Neville, 28 May 1870.
The Robust Invalid	(from Molière's *Le Malade imaginaire*): Adelphi, George Vining, Mrs Seymour, and Florence Terry, 15 June 1870.
An Actress of Daylight	(from Fournier): St James's, Mrs John Wood, 8 April 1871.
Shilly-shally	(from Trollope): Gaiety, 1 April 1872.
The Wandering Heir	Queen's, Mrs John Wood, 15 November 1873.

Rachel the Reaper	Queen's, Ellen Terry, 9 March 1874.
Griffith Gaunt	Queen's, Ellen Terry and Charles Kelly, 1874.
The Scuttled Ship	Olympic, Henry Neville, 2 April 1877.
The Lyons Mail	Lyceum, Henry Irving, 19 May 1877.
Jealousy	(from Sardou's *Andrée*): Olympic, Henry Neville, 22 April 1878.
Drink	(from Zola, Busnach, and Gastineau): Princess's, Charles Warner, 2 June 1879.
Nance Oldfield	Olympic, Geneviève Ward, 24 February 1883.
Love and Money	(with Henry Pettitt): Adelphi, John Ryder and Sophie Eyre, 18 November 1882.

The following plays were produced in the provinces, but never in London:

The Hypochondriac	(original version of *The Robust Invalid*): taken on tour by Mrs Seymour, 1858.
Our Seaman	(original version of *The Scuttled Ship*): taken on tour by Ellen Terry, 1874.
Joan	(from Hodgson Burnett's *That Lass o' Lowrie's*): produced at Liverpool, September 1878.
Singleheart and Doubleface	produced at Royal Princess's Theatre, Edinburgh, 1 June 1882.

BIBLIOGRAPHY

Malcolm Elwin, *Charles Reade* (London, 1931).
John Coleman, *Charles Reade as I Knew Him* (London, 1903).
Walter C. Phillips, *Dickens, Reade, and Collins* (London, 1919).
Morris L. Parrish, *Wilkie Collins and Charles Reade* (London 1940).
Charles L. Reade and Compton, *Charles Reade* (London, 1887).
Charles Graham, *The Late Charles Reade* (London, 1884).
Ellen Terry, *Story of my Life* (London, 1908).